Design for New Media

We work with leading authors to develop the
strongest educational materials in **multimedia design**,
bringing cutting-edge thinking and best learning
practice to a global market.

Under a range of well-known imprints, including
Addison Wesley, we craft high quality print and
electronic publications which help readers to
understand and apply their content, whether
studying or at work.

To find out more about the complete range of our
publishing, please visit us on the World Wide Web at:
www.pearsoned.co.uk

Design for New Media

Interaction design for multimedia
and the web

Lon Barfield

PEARSON

Addison
Wesley

Harlow, England • London • New York • Boston • San Francisco • Toronto • Sydney • Singapore • Hong Kong
Tokyo • Seoul • Taipei • New Delhi • Cape Town • Madrid • Mexico City • Amsterdam • Munich • Paris • Milan

Pearson Education Limited
Edinburgh Gate
Harlow
Essex CM20 2JE
England

and Associated Companies throughout the world

Visit us on the World Wide Web at:
www.pearsoned.co.uk

First published 2004

ISBN 0201-596091

British Library Cataloguing-in-Publication Data
A catalogue record for this book is available from the British Library

10 9 8 7 6 5 4 3 2 1
08 07 06 05 04

Typeset in Caslon 224 Book by 35
Printed and bound by Henry Ling. The Dorset Press, Dorchester, Dorset
The publisher's policy is to use paper manufactured from sustainable forests.

for Wendelynne
five years on

Contents

Preface

The 'big picture'

New media design is like a giant jigsaw puzzle: a combination of different media and skills. We know about all the pieces – some of them we have known about for a long time and others are very new. However, although we know about the pieces, the problem is putting them all together to get the big picture of new media design.

Many 'new media experts' are experts with roots in one of these existing media types or fields, and often they lack the overview of the whole subject area: the 'big picture'. Similarly, many new media courses (or multimedia, or digital media or whatever) adopt an approach that builds up expertise in each of the underlying parts in isolation, but that lacks the conceptual 'glue' to bind them all together. Partly this is due to an existing design philosophy within the institute, and partly it is cost-management – creating new courses from existing modules.

WEBCODE
courses

A unified approach

What is needed is a *unified* approach. An approach that covers the separate elements, but that covers them in the context of the role they play in new media design as a whole, an approach that provides the elements and also the 'big picture' about how they all fit together.

New media = multimedia + the web + more

The scope of the term 'multimedia' has shifted since the mid-1990s. 'Multimedia' used to mean the design of systems authored with tools such as Macromedia Director and distributed using cd-roms as a carrier medium.

In the mid-1990s the developments surrounding the internet and the web (I shall be explaining both of these in detail later) meant that the focus of multimedia development shifted from the static, physical carriers like the cd-rom to dynamic and updatable delivery methods on the web. Even now this shift is getting more and more pronounced, pushed along by the developments on the web, the increase in the bandwidth available and the explosion in access by the public. Distribution based on cd-roms will always have a niche in the market, but the main focus of multimedia will be online content on the web.

A large part of the jigsaw I mentioned above is connected with the web. Many elements of web design are similar to cd-rom multimedia design. There is an overlap in the skill sets, but there is also much to learn about design for the web that was never possible with cd-roms and could never even have been imagined. This change is being mirrored in the skill sets being demanded by employers and offered on courses. Many classical multimedia courses are introducing their students to the web and including web design and construction as part of the curriculum. This trend will gather pace as courses restructure to follow developments on the internet.

Goals, audience and scope of the book

There are interesting parallels between designing a book and designing a new media system. Fundamentally both are concerned with presenting content to an audience. One of the common ideas is deciding the goals, audience and scope (GAS) of the system. This will be dealt with later in chapter 9, but here I will apply the analysis to this book.

Goals

The goal of this text is to give the reader a solid grounding in new media design; to introduce them to the factors that play a part in the design of interactive digital systems; and to provide them with a design vocabulary to enable them to come up with their own solutions in this new area.

Audience

This is primarily a course book for studies in, or relating to, the design of interactive digital media. However, the nature of the digital world is such that the boundary between educational texts and professional texts is a very blurred one indeed, so let me deal with the different readers that may make use of this text, in particular lecturers, students and practitioners.

For the lecturer

WEBCODE
lecturer

Lecturing on the subject of multimedia design, interaction design, web design or any of the other overlapping disciplines that make up new media design can be a difficult process. There are no recognized curriculum structures, there are no books that define the area, indeed the area itself is constantly changing and evolving.

New courses are being offered at all levels, incorporating the words 'multimedia' and 'design' in their titles, and the coverage and quality is wide ranging, from the technical 'how to do this effect with this tool' to the purer, design-oriented courses. All too often these design-oriented courses are spin-offs from visual design courses and tend to accentuate the visual aspects of multimedia design while not giving enough coverage to other issues such as sound design and interaction design. A further criticism is that they lack exactly what the computer scientist has too much of: formal methods – rigorous approaches to thinking and structuring the design that help in any technical, production-oriented design discipline.

Such multimedia design courses are frequently amalgams of modules from existing courses and while each module is taught by an expert in that particular field, the courses sometimes lack a good overall cohesive approach to bind the elements together. The purpose of this book is to provide that cohesion and conciseness and to support the teaching of multimedia design at art and design colleges and universities.

Lectures

This book is based on my own experience of lecturing in new media design, primarily during my five-year involvement with the Interaction Design course at the Utrecht School of the Arts (HKU as it is called in Dutch). The separate chapters have a one-to-one relationship with lectures and can usually be covered in about an hour, depending on the level of detail and the amount of interaction with the students during the lesson.

Translating the chapters into lessons is a fairly easy matter. When I give the lectures I usually accompany them with a Tony Buzan-style bubble diagram ('mind maps' as he calls them), putting down the key concepts and their relationships on one sheet of paper with a few pictures on it. This makes the handout a bit more fun and, more importantly, allows the

WEBCODE
handouts

student to add annotations as the lecture progresses. On the accompanying web site (www.booksites.net/barfield) there are bubble diagrams for the chapters and also the more traditional bullet point slides.

The design of a lecture itself has overlaps with the design of an interactive system: both are essentially concerned with communication – admittedly the lecture is largely one-way with only a bit of interaction but then so are a lot of other interactive things.

Resist the dark side

Designing new media as a subject can be difficult for students to grasp. The emphasis is not on graphic design but the interactive elements of the design. It is always too easy for a student to 'lose the plot' a bit with the interaction design and become more engrossed with the more tangible and more 'trendy' graphic design. This is the equivalent of succumbing to the 'dark side of the Force' and all attempts should be made to steer students away from this. One way of doing this is to give examples and exercises that emphasize the interaction with little, or no, graphic design.

A few notes on presentation

Giving a lecture is a lot like giving a performance. One way in which they are similar is that it is important to get the audience's attention within the first few seconds of the talk (see chapter 15 on narrative for a further discussion of this). Start with something to whet the appetite, a quick demo (make sure it is quick – anything involving computers and beamers can end up taking half the lesson), hand something tangible around and tell an anecdote about it, do anything else that can attract the audience's attention. For a lecture on 'sound' start off with something that makes a loud noise; for 'user models' start off with something that does not fit in with their user model of a lecture; for 'contexts' start off with national cultures and insulting gestures from different countries; for 'layout' give out some fake handouts with 8 point type in a strange font and wait for complaints. Make it fun!

For the student

WEBCODE
student

New media design is a part of the future of design and it can be an addictive subject. Once you do manage to get hold of the big picture it can become difficult to let go. Becoming a designer of interaction is not about learning a few guidelines parrot fashion; it is about a paradigm shift in how you look at what is around you – both the technology that you and others interact with, and interaction in general, between people and the world around them.

The subject area is not set in stone. Although this book does take a big step in defining a structure to hang everything on, there is still much scope for change in the discipline, even in the classroom. If you study physics then you know that everything you learn about has been done before. With new media design it is still being done, and new people can still contribute to the area. It should be borne in mind that, even though this is a textbook that sets out the structure of the discipline, it is a textbook that was made possible in part by the lecturing process itself and by the input of many hundreds of students studying this new subject area.

And for the practising designer . . .

WEBCODE
designer

Nowadays, in the Western world, our life is lived in a bubble of design. Design is always between us and the outside world. We do not sit on trees and roll in the grass or catch our own food. We live surrounded by manufactured things and systems. Even when we do finally get out into 'nature' we get there by a designed car, we wear our designed outdoor clothes and we usually take a few designed gadgets with us (mobile phone, Walkman, camera).

Whether or not you agree with this way of living, it is what happens and because people live their lives in this bubble of design, the quality of their life is directly influenced by the quality of the design. This quality of design is not the 'swoosh' factor of making things look cool and stream-lined, it is about designing them with the user in mind. True design is about just that, designing for the user, and if you look at the things that have become design classics, they are the things that were designed with this in mind – not designed to look like a classic or to be really different, just designed to do what the user wants in an efficient, usable way.

Recently the nature of our 'bubble of design' has changed: there is less that is material and more that is digital and new medial in nature. We spend more hours on the web, using computer games; and interactive television is becoming more and more popular.

WEBCODE
time stats

This book is about extending that design-for-use ethos to include this new, interactive world of new media.

Scope

We have looked at the goals and the audience; the final part of the GAS analysis is the scope. The book covers the ingredients of new media design and the process necessary to combine them in design practice. It is divided up into four main parts, described below and shown in Figure P.1.

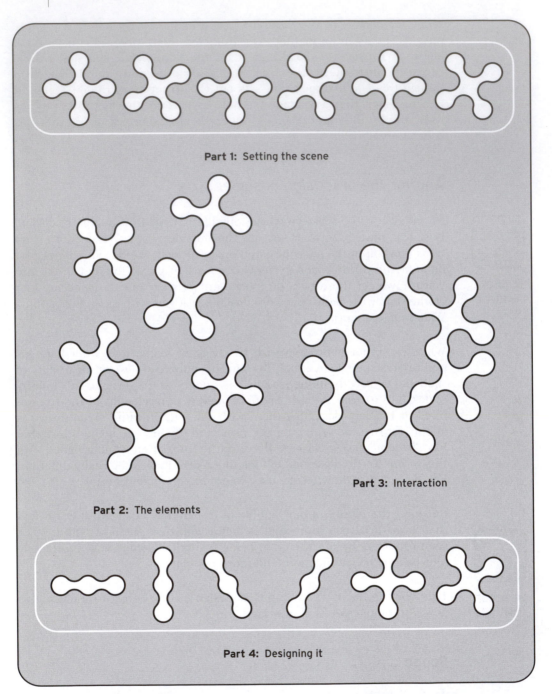

Part 1: Setting the scene

Part 3: Interaction

Part 2: The elements

Part 4: Designing it

Figure P.1: How the four parts of the book relate to one another.

Part 1 Setting the scene

The book starts with a look at what new media is – multimedia, web design and interaction design (designing the interactivity) – and considers some the issues that arise from designing with new and developing technology.

Part 2 The elements

What I call the 'elements' are the basic building blocks of new media: sound, color, animation etc. Each is given a thorough examination and all aspects of its role in the design of a new media system are explained.

Part 3 Interaction

The next part covers interaction design: the design of those elements of new media that are connected with use and understanding of the system and the bringing together of the elements into a coherent and usable whole.

Part 4 Designing it

Finally the process of design itself is considered, not in an abstract but a practical way how: do you take the first step and how do you go on designing until you have a design down on paper?

Examples, exercises, guidelines and rules

The main thread of the text is accompanied by many illustrative examples from interactions in the real-world. I have added these examples in order to clarify the points I am making. The fact that many are non-digital examples means that they should be more familiar and approachable while showing how much can be learned from studying real-world interactions.

Design is not just about 'knowing', it is also about 'doing', and knowing what to do. Learning about design is not passive; it is not just about reading and clicking. Design is active: learning about design is taking action and trying to design things. To support this, the book contains many exercises. Some are well-defined 'exam quality' questions, while others are more open-ended and intended as group-design projects. To support and guide the readers with these exercises there are selected guidelines on the accompanying web site accessible with the 'webcodes' described below.

Scope: what is not in it

A vital part of defining the scope of content is to specify those areas that will be covered and also those that will not. As far as this book is concerned the following areas will not be covered.

Pure technological content

An architect has to know that their buildings will not fall down but they do not have to know how to make steel. Similarly a new media designer should be aware of technology but not be a slave to it. This book will deal with technology only in as far as it is relevant to the design.

If you want to know how to set up an application with Enterprise Cappuccino Beans++ or what steps to follow to get a jazzy, chrome effect with PaintyPack4.2 then buy another book.

Separate media: film, photos, video etc.

There are a wealth of experience and excellent books covering good practice in the separate media worlds of photography, movie making, sound recording etc. While such areas may be brought together in a new media system, new media is about multiple, digital media types. This book does not deal with building up proficiency in each of the media types independently. It deals with those aspects of each medium that play a key part when that medium is integrated with other media into an interactive, new media whole.

If you want to become an expert in digital sound recording and digital sound recording *alone* then buy another book.

Building new media

This book focuses on new media *design*. There is some acknowledgment given to the building process in the book since you have to know something about building in order to design a system. However, an in-depth look at building and project management applied to new media projects is inappropriate.

The accompanying web site

This book is accompanied by a web site:

www.booksites.net/barfield

One role of the web site is to promote the book, the other is to support those people who have bought it. It is not a totally dynamic site updated every minute of every day, but a useful collection of resources to accompany and expand upon the ideas in the text. It is not worth visiting daily, but certainly worth browsing if you find the subject matter interesting.

Webcodes

Various organizations are currently undertaking research on link-ups between the printed world and the digital world. One example was an early system of paper-based television listings where each program was accompanied by a barcode and, if you had the right video recorder with a light pen, just stroking the pen on the code would read it and program the video to record the program. A more recent idea was a free newspaper given to commuters which had barcodes so that you could read more about certain news items when you scanned the barcode with a light pen.

Similarly, in the education field there are printed class materials that contain digital references, again in the form of barcodes. These are read with a computer light pen to access the appropriate web page or section on a cd-rom.

From the outset of writing this book I wanted to accompany it with a web site, but there was the question of how to tie the two together. Rather than forcing everyone who buys the book to buy a light pen, I opted for a simple, textual access code system. At certain points in the text a link is made to the web site by means of a short textual code. If you go to the web site and type this code, you will be shown the information appropriate to that point in the text.

This approach is starting to be used on some commercial web sites as well. Rather than have a separate URL for each short-term offer they run, each offer has a reference code and entering that in the text field on the home-page takes you straight to the relevant information.

WEBCODE
paper and
web

For example this part of my book has a webcode 'paper and web'. Type this in and you get a short overview of research in the area of paper/

digital tie-ins with links to several examples of the technology – current developments, barcode readers, even the ancient SoftStrip reader from the 1970s is there!

Terminology

WEBCODE
terminology

As I pointed out in the opening paragraphs, the term 'multimedia design' is usually taken to mean 'classical' multimedia design for cd-rom. To avoid any confusion I shall use a different term, 'new media', to cover interactive, digital media for both the cd-rom and the internet. I shall go further to include all other forms of interactive, digital media and any forms that have yet to be launched.

As well as this definition there are a number of other terms that should be pinned down before I start. Do not worry if these definitions seem a bit short as they will all be covered later in the book.

The web

The internet is the global network of computers through which data can be transferred. The term 'the web' is short for the world-wide web. It is the collection of text, graphic and multimedia information in a particular format that is accessible using the internet. There are other services available on the internet besides the web, but most of them are of a more technical and less useful nature, with the exception perhaps of e-mail.

New media

New media is a collective term for the many types of interactive, digital media that have been or are being developed. Primarily it includes classical, cd-rom-based, multimedia and web design, although much of what follows is applicable to new, up-and-coming media areas such as interactive television, WAP services (web for mobiles), interactive phone services and complex interactive technologies in general.

New media systems

The terminology to describe a new media 'thing' is always difficult and the choice usually depends on the background of the writer. A new media *production* makes it sound very much like a film production or some other form of traditional arts medium. New media *products* also sounds rooted in the physical rather than the digital. New media *documents* sound static. My choice, therefore, is new media *systems*: this seems to steer a good line between physical products employing a degree of digital interaction and purely digital interactive services.

Users

There are a great number of terms to describe the people sitting in front of the new media systems, be they cd-roms or web sites. They can be 'viewers', 'readers', 'visitors' etc. The most neutral and appropriate term, I find, is 'users'.

Interaction design

This is the design of the interactive elements of systems, be they drinks machines or new media systems. It is known under many names: human–computer interaction, user interface design or just plain interface design. It is the main building block of new media design.

Pages and home-page

In some new media systems the interaction is divided into discrete units, each one visually different in some way from the one before it. In presentation multimedia one often refers to 'screens', while on the web they are 'pages'. A good cd-rom production avoids this jerky progression from one screen to the next and good multimedia extensions to the web are also starting to soften the page-by-page nature of web sites. However, for the times when we will need to refer to this idea I shall use the web-based terminology as the web is more page/screen oriented than classical multimedia. Thus I shall refer to 'pages' and 'the home-page'.

Acknowledgments

My thanks go to the staff and especially the students on the Interaction Design course at the HKU in Utrecht (Utrecht School of the Arts), for testing, refining and in some cases supplying the content of this book during a wonderful five years spent there. Also to my colleagues at 'General Design, Internet Solutions', for the roller-coaster ride of the dot.com years.

At Addison Wesley my thanks go to Karen Mosman for initiating the project in the Ijsbreker cafe one foggy day in January, to Karen Sutherland for taking it over and to Kate Brewin for steering it to completion.

And of course thanks go to Wendelynne, Morgan and Keiran.

Part ONE

Setting the scene

■ How this part relates to the other three parts

What I want to do in this first section is get an overview of new media, what it is, where it came from and a little bit of where it is going. I want to map out the boundaries of what we are going to be discussing throughout the rest of the book and I also want to consider the justification of *why* we are doing it.

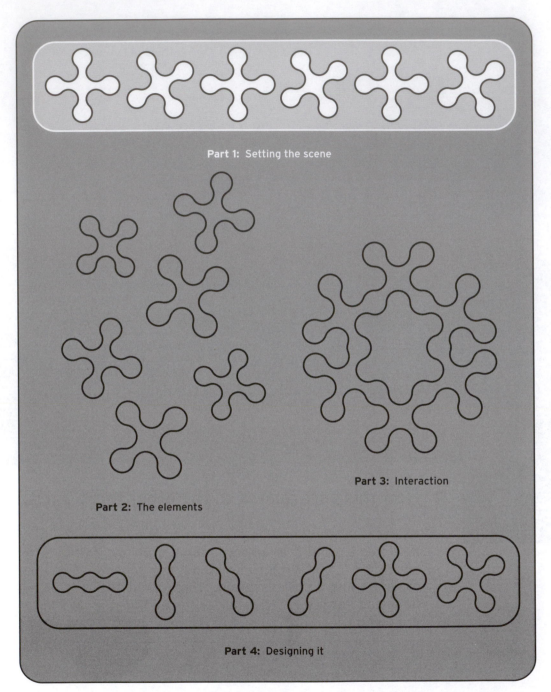

Part 1: Setting the scene

Part 3: Interaction

Part 2: The elements

Part 4: Designing it

Figure Part 1: How this part relates to the other three parts.

New media and interaction design

New media, new design

From flint to mass-production

The making of artifacts for human use goes back millions of years. Indeed, one could say that it goes right back to when *Homo habilis*, one of our ancestors, first bashed chunks of flint to give them a sharp edge on one side that could cut through animal flesh.

Nowadays, products are mass produced; a prototype is created and, when it is deemed OK, hundreds of thousands of copies are made. This has resulted in two big changes in the way things are designed and made. First, things must be designed before they are made; you cannot gradually put something together bit by bit, you have to have a precise design that is then produced. Secondly, the design cannot be altered once the products are in use; there are just too many of them to make this possible. The product has to be designed until it is correct and then never changed again.

Ergonomics

The result of these two factors has been that design became a separate discipline from the actual production of products, and that the product has to be well suited to its use and its user before going into production. Today this discipline of designing and creating artifacts for human use is called 'ergonomics' (or 'industrial design') and it embraces a great many issues and ideas.

Here is a a quote from an article written by Reyner Banham, one of the great design gurus in the 1960s. The article was a snapshot of the current state of design at that time across a wide rage of fronts. Amongst the different areas discussed was the area of ergonomics. This is what he had to say about it:

> *Ergonomics has generated little facile optimism, except for a faith that by patient and painstaking research the relationship between men and their tools can be improved. At one level this has meant quite simply the reshaping of the handles of traditional tools, but at other levels it has meant exercises as abstract as the devising of new sets of symbols for the keys on the control panels of computers.*

WEBCODE
banham

That last sentence is interesting from the point of view of new media design because it shows the lengths to which this area has changed in such a short time. Banham talks about designing the symbols for computer keys: 'icons' in today's terminology. In the 1960s this was a highbrow area on the leading edge of ergonomic design, but today it is something that the majority of Mac-using students do in their coffee break, designing their own icons for folders on the desktop.

Interaction

Our technology has moved on from the flint tools and mass production mentioned above, indeed it is no longer just composed of solid objects that are grabbed and moved. Today's products have conceptual complexity: many of them now involve an element of interaction – interaction be-yond getting hold of them and picking them up. As technology evolves and becomes cheaper, our interaction with complex devices involves more new media. Mobile phones, personal music systems, digital cameras and video recorders all have a little color screen and sometimes sound to sup-port the user's interaction with the system. They can be said to exhibit behavior and they can carry and communicate information. With techno-logy such as this, the outer form – the materials, the size and shape – is important, but it is only a small part of the story. How the product behaves and interacts with the user is becoming the main design issue.

New media

The final step in this progression is the one from these complex interact-ive products to complex interactive *digital* products – products that have no physical shape, that cannot be picked up and put into a box, products that exist only within the computer: software, web sites, games, cd-roms.

The struggle I had with terminology in the preface gives some indication of the turbulent nature of the developments in this world. Cd-roms, interactive television, the web and complex hybrids of all media are leading to a real melting-pot of terms and ideas. The things that remain the same throughout are those aspects of interactive systems that are basic and underlying, ideas that will be covered later in the book such as efficient, coherent presentation and good feedback. However, there are also new areas that have arisen from the usability problems associated with media such as the web, in particular the areas of condensing and structuring information and supporting user navigation through the structure.

New media design and interaction design

As we shall see, the main ingredient of new media design is interaction design. Figure 1.1 shows that the two areas are very closely related. What I shall do in the rest of this chapter is consider new media design and then interaction design, spending more time on interaction design because it is the key ingredient and because it is an area that is wider than just its role in new media design.

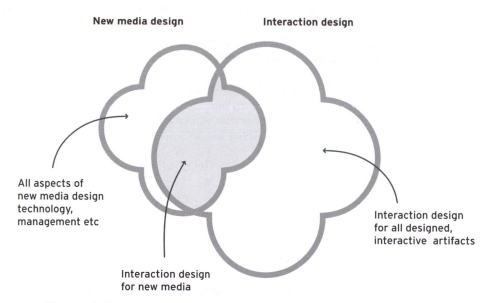

Figure 1.1: The overlap between new media design and interaction design to give us interaction design for new media.

New media

New media: the term

New media is a follow-on from multimedia which is a follow-on from hypertext. That was first put into words by Vanevaar Bush who defined a new concept in the 1940s: the ability to click on a word in a piece of text and have the focus immediately shifted to another page dealing with that word. Although he outlined the idea, Mr Bush failed to give a name to it. The idea lay dormant and only really started catching on when the technology came into being to make it possible. Around this time of burgeoning technology the term 'hypertext' was coined by Ted Nelson. It soon started to develop beyond just text and it was not long before the technology could support pictures, animation and sound. At this stage people began to talk about 'hypermedia' (another Ted Nelson term). Then Apple assembled a group of people to investigate hypermedia further, but the head of the group, Sueann Ambron, found the term 'hypermedia' too technical sounding and instead coined the term 'multimedia'.

Eventually, a means emerged of distributing the large amounts of data associated with multimedia, the cd-rom. Cd-roms became widespread and were only really pushed out of first place when multimedia met the internet. The internet had been around for a while but was a predominantly techy and texty means of communication. The world-wide web changed that by allowing more detailed documents to be put together and connected to the internet so that other people connected to the internet could access them in a more user-friendly way.

Soon it all went commercial and developed its own services, its own way of laying out information, and its own vocabulary. It was quickly joined by other developments as web content became accessible on mobile phones, personal organizers, street kiosks and interactive television sets.

The term 'multimedia' was stuck with clunky cd-roms and no longer seemed to encapsulate what was happening on the web and beyond, so the term 'new media' started to take its place; the 'new' being a catch-all phrase for the fast way that media was changing and broadening.

New media: what it is

As I pointed out in the preface the terms 'new media' and 'multimedia' are pretty interchangeable. I am using 'new media' mainly to emphasize the point that I am talking about cd-rom-based multimedia *and* multimedia on the web. As new media is multimedia combined with the dynamic communication possibilities offered by the internet to get to the roots of new media we must start by considering multimedia.

The more classical term 'multimedia' is made up of the terms 'multi' meaning more than one and 'media' meaning some distinct carrier of information. So multimedia is something that is composed of more than one medium. Here is an example to counter this definition: a prehistoric cave dweller wants to warn his fellow cave dwellers of the approaching woolly mammoth. He grunts the noises that are the approximate equivalent of 'hey guys there's a woolly mammoth coming over that hill' and points in the direction of the approaching beast. This is communication involving more than one medium (visual signs and spoken word) and so by our definition the cave dweller's warning was a multimedia system. Quite clearly this is not what we mean. As most people use more than one of their senses when they are taking information in, every sensory experience can be described in this way as multimedia.

If we look to the world of the arts then multimedia usually means a work of art realized in more than one medium. So a combination of eight slide projectors, music and rotating firebricks would be multimedia. But that fails to address the interactive element. In the same way I could also state that watching the television is multimedia since it is realized in both sound and pictures. Again this is not what we are talking about.

So here is a definition of multimedia:

> **A multimedia system is a system that is interactive and uses more than one medium in an integrated way. The media are rich media and are stored media.**

Let us break that down and look at the points in a bit more detail.

Interactive

Multimedia systems are dynamic, that is, they change with time: the images we see on the screen and the sounds we hear change. This change can be initiated by the system itself or it can be changed in response to some action that the user performs. Interactive, in this context, means that the user can interact with the system and through that interaction influence the behavior of the system.

Integration

Demonstrations of early multimedia systems were like watching latter-day engineers tending to steam engines. The demonstrator would be running around tweaking knobs and checking cables to make sure that the frame buffer was connected via the tilting engine to the screen with the video connection and the 12 track . . .

Nowadays everything can be digitized and stored on one large hard-disk. As everything is digitized and handled in a similar way by the computer the media are all integrated to a high degree and they can be easily combined and manipulated together. This is also reflected in the authoring systems for creating multimedia; users can insert video, sound, pictures, 3D models or whatever they want into the multimedia system.

Rich media

Another key factor is that the media involved are (or can be) rich media – not just plain text, but layout, colors, photo-quality graphics, animation, sound and video.

Stored media

If we think back to the transience of the mammoth message given by the cave dweller introduced above, we can see that the whole idea of a medium is that it holds a fixed representation of something. This fixed representation can be stored and then played back and reviewed when required.

The key point from this list of qualities is the first, *interaction*. Let me move on to consider that in more depth.

Interaction design

The important factor in book design is certainly not the fact that the pages are made of wood pulp. In a similar way, the key factor in new media design is not really the fact that everything is digital, but the fact that because it is all digital and stored on a computer it is all *malleable*. Things can be made to react to the user; in other words, the system is interactive.

The design of this interactivity, so-called 'interaction design', is the heart of new media design, and interaction design is a very broad area. New media design is just the latest addition to it but even though it is a latecomer, new media design as a discipline involves a much greater input from interaction design than other disciplines do, simply because the interaction is pretty much all there is.

When you learn about interaction design for new media it is difficult to restrict yourself to learning only the bits of interaction design that are applicable to new media design: you must learn much more about interaction design, appreciate it and understand how and when to apply it to new media design. So let's take a longer look at interaction design, starting with the term itself.

Interaction design: the term

WEBCODE
terminology

Interaction design is the design of those aspects of a system that the user perceives and communicates with. It is a relatively new discipline and an indication of its novelty is given by the many different terms that are used to describe it, ranging from the hype-buzzwords (I love 'design for unstable media'), through to the downright old fashioned ('the man–machine interface').

If you are in a bookshop looking for the shelf with books on interaction design then it may not be immediately clear where it is. Interaction design is such an overlap area and goes under so many different names that it can be confusing. Indeed I have had several discussions with the publishers to pin down a good set of terms to use throughout this book.

Another interesting source of differing terms for the area can be found by scanning the job adverts in the newspapers and on the web. Companies are asking for information engineers, usability experts and such like. This is interesting not only because it shows that the area is still in a state of flux but also because it shows that the commercial world is aware of the area and that they are in need of people to carry out interaction design tasks.

Things are not as chaotic as they may appear, though. Now that interaction design and usability are becoming more appreciated by the commercial world, efforts are being made to define things a bit better. We already have a definition for 'usability' in one of the ISO standards (ISO 13407). It states:

> *The usability of an interface is a measure of the effectiveness, efficiency and satisfaction with which specified users can achieve specified goals in a particular environment with that interface.*

Interaction design is about designing with the focus on this idea of usability.

Interaction design: what it is

The best way to explain the nature of interaction design is not to carry on with more terminology but to use a concise illustration, a simple real-world example – the cockerel alarm clock.

I have an alarm clock that someone gave me as a gift. It is shaped like a cartoon chicken and when it goes off it makes an awful 'cock-a-doodle-doo' sound. However, the interesting point from an interaction design point of view is the on/off switch or, to be more precise, the switch that arms or disarms the alarm. This is controlled by pressing its head down; click to arm and click again to disarm. The problem is that the head always remains in the same position: you cannot see whether it is pressed in or out like you can with a radio button. There is no indication from the head as to whether the alarm is armed or disarmed; see Figure 1.2. To find that out, you have to look at the eyes of the chicken. When you click the head down they change from open to closed. Click and the eyes are open, click and the eyes are closed. The question is, which is which? When is the alarm armed and when is the alarm disarmed?

I have demonstrated this clock to audiences and whenever I have posed that question and counted a show of hands the audience is split roughly in half. Half the people think that 'eyes open' means that the chicken alarm is armed and will wake me up in the morning, while the other half think that 'eyes closed' means that it is armed.

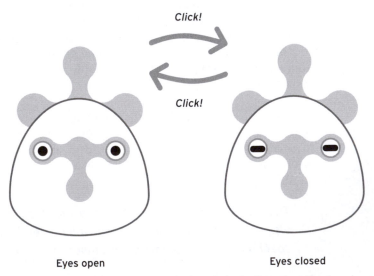

Eyes open   Eyes closed

Figure 1.2: The head of the cockerel alarm clock. Pressing the head arms or disarms the alarm. The eyes show which.

WEBCODE
alarm clock

Although completely non-digital in nature this is a splendid example of the disruption that can happen with even the simplest of interactions. Interaction design is about paying good attention to the design of the interactive aspects of a system (even a clock is a 'system') so that users are not left confused about what is going on. We shall be revisiting this alarm clock in chapter 11.

Physical ergonomics, matching the body

The best way to analyze what interaction design is all about is to set it in an ergonomic context. Let me start with physical ergonomics. This is the ergonomics that most people are familiar with. It is the ergonomics of well-designed office chairs and control panel layouts. Let me define it before we go any further:

> **Physical ergonomics is the design of the physical aspects of a system to fit with the physical parameters of the human body.**

A good example is a standard wall-mounted light switch. It is mounted on the wall at about chest height. If it were 2 meters up it would be difficult to get at; impossible for some people. If it were 50 centimeters off the ground it would be an effort to use it and it could be activated accidentally by things knocking against it. So the height above the ground is chosen to fit in with the physical parameters of the average person. In a similar way the spring built into the switch could be made really strong, but then old and infirm people may not have the strength or coordination to activate it. Similarly, a weak spring would mean that it could be activated just by brushing against it with something – a coat or a duster. So the strength of the built-in spring is also designed to fit with the physical parameters of the average human.

Mental ergonomics, matching the mind

Now let us adapt the definition for mental ergonomics, what we are calling interaction design:

> **Mental ergonomics is the design of the interactive aspects of a system to fit with the mental parameters of the human mind.**

The physical parameters in the first discussion are fairly obvious. They are tangible things such as height and strength exerted by the arm, but what about the mental parameters? What exactly are they and how are they measured? To start with, they are a lot more vague than the physical parameters. They cover such issues as what people expect, how they communicate, what they see, what tasks they want to do, how they organize information and how they think and approach problems.

Spiritual ergonomics, matching the heart

Finally, we will adapt the definition for spiritual ergonomics:

> **Spiritual ergonomics is the design of all aspects of a system to fit with the spiritual parameters of the human mind.**

If the mental parameters were vague and intangible then the spiritual parameters are even more so. However, that does not mean that they are not important, indeed they are probably the most important of the three. They are connected with the deep aspects of what it is to be human: enjoyment, game playing, humor, fear, prestige, pride of ownership etc.

**WEBCODE
tufte**

**WEBCODE
memorial**

The author Tufte gives a wonderful example of spiritual ergonomics in the design of information: the Vietnam Veterans' Memorial in Washington. This is a set of granite tablets with the names of all the US servicemen and women who lost their lives in the Vietnam War. The issue was how to organize the list. First ideas of alphabetical order of surname were thrown out – admittedly it was the most efficient way of organizing the list but it was too brutally efficient and unfeeling, because it would result in the equivalent of a granite phone-book. Anybody called 'Smith' who lost a son will find he is just one of very many Smiths in the list. In the final design the names were ordered on the date that they died, decreasing the informational efficiency of the monument, but creating a history carved in stone telling of the development of the war, the big offensives and the part played by each person in the campaign.

An example

To contrast all three types of ergonomics let us consider the design of the emergency-exit doors in an aircraft.

Physical ergonomics involves design issues such as ensuring that the door controls can be operated by someone with average muscles and ensuring that the door is big enough to fit even the largest of people. Cabin crew will sometimes move passengers around so that those who are closest to the door are fit enough to open it.

Mental ergonomics covers issues such as being able to quickly find the door in an emergency situation and to understand how to operate it and (even more importantly) realizing that there is a door there in the first place. Also the important trade-off that it must be easy to open in an emergency but difficult to open by accident.

Spiritual ergonomics deals with the aspects of user well-being in the face of possible mid-air disasters. Users need to be aware of the safety features without being allowed to dwell on the reasons that they need those features. They need to be aware that adequate provision has been made for emergencies without feeling that the plane is doomed.

Which bits are interaction design?

I have given examples of interaction design and I have given a bit of analysis. Here is another way of tackling the question of what interaction design is: a list of some of the key factors of a system whose design falls within the scope of interaction design:

- How the information is organized, and how it is presented.
- What buttons and functions are available to the user and when they are available to be used.
- What the underlying behavior of the system is.
- Which information and controls are available to other users, such as admin. staff, super-users, supervisors, executive overviews etc.
- The content and layout of standard print-outs available from the system (see the exercise at the end of the chapter on book sales).
- The printed material accompanying the system, especially the cover if it is cd-rom based.
- Also, other external sources of information related to the system such as the manuals accompanying the system (both online and paper/cd-rom based), the training packages (cd-rom or real) etc.
- And much more, as we shall see in the rest of the book.

Why bother with all this design?

Interaction design is the main ingredient for new media design, but does that necessarily mean that it is worth devoting large parts of this book to it? Is it really all that important? Perhaps interaction design is a bit like the recent craze for feng shui. Devotees believe that it is important and it can change your life in a big way, but to many other people it seems to be a hybrid of common sense (obvious points such as not putting your chairs facing the walls), combined with rather vague and fluffy things such as where to hang bells to stop good fortune in its tracks. Isn't interaction design just the same thing – an excuse to sell books on interaction design? With feng shui one could argue that it is unnecessary because people can live just fine in a house that is a bit disorganized and messy. In a similar way one could argue that people can live with a badly designed new media system; they just have to do a bit more training and be a bit more careful when they use it. Why bother with all the investment in interaction design? Why not invest it in the other parts of new media design such as sound design, speed of delivery and cool graphics with little animated bits?

Why indeed? Well let's have a look at some of the advantages good interaction design has to offer for new media design or the design of any other interactive system for that matter.

Advantages in production

Even before the user gets anywhere near the system there are advantages to be had. Thinking about the user and defining the user side of things has spin-offs in terms of good project management.

Defining the interface first and showing it to the client means that you rarely get met with comments such as, 'Wait a minute, that's not what we meant!' when the system is finally rolled out. Also, better interface design means that you can design for now and for the future, so that extensions to the system are easier to design and build.

Advantages in marketing

WEBCODE
marketing

Some large companies are investing in interaction design for purely financial and marketing reasons. Although this is somewhat dubious motivation, the end results are nonetheless good. Interaction design is useful in marketing for several reasons. First there are various prizes and awards associated with usability, always a good thing for advertizing copy. Secondly, as technologies mature there is more need to differentiate your system from that of the competitors. One way of doing this is to give your system better interaction design. Several years ago a leading producer of high-tech equipment made a big thing about the usability of their new phone incorporating a digital address book. They even went as far as to call it 'user friendly' and then claim 'user friendly' as their own trademark!

Finally, a part of software selling is giving demos to companies and on stands in exhibitions. If the system is easy and intuitive to use then it will sell better. I once visited a reseller of a leading computer-aided design (CAD) package for a full-scale demo. One of the features was a 3D viewing system where you could construct a model then do a virtual 'walk round' view of it. The interface was awful, with the result that, as the poor salesman struggled with the on-screen sliders, the house he had built whizzed this way and that way, sometimes upside-down, sometimes on its end. In the end he gave up trying to get a normal house-like view and finished with a weak 'well, you get the general idea don't you?' Indeed I did!

Advantages in use

Of course the very fact that interaction design is concerned with the use of the system means that there are also advantages in the use of the system, both for the client (the users) and the company providing the system.

Less support
Once a system is released into the market there is still a lot of investment required from the company. Courses need to be organized to assist staff in using it. Help desks need to be set up and staffed to ensure that users have help if they having difficulty with the system.

This investment can be kept to a minimum if the system has a well-designed interface. It will be easier to learn and people will have fewer problems using it, ensuring that support is minimal.

It is interesting to note that many companies make a lot of money with their training and help systems so there is a real commercial logic in supplying systems that are cryptic and difficult to use. However, as markets mature and as users become more knowledgeable and discerning in this area, this logic is becoming weaker and weaker.

More efficiency
A system with a well-designed interface will be a system that is efficient in terms of its use. Users will be able to learn to use it quickly and be able to use it faster than a system without good interaction design.

Fewer errors
In a similar vein, systems with good interaction design will be less prone to errors in their use. The results will be more dependable, less will go wrong, and if it does go wrong users will quickly be able to rectify the situation themselves.

Improved safety
In mission-critical systems, errors are not just about going back and correcting something, but they may involve non-undo-able actions such as submitting e-mail, ordering furniture or booking an airplane seat. Here, the role of interaction design is a vital one in preventing errors from happening.

Making web sites 'sticky'

In the world of the web, users are very discerning. If your web site is difficult to use or confusing they will not spend hours trying to understand it; they will immediately click on to another site supplying the same service, but faster and more efficiently. Ensuring that your web site is clear and usable will maximize its 'stickiness'. Users will stay longer and return more frequently.

The past: where did new media design come from?

Now that we have looked at the relationship between new media design and interaction design, let us have a look at the bigger picture: where these disciplines came from, and where they are going. What follows is not a linear history of new media design but rather an overview of the different 'nesting grounds' that have given rise to this new discipline.

Ergonomics

Ergonomics was born in the 1950s with huge percentile studies of human physical abilities, usually of men tall enough to make it into the military. These results were then used to shape the design of products designed to fit the human form, usually average-sized women working in offices.

Industrial design

Industrial design covers the design of products that people will use. Modern-day products are getting more and more complex and to support their use everything seems to have a tiny screen built in. The division between product interfaces and computers is starting to blur and industrial designers are getting more and more involved in the interaction that takes place between the user and the information that the product is presenting to them.

Graphic design

New media design is a new area but it involves elements from other existing areas, in particular graphic design and copy writing. If someone cannot design a good newsletter on paper, then they are not going to be able to design a good web newsletter. However, an expert DTPer (desk top publisher) is not necessarily a good new media designer. You need a grounding in existing skills coupled with a good grasp of the new skills.

Computer-human interaction

The most advanced piece of technology around today is the computer. Now that the computer is migrating into areas where it is being used by non-computer people, usability aspects are becoming paramount. Early computer interaction design revolved around designing software commands and textual dialogues between the user and the computer. With the addition of high-quality graphics screens and the mouse, interfaces became more visual and spatial.

Multimedia and web technology

The developers of the actual technology also got involved with user interaction with richer media. They built systems around new technical developments and, as they gradually built outwards towards the user, they were confronted with usability issues.

The present: the current scope

So now we have a definition of new media/multimedia and we have looked at the different threads that have been woven together to form the discipline of new media design. Let us look at the *now* of new media design. What are the current areas of activity that can be described as new media design and what sort of people are doing the design?

Classical multimedia products

Usually when people use the term multimedia today they are referring to rich media on large static carriers such as cd-roms involving high-end graphics, sound and some video sections. These products cover a wide range of applications including games, encyclopedias, educational titles; even user manuals for products are now becoming more multimedia-oriented.

Web sites

The conventional view of a web site is as a collection of related information documents. However, internet technology can offer far more than this. The more recent wave of web sites includes complex interactive systems and services supported by databases and coupled with web-based interfaces.

Pure software interfaces

In the 'olden days' the user interfaces to computer systems were basic and text oriented. Nowadays, the display and interaction possibilities allow programming with highly visual interfaces. Programmers build up screens of buttons and read-outs and couple these to chunks of program code to build programs with visual and spatial control panels. Complex layout, colors, fonts and occasionally sound are used in the separate screens that form the front-end to the programs.

Advanced hardware interfaces

More and more complex products now include an LCD (liquid crystal display) screen as part of a complex user interface, including personal organizers, mobile phones, MP3 players, digital cameras and photocopying machines. Although the screen quality is usually limited in comparison with stand-alone computers (smaller, lower resolution and fewer colors), user interfaces involving such screens can be classified as part of new media design as they incorporate combinations of text, graphics, animation, color and sound.

Current new media designers?

With all these areas falling under the definition of new media design, is there just one sort of new media designer? The answer is 'no', although a more accurate answer would be 'not yet'. The design of these products is carried out by a variety of professionals, usually where the skill of new media design is part of a larger skill set. Complex products where a great deal of the interaction takes place on screen are the realm of the industrial designer; many industrial design courses are now integrating more of the 'soft' industrial design areas to do with psychology and communication.

Another well-established discipline that is embracing interaction design is computer science. Here the emphasis is less on design and more on function and formal methods. Although this area is full of obscure formal tools for dealing with interactions (which are in themselves more difficult to use than the system they are describing), there is a growing body of empirical results governing the fundamentals of interaction.

The future: education

WEBCODE
courses

Finally on to the future. The future is defined to some extent by the shape of education for new media design. So let us have a brief look at developments in that area.

Condensing the cloud

Setting up any course early on in the development of a new discipline usually leads to a desperate search for three years' worth of content. New media design has now matured to the point where there is a huge cloud of ideas and themes and a healthy overlap with chunks of other related disciplines and technologies. Designing a course is thus a question of condensing this cloud down to well-defined set of contents that satisfy two key requirements. First, the contents must have a definite relationship to each other – there is no room for 'jigsaw courses' where the student is served up a pile of recycled modules from other courses and has to make sense of it themselves. Secondly, the course must have a definite goal in terms of the profile of the person that they are eventually going to produce.

Following market developments

In an area that is changing constantly, the curriculum of such courses needs to be well structured for change; it needs a core set of subjects that are technology independent and that will remain applicable as things develop. This core is then ringed with courses dealing with technologies, both those in mainstream use and those that are on the horizon and could be in mainstream use by the time students hit the commercial world.

New media extension to existing courses

Often what happens is that institutes build on their existing strengths and devise new media extensions to their existing courses or separate new media courses based on their existing in-house skills. Ideally new media design is a neutral discipline, bringing together elements from a number of different fields, but this approach of course extensions usually results in a course that is spun towards the existing discipline. In this way there are new media courses that are heavily technical, heavily video production oriented, heavily screen-design oriented and so on.

Perhaps putting together a truly non-partisan, new media design course is an impossible ideal, since it will always be instigated by an existing department and so will always have some degree of bias towards an existing discipline. Still, it is no bad thing to have such ideals.

Exercises

Bad ergonomics

Consider the ergonomics of things around you in your everyday environment. Imagine redesigning some of them so that they fail miserably with respect to the physical, mental or spiritual ergonomics. Come up with some examples and explain why they fail.

For example, re-design the manager's desk so that it is 2 feet square and made of chipboard, it would be practical and lightweight, cheap to replace. Redesign the desk lamp so that the shade is very close to the bulb and the user has to grasp the shade to reposition the lamp. Redesign the swing door so there were no clues as to which side it swung on. And so on.

Searching job sites

Go on the web and access a few job sites, then carry out searches for some of the terms I have discussed here. See what sort of terms are popular in the industry and see what different sorts of interpretations there are for them. Put a list together and indicate which ones sound interesting and which do not.

Printed overviews

Every six months I used to get a statement from my publishers about how well (or otherwise) my first book was selling. The statement covered four pages of paper. It was covered in figures and it took me half an hour to answer the one question that was important for me (and other authors): how many books had I sold since the last statement?

It was so cryptic that I used it in lectures, I would hand it out and ask the question, 'If you were the author what would you want to know, and can you extract that information from the statements?' Sometimes it took up to half an hour to sort out.

Imagine you are an author. What would be the key bits of data you would want to know? What would be the other things you would like to know? How could they best be organized on paper? What about an on-screen layout for a future web-based system where authors could watch their book sales like stockbrokers watching stock prices?

Remember that authors live in many different countries and may have several titles on sale at once. Also remember that academic books have sales, but they also have returns (where people return them and get a refund).

I should add that the publishing company in question has since redesigned the form with pleasing results.

WEBCODE
bad
ergonomics

WEBCODE
searching
job sites

WEBCODE
printed
overviews

Design and technology

Let us move on briefly to talk about the technology. This is actually a dangerous thing to do; even before a book makes it through the publishing process, any technical content is outdated. Therefore I shall try to steer the discussion away from the fine detail of technique and concentrate instead on the more abstract ideas involved. This should result in a chapter that is useful and relevant and that remains so for some time. Any reader with a good grounding in either multimedia distributed on cd-rom or the internet should feel free to skip sections of this chapter that they already know about, although the last part on 'design vocabularies' should be read by all.

This chapter starts off with more conventional media and then, with the appearance of the computer, it moves on to digital media, typified by the cd-rom. The paradigm shift that the web embodies means that there will be a fairly detailed introduction to the capabilities of the internet. The chapter rounds off with a consideration of the process of design within this new world of multimedia technology and a look at one of the many ways of searching for direction in new media design.

Conventional media

For the purposes of this book on new media, conventional media (non-digital) can be seen as being made up of two elements. First, the carrier, the thing that carries or holds the information for storage and distribution purposes: magnetic tape, light-sensitive film, paper etc. Secondly, the nature of the information itself in an abstract way such as film, music, sound etc.

Some carriers are intended for storage of information: just keeping one or two copies as part of the creation and production process. Some carriers are used for distribution of the information on a large scale. Such carriers are permanent such as print or cassette tape while others are the transient, broadcast carriers of encoded video and sound signals.

Up until the advent of the computer, things were fairly clear-cut; film was film, sound was on analog recorded tape, and so on. When the computer came along, something strange happened: things started to go digital.

Digital media

Basically, a digit is a number. Representing things digitally means representing them as numbers. Computers have always worked in this way and as the computer increased in power you could track the complexity of the things that it could represent with numbers. Initially it was just simple text – number codes saying 'here is the letter A then here is the letter N', no information about fonts or layouts or colors or anything else. Such text coding is referred to as 'flat-text' or 'ASCII text' after the coding system it uses.

With more storage and more powerful systems came black-and-white pixel-based screens. These were screens made up of lots of little points that could be colored white or black (pixels). The whole screen was represented as a mass of numbers; for each point on the screen there was 1 for black or 0 for white. Now text could be shown in different fonts, each letter made up from a pattern of black points against a background of white points, pictures and animation were possible and on-screen controls started to appear. This paradigm shift was typified by the lovable Apple Macintosh.

Further increases led to higher-quality graphics (more pixels per screen, more colors per pixel). Instead of just a 1 or a 0 meaning black or white for each point on the screen, computers could say 'this point is colored a sort of purple color made with a mix of 25% red and 75% blue'. Taking the progression still further we hit the time-based media: sound and video. Video is not just one still image but can be thought of as many images one after the other, so obviously it requires more capacity even with the advanced optimization techniques available.

Complex combinations of all these media, coupled with other advances such as three-dimensional models, led to the first multimedia products. Once again with so many different media being packed together, the requirements on capacity were even greater.

Cd-roms

The need for extra storage on the carrier medium was met by increasingly larger ways of storing multimedia data. Initially the internal hard disk of a computer was the only reasonable place to store large amounts of data, but eventually the breakthrough in distributable media came in the form of the cd-rom. What made it unique was the fact that it could store a relatively high amount of information at a very low price. Also it could be mass-copied and mass-distributed easily. For these reasons it quickly became the main distribution medium for conventional multimedia.

WEBCODE
cd-roms

It is a measure of its ease and low cost of production that cd-roms now crop up all over the place: stuck to magazines as free gifts, included with hardware as a carrier of demo programs and documentation, even digitized video-clips showing the correct use of the product. Cd-roms come through the post and are given out free at shops to promote internet access providers, they contain internet connection software and glossy multimedia demos of services and what the web has to offer. Indeed the marketplace has become so saturated that old cd-roms occasionally turn up as shiny decorations or parts of fancy dress outfits.

Despite the penetration of the internet into the new media marketplace, cd-roms have not been left behind; they have simply become a very appropriate niche area. New data formats such as DVD and smaller-sized 'credit card' cd-roms have meant that the cd-rom continues to play a useful role in new media.

Shifting to the internet

The internet is a more recent development, commercially speaking, than the cd-rom, and it is more of a paradigm shift than the cd-rom was, so it needs a bit of time to get used to the enormous possibilities that it has to offer. For these reasons I shall devote a bit more space to it than to the cd-rom.

Initially the internet was a way of connecting computers together that was primarily a defense project. It did not take long before it migrated into the academic world and from there into the commercial world. Just as we saw earlier how the storage of digital media supported richer and richer media types, a similar progression happened with the internet. Initially it was used for purely text-based applications but it gradually came to support richer media, eventually being used as a channel for delivering audio and video. To make things clearer let me explain the difference between the internet and the web.

The internet network

In physical terms the internet is the computer equivalent of the telephone system. It is the network of computer connections that encircles the globe. Indeed a lot of it actually does use the telephone system. The computer I am using to write this book is connected to a large computer in the same building; that computer in turn is connected to a computer in a research lab, and that is connected to computers throughout Europe and the rest of the world. Anybody sitting at a computer on this vast network can quickly transfer information to any other computer on the network . . . if they know how to do so.

One of the reasons for the fast growth of the internet was that most of the hardware was already in place. In the early days of the telephone if you wanted a connection you had to have a cable installed to your house and purchase the telephone hardware. With the internet there were already millions of people with computers and there was already a huge global network in place in the form of the telephone network. In its simplest form, getting on the net was just a matter of connecting your computer to the phone line.

Internet services

The internet is more than just the network, more than just the physical cables and the communication protocols that use them. Once the internet is in place, people connected to it can use services that are supported by the internet, in much the same way that once you are connected to the telephone system you can use services such as the speaking clock. As far as the internet is concerned the two key services are e-mail and the world-wide web (web for short).

E-mail

E-mail was around on the internet long before glossy (and even not so glossy) web pages started appearing. E-mails can be sent to other people's e-mail addresses, or to mailing lists containing many e-mail addresses. The e-mails usually contain text but they can also contain computer files of things such as word-processor documents, images and anything else that is digital. They can also be sent out automatically by computer programs to alert people to things or bring them news.

Nowadays e-mails can be supplemented by richer forms of layout and graphics so that they can look more colorful and interesting, more like magazine articles and less like typewritten notes.

The web

As well as e-mail, which was primarily a directed communication service, there were early services for information servers: putting together collections of information on the internet and allowing other users to access it, something similar to a sort of digital library. These services had obscure names such as bulletin boards, FTP servers and Gopher.

Eventually, a really good way of doing this was devised and it became the standard means of providing information on the internet. It was dubbed the 'world-wide web'. When a web site is designed, built and installed on the internet any user from around the world can connect up and browse the information in the documents. On the web it is possible to present this information using a variety of media. The most common is formatted text – text shown in a particular style with different level headings, indentations and so on. As well as this, web sites can contain pictures in black and white or in color. Multimedia-type information can also be incorporated such as sound files and video clips.

The key to the web concept is 'hypertext', the ability to include links in the documents. A word or graphic in a page of material can be set up so that when the user clicks on it they jump to another page of the document. It is even possible to configure the links so that when the reader clicks on it they jump to a web document from some other part of the world.

The medium also offers interactive services. The person reading the web page can fill information in and this is then stored and processed within the web site. This idea can be used for things such as interactive order placing: a customer thousands of miles away can fill in their name, address and credit card number and then with just the click of a button on the screen they can place an order for artists' materials, books, CDs, plane tickets, whatever. Some products such as electronic fonts and digitized images can even be delivered to the customer over the internet.

In short, the internet now offers most of the things that the cd-rom offers, with the added features of updatable information and connectivity to many other users and the drawback (for the time being at least) of slower access times for richer media.

The paradigm shift

Why is the internet such a new phenomenon? Fax machines have become cheaper and more widespread in the last ten years, all offices have got one and some people have one at home, but there has not been the same hype about fax as there was about the internet. The reason is that the fax machine was a new way of doing an old function. Fax technology was new, but the idea of sending information on a bit of paper to someone else to read is a pretty established idea.

The internet is different because it is a new way of doing a new function, and nobody is even too sure what that function is yet. The internet is continually regarded in relation to existing media: the phone companies see it as the future for telecommunications; the publishers as a new avenue for publishing; the broadcast companies talk about webTV, and so on. The fax machine is no parallel for this, but perhaps the telephone is.

The telephone as a parallel

When the telephone was first invented there was no technological parallel as with the fax. Granted, it was just a means of carrying out conversations at a distance but this was such a new idea that there was a big struggle with the whole concept and what it would be used for in a commercial context.

Different applications of the technology were tried and different customer services were tried using this new piece of technology. Some technical observers of the time were skeptical:

> *The telephone is probably a good thing for the Americans, but here in London we have enough messenger boys.*

Others were more visionary:

> *The telephone is such an important invention ... that there will come a time when every town and city will have one.*

WEBCODE
phone quotes

It was a long development route and learning experience for society as a whole to reach the point today where we have a large network, a huge array of telephony services and are starting to see the merger of the telephone with the internet. Who could have guessed at these services in those early days when the medium was still being developed? In a similar way how can we now guess at the direction that the internet will take in the future?

Design and technology

How does design fit in with this fast-moving world of technology? Design and technology have always had a difficult relationship with one another. The division used to be less distinct; the master builders of old used to incorporate the essentials of today's architects and engineers. Today there is a fairly distinct separation between the people who design the system and the people who build it. However, the designers still need to know something of the technique in order to design within the parameters of their chosen medium.

If I am an architect designing a bridge then I need to know something about the strength of steel and how far I can build a span, and about the vibrational effects of people walking on it. If I am designing a TV advert I need to know what sorts of things are possible with special effects and how much they cost to do. And if I am designing a web site I need to know what sorts of possibilities are available to me with the latest technology and what part of my audience will have access to that technology. But how much do I need to know?

Too much or too little?

The critical issue here is not the simple question of *whether* the designer should know about the technique or not. It is the question of *how much* they should know about the technique.

Having a lot of knowledge about the technical side of the medium can mean that a designer can come up with amazing products by skilfully combining elements of what is possible with the medium. Alternatively the designer can become too rooted in the possibilities of the medium and not do any 'pushing of the envelope' to achieve new solutions.

If the designer has little knowledge of the technical side of the medium then the upside is that they can can come up with incredible designs that act as a challenge to the technical people trying to build the system. The designer says 'can we do this?' and the technicians say 'not quite, but we can do this and if we add a bit here we can do this . . .'. Of course this dynamic 'pushing the envelope' depends on a good interaction between the design staff and the technical staff. All too often the designer says 'can we do this?' and the technicians just say 'no, don't be daft'. The downside of too little knowledge on the designer's side is that designers are unable to design for the new medium because their designs are not rooted in the possibilities of the new technology.

New media, old ideas

A more dangerous variant of that last point is that designers with little knowledge of the new medium can tend to design for the new medium using what they know about another old medium. They fall back and design in terms of things they do know and come up with designs for the new media that are just copies of designs for the old media. Examples are web sites that are modeled on paper brochures, interactive web-based discussion groups that are modeled on old text-only discussion groups and even web sites that are based on multimedia cd-roms involving huge amounts of gratuitous sound and graphics.

Old media

This idea of designers having knowledge of the technique is not a new idea. When any new medium is introduced, the first things to be produced are produced by the technicians, for the simple reason that no one else knows what is going on. Then you get designers who know about the technicalities of the medium, and finally you get appropriate tools.

This was the case with, for example, the film industry. Initially the film camera was seen as no more than a device for recording plays. A play would be staged, the movie camera set up and the whole thing would be recorded from start to finish. Early film-makers were very much technicians, although to get anything worthwhile out of the process you had to have the right mix of technical competence and creativity. Walt Disney understood this when he set up his animation studios. The focus was not just on making cartoons, it was on bringing creative artists together with good technicians to push the boundaries of what was possible with the art.

A design vocabulary

The previous section brings us on to the subject of design vocabularies. A vocabulary is a set of terms that can be combined in different ways in order to express ideas. A *design* vocabulary is something similar in the world of design, a collection of conceptual building blocks that can be combined creatively in different ways to achieve certain goals.

Designers have to build up a design vocabulary. They have to know what they can do with a medium, they have to understand what is possible and what the building blocks are, and then they must design creatively using those building blocks. Designing new media is about understanding this vocabulary of concepts and of combining them creatively in solving a design problem.

Classical multimedia and, to a greater extent, the web involve a strange mix of incredible possibilities coupled with frustrating technical restrictions.

Technological influences

This part does get slightly technical, but the technical stuff is there only to illustrate the points I am making. If you cannot follow the technical stuff then do not worry; it is the non-technical stuff that is really important.

Everything is possible

The wonderful thing about the current state of digital media is that at the bottom level everything is theoretically possible. Computers are fast. Visual and sound systems are high quality in terms of human perception, and the internet is making things more connected: real-time, full-color, 3D environments are readily available. In theory you could do anything you want to on the screen – it is like having a blank sheet of paper and being able to write anything and everything.

The limitations to this wonderful state of affairs come in the technical restrictions of the systems associated with these resources. These restrictions help define the design vocabulary that designers have to work with; the building blocks of what is possible with the resources. Below, we consider some of the key restricting influences. The discussion is summed up in Figure 2.1.

Physical medium

The physical medium has its own built-in restrictions. The two principal restrictions are the limitation to the amount of data that can be stored on it and the speed at which that data can be accessed.

The amount of data that can be stored is of course a restriction of physical data-distribution methods. Floppy-disks, cd-roms and DVD cd-roms all have an upper level to how much data they can store. When it comes to the internet, there is no limit.

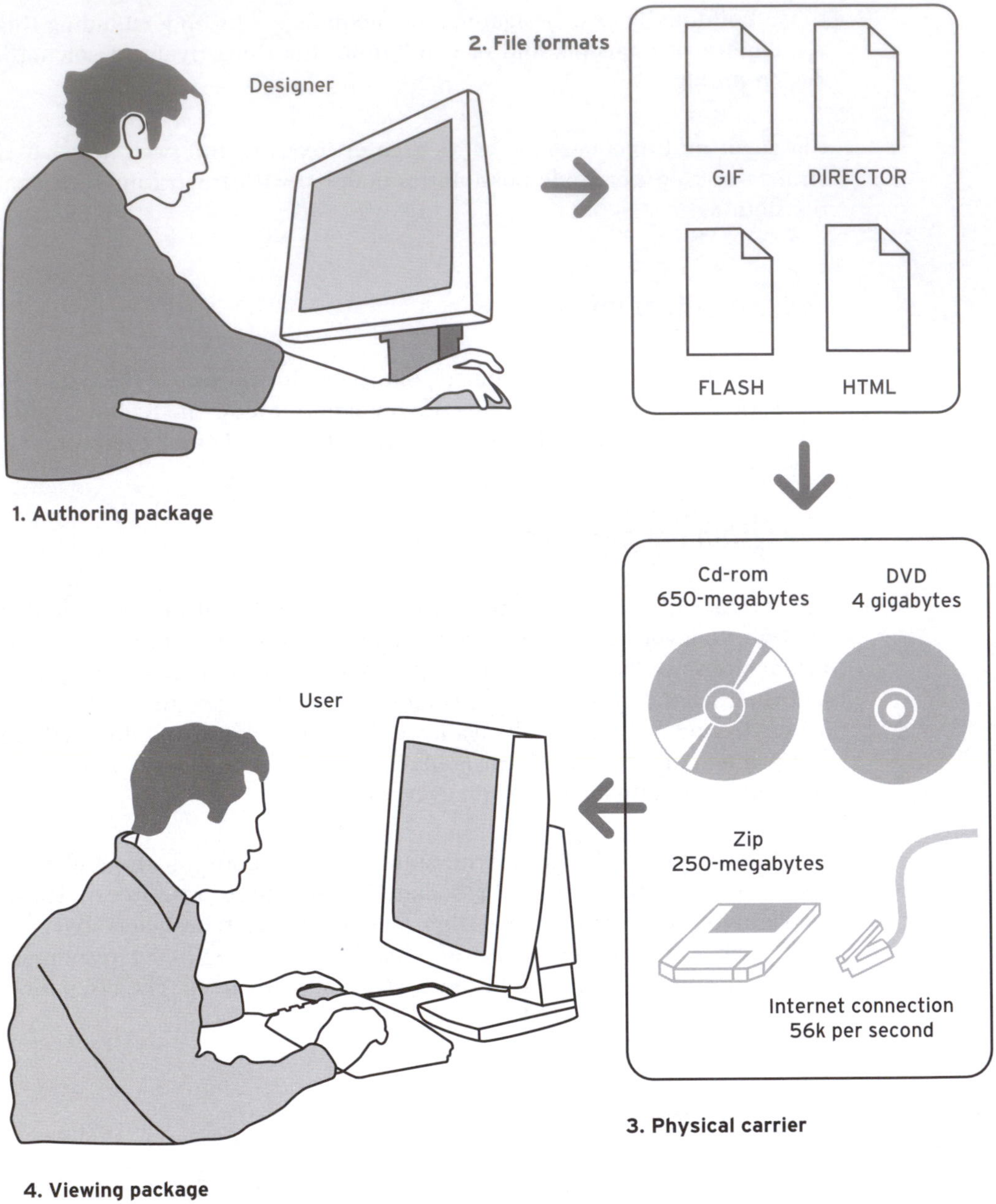

2. File formats

Designer

GIF   DIRECTOR

FLASH   HTML

1. Authoring package

Cd-rom
650-megabytes

DVD
4 gigabytes

User

Zip
250-megabytes

Internet connection
56k per second

3. Physical carrier

4. Viewing package

Figure 2.1: Four things that can restrict the design vocabulary.

However, a common problem, albeit for different underlying reasons in the different media, are delays associated with the transfer and display of the information. The cd-rom and other data carriers have delays in accessing the content, while the internet has delays in downloading the content through the computer connection with the internet.

File formats

Even with the simplest tangible thing such as a picture or a chunk of text there are many different ways of storing it digitally. Each of these ways has different pros and cons and can support different features. Consider pictures: there are many different file formats for storing images (JPEG, PNG and GIF to name but a few). Some of these formats just say: 'here is a picture made up of these colors in these places', while other picture formats can support more interesting possibilities. For example the GIF image format also supports extras such as transparency; you can say: 'here is a red line on a white background and I want the white background to be transparent so that wherever I put the picture of the line you can see the background through the bits that were white'.

In these and many other cases the file format is one of the things that defines what is possible with the medium. If the file format does not include a certain effect or property, then to all extents and purposes it is impossible. The possibilities become part of the building blocks available to the designer; they are part of their design vocabulary.

WEBCODE
early html

HTML, the web layout language
The language used for the layout of web pages is also a way of encoding information that possesses certain features and not others. Learning to use HTML is partly a case of learning the special codes (tags) to do things in the language and partly learning what the things are that you can do.

Authoring programs

Authoring programs are the software packages that are used by the designers to design and build things using certain file formats as discussed above. As an example of how file formats and authoring programs work together, let us look again at the GIF image format. There are many authoring programs for making images and the majority of them can save an image as a GIF image. Although many authoring programs allow you to save the image as GIF, not all of them offer you tools to use the transparency option. So you have a case of the authoring program allowing you to get to grips with only some of the things that are possible in the file format.

Let us look at another example – a word processor. My computer screen can display all sorts of different colors and thus in theory I could display the text in my document in green. However, if that is not supported by the file format that my document is saved in then I will not be able to take advantage of green text. Furthermore, it could be a property of the file format but if control of that feature is not offered by the word processor then that possibility is again closed to me. The end result of my work, the document I am writing, is limited by the restrictions of the file format and the limitations of the word processor.

The same is true of multimedia authoring tools: if either the file format or the authoring tool does not allow me to play two different sounds at once then I cannot create a system where two different sounds are played at once, even if it is possible with my computer hardware.

Viewing it

As well as the limitation to what the designer can create discussed above, there is sometimes a limit to what the user can see. This is more subtle: designers are painfully aware of what they cannot make, but they often dash out complex designs with little thought to what the end-user can actually perceive of their designs.

Black and white television

In the early days of television, when color sets were just starting to replace black-and-white sets, you had a situation where programs were being broadcast to a public who had different viewing hardware with different capabilities. Since the majority of content being broadcast was not of a functional nature, there were not many problems associated with this mismatch. The only time the difference had a real impact on the viewers was in sports events making use of color coding. In this cross-over time between monochrome and color, the commentators reporting on sports events would often adapt their commentary to reflect this mix of viewers, taking time to give assistance to people unable to see the different colors of the players' shirts, the balls or anything else that was color coded.

That was a long time ago, but the same thing has happened with new media although in a much more pronounced manner. Information is distributed and there is no guarantee about what hardware and software people will be using to view it.

WEBCODE
fridge
browser

The boom in web services has also meant that all sorts of companies are keen to incorporate web access into their products in an effort to make their product the digital hub of the home. As well as computers and organizers, WAP-enabled mobile phones offer web access, cable TV services offer you internet on the television, ordinary land-line phones sometimes have e-mail access, game consoles let you browse the web and you can even buy fridges with built-in web browsers.

With cd-roms, differences in the users' technological base in terms of screen size/resolution and the speed of their computer meant that users

WEBCODE
hardware
and browsers

with different systems had very different experiences of the new media systems. That situation is far worse with the web, where there is a concerted effort to separate the content from the way that content is displayed, making the display of web-based content on different systems fraught with problems and quirks. Suffice to say that I am not going to go into all the details here but there are plenty of web sites where the differences in hardware and browsers' capabilities are well documented.

New technology = old restrictions

With an eye on the future it should be borne in mind that even with the apparent advances in technology solving all the restrictions, there is always some new form of technology just around the corner that is going to have the same restrictions all over again. The shift from black and white to color screens on personal computers happened years ago; later on it was followed by the same switch in laptop computers; another pause and the black and white screens of personal organizers have also made the switch to color. Most recently of all, mobile phones hitting the market now have color screens. In each case, designers had to design for a non-color display of information before color arrived.

Creativity with restraint

In conclusion then, new media is a strange mixture of frustrating restrictions and amazing possibilities. Coping with the restrictions is one thing but surely the amazing possibilities are a boon. I want to finish this chapter with a word of warning about those amazing possibilities. The key aspect of new technology is using it appropriately, with restraint. That means only using some new feature if there is a measured and arguable case for using it.

We can look back to the introduction of desk top publishing (DTP) for a parallel. With word processing, people could make a few mistakes in the layout and in alignment and the like, but when DTP arrived it offered them so much scope that awful graphic design became common-place. People felt they had to use all the tools and fonts at their disposal even if it resulted in annual reports that looked like the floor sweepings from a run-down letter factory.

By all means be creative, but remember that the phrase 'because it was there' may be a good line for mountain climbers but it is no justification for designers of new media.

Exercises

Creativity with restraint

Try to come up with examples of creative technologies where the technology offers the user a restricted vocabulary. I can think of two good examples. The first are filters for photography – round pieces of colored glass that are fitted onto the camera lens. There are lots of different types of filters, but at the end of the day you always come out with photos that look as if they have been taken with a filter.

Children's toys yield interesting results, and the second example is a child's sculpture kit I once saw, consisting of blocks of soft plaster containing pre-made sculptures in very hard plaster. The child could chisel away at the block of soft plaster and create . . . whatever it was that was buried inside.

WEBCODE
restraint

DVD-rom possibilities

When the cd-rom came in it was not just a new way of storing lots of data; it suddenly meant that large multimedia projects could be developed and distributed cheaply. The new DVD-rom way of storing stuff on cds means that we can now fit almost ten gigabytes onto a cd-rom (in the double-sided format). Will this just mean more data, bigger multimedia productions, or will it open the door to something completely new? Discuss . . .

WEBCODE
dvd

Technological cocktails

Often a new idea will emerge because of the combination of two or more types of existing technology. Consider the following three technologies that can be built in to mobile phones: digital cameras, internet capabilities and GPS (global positioning system – the phone effectively 'knows where it is' on the earth's surface).

Do some group brainstorming and see if there are any interesting ideas that arise from this combination. Have a look at chapter 16 on generating ideas as well.

WEBCODE
cocktail

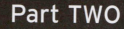

Part TWO

The elements

■ How this part relates to the other three parts

Elements are fundamental building blocks. Early alchemy revolved around the idea that everything was made up of the four elements (earth, water, fire and air). Modern chemistry expanded this to today's understanding of the chemical elements and the periodic table. Architects talk about the elements of building design. The artist John Ruskin wrote about the elements of drawing.

The elements of new media are the building blocks that combine together to make a new media system. In any medium, creative design also depends upon other factors, such as inspiration, enthusiasm, skill with the medium, knowledge of the medium, time to achieve the desired level of quality, access to the necessary resources and so on. However, all this is useless unless you have a good grasp of the building blocks, the elements in the field you are designing in.

What I want to do in this part is introduce the key building blocks of new media. I do not want to deal with them in great depth because there is not enough room for that. I want to deal with them in the wider context of designing new media. I want to show what layout is and what is important about it for new media design, and I want to do the same with color, animation and the rest. This is an extension of the ideas developed towards the end of the previous chapter about design vocabulary.

At the end of this part you will have the pieces to the puzzle and you will be aware that they are all part of something larger, but you still need the frameworks to put them all together to start making that 'big picture'. That will come in Part 3.

Media and the five senses

Before starting on the elements let us have a brief look at the five senses, since there is a degree of overlap between the elements and the senses. The senses can be divided into the 'remote senses' – those that operate at a distance – and the 'intimate senses' – those that normally operate at close range. I shall begin with the remote senses.

Vision and sound

Vision and sound are the senses that are used for things at a distance. I should, of course, point out that they can also fall into the category of intimate senses if the stimulus is of a particularly low level; consider listening to hear if a wrist-watch is ticking or looking at a very small object. However, in general they are the senses used at a distance and the senses that do not require actual contact with the things being sensed. This is one of the reasons why they are the two senses that are easiest to reproduce; thus they are the two key senses used in new media. They will each be dealt with in depth in the following chapters. However, the remaining intimate senses will be dealt with below as they are not broad enough in the new media context to warrant chapters of their own.

Smell

WEBCODE
odorama

There have been occasional attempts to create smell reproduction systems. One or two involved films with accompanying scratch-and-sniff cards for the cinema visitors who were instructed to scratch and sniff the numbered areas on the card following the numbers that appeared in the corner of the screen. The most renowned one was John Waters' 'odorama' film *Polyester*. Personally I don't think the idea will catch on quite yet though ('...and the nominations for the Oscar for Best Aromas are...').

Having said that, there are several examples of non-complex/non-digital use of smell for feedback. In the Netherlands the millers used to grease the main axle of their windmills with pig fat. As well as making it run smoothly this had an extra bonus – the smell. When a miller is working in his mill he has little visual feedback about how fast the sails are turning. This information has to be built up from other forms of feedback. One of these is the smell of the fat. As the axle turns faster, the fat starts to heat up and burn, and this smell provides a good indication of the speed of the mill.

The second example are the 'stench alarms' used in some mines in South Africa. If there is a gas or water leak resulting from a pit fall then there is a good chance that any electrical method of sounding the alarm deep below ground is also out of action. The stench alarm mixes a pungent smell with the air being circulated through the mine. This spreads very quickly and is totally independent of complex technological systems such as radio, cabling etc.

One day smell will become a part of new media systems – initially as part of large entertainment presentations in

WEBCODE
smell

cinemas and museums and then later as part of systems at home. But for that to happen researchers will have to do three things: isolate the building blocks of smell, find a way of reproducing them and finally find a way of doing it all in a commercially viable manner.

Taste

WEBCODE
natural
history

The situation I have described above is more extreme for taste. It involves a more direct contact, limited to only a few areas of human activity, and a solution is even further in the future. While a full investigation of the role of taste in our interactions with the world around us is inappropriate for the scope of this book, it is nonetheless a fascinating subject and the reader is referred to Diane Ackerman's wonderful book of sensory perception *A Natural History of the Senses*.

Touch

There are three important aspects to touch. First there is texture: what things feel like against your skin. Secondly there is shape: the fact that you can build up an idea of the spatial form of something by exploring it with your hands. Finally there is haptic information which stems from the muscular resistance that you feel when you press or move physical objects.

Textures are notoriously difficult to reproduce; only in the last decade have designers started to get visual textures right with computer graphics. Tactile textures are far more subtle in nature.

WEBCODE
touch

Shape may seem impossible, there are three-dimensional output devices that can create three-dimensional models from computer data, but they take hours to produce anything and are used for model making, not real-time, interactive feedback. However, limited things can be achieved in this direction with tactile mice – mice where a small pad of pins under the finger tip moves up and down as the user moves the mouse over things on the screen.

Accessibility

Any discussion of the five senses must include the issue of what happens to design when the users have problems with those senses – so-called 'design for accessibility'. This is a tricky area; it is a valid part of usability design but is bound up with complicated issues such as our own prejudices and fears and uncomplicated issues such as failing to realize that the issue even exists.

I have a slight disability. I have problems inputting proper text on the computer. In days gone by I used to have to get someone to assist me. Nowadays, thanks to advances in computer technology, I have computer-based aid to help me with my problem . . . it's called a spell checker. Amusing, and flippant perhaps compared with someone who is blind, but the point I want to make is that disability is not clear-cut, it is a sliding scale. To some extent, many of us are disabled, there are just different degrees. Around 8% of all male users are color blind, huge numbers of people have poor eyesight, many people cannot spell, some cannot read or write very well. As we get older we may still possess all our faculties, but they are all a bit slower/weaker than they used to be. One person has suggested that instead of the term 'disabled' we should introduce a term for the opposite: 'temporarily able-bodied'.

What is it then that makes this sliding scale of ability seem so clear-cut? The answer is *design*. If I design something where someone with a certain degree of visual ability cannot read it, then the design *itself* creates the border between those that are able to read the information and those that are unable (disabled). It is in effect the *designer* that has rendered the user disabled.

WEBCODE
accessibility

Currently, much of accessibility for digital media is tied up with the guidelines and laws connected with disabled access to information. The area is getting sorted out, although the guidelines still vary from country to country. As this is an introductory text on new media design, accessibility in design is one of the specialist subjects that is outside the book's scope and it is enough that the reader is aware of the issue and can track the latest developments and guidelines on the web.

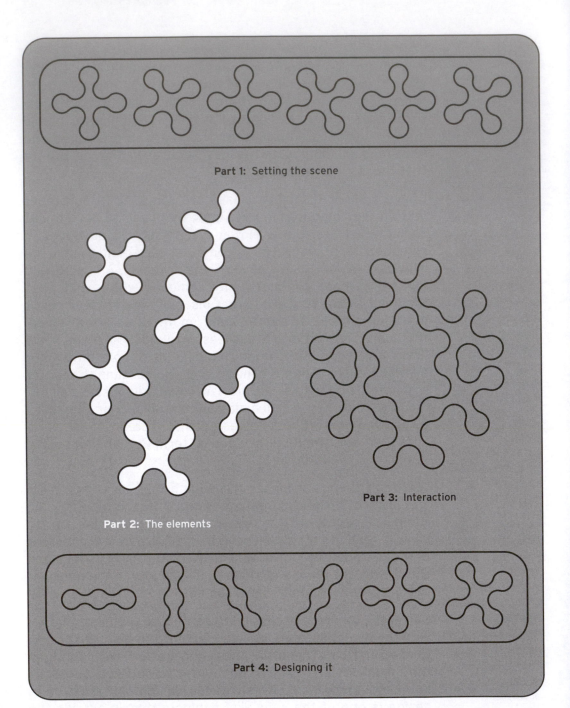

Part 1: Setting the scene

Part 3: Interaction

Part 2: The elements

Part 4: Designing it

Figure Part 2: How this part relates to the other three parts.

Text

Introduction

This chapter is aimed primarily at the design of web sites or other text-rich new media applications, but it is also of relevance to more classical multimedia with a high degree of text content. Certain points, such as consistency, are vital even if the new media system has a minimal amount of text in it. It also has a high relevance for applications that do not use text but that use speech fragments embedded in an interactive structure, for example interactive telephone services.

The next chapter will deal with text from the point of view of pure layout: paragraphs, fonts, legibility and so forth. This chapter is going to concentrate on what the text is actually saying: the functional and stylistic aspects of the *content* of text, from writing scannable text through to writing for dynamic content.

A new skill

In modern-day life there is an assortment of different media and each of them demands its own style of writing. There are writers skilled in writing for the theater, film scripts, brochures, novels, adverts and many other areas. These writing styles are often very different from one another and it is dangerous to assume that one can employ an expert in one area to produce text for another area. For example, the chances that a good brochure writer would be able to write a winning film-script are quite low.

When we come to producing textual content for new media systems it becomes apparent that this is yet another area demanding specialized text-writing skills and it should not be assumed that an expert in advertising texts or scripts will have the necessary skills to do the job.

The roots of text for new media lie in 'hypertext': collections of text documents that are interconnected with links, so that the user can follow links from one chunk of information to another. Until recently, large-scale development and research in the area was hampered by the lack of a general, widely used and easy-to-author hypertext system. With the advent of the web all that has changed; authoring hypertext and hyper-media (hypertext mixed with other media types) is now well and truly out of the research world and into the commercial world.

The internet and the web have provided a global platform for hypertext and hypermedia information. The impetus given by this development, and the ability of the internet to capture popular attention, have resulted in a huge increase in this sort of information. The audience is expanding, the amount of information available on the web is expanding, and finally the medium itself is becoming more mature, supporting more possibil-ities for layout, animation and interaction. In short it is high time that writing text for new media applications was recognized as a specialized task in its own right.

Writing text for new media properly requires the investment of having it done by a specialist. However, there are lower investment approaches, namely training existing text-writing staff to do the job or, as a last resort, simply copying text from a different medium into the new media system, having first made any changes necessary to ensure the text is suitable for the web or other new media systems. Basically it is a question of apply-ing the guidelines described in this chapter. Bear in mind, though, that taking a large chunk of textual material and spending time changing it to make it suitable for the web could end up taking more time than writing it from scratch.

Text: the king of content

The world of new media is dominated by flashy graphics, animation, video and sound. Why should anyone concern themselves with the design of the textual content? There are a number of reasons why text is still the king of content.

It is the first step with new technologies

Textual characters are simple; they do not need much technology. As a result new digital media usually start off with text-only information before progressing to black and white graphics, color graphics, and then sound and video.

This progression has been followed with computers, starting with the old alphanumeric terminals, then the bit-mapped screens (loads of little black and white dots) of the early Macs and Suns, then color screens, then sound reproduction and video capture and encoding. We are also nearing the end of it with the web; initially the internet was used for simple text communication, then images and text with layout, gradually richer media and more possibilities and now it can be used with ease for sound, music and video. The same route is also being followed by information on mobile phones and there are bound to be technologies yet to be invented that will also tread this path.

Its content is easy and open

Flat text is a very easy medium; it is easy to generate in comparison with other media. Few people can make an animation or a graphic presentation but many can quickly produce text content. You do not need expensive technology, you just need a keyboard.

Text is an open medium; it can easily be split up (chunks and pages) and given structure (links). The richer varieties of media in new media are the time-based ones of video and sound and these are linear in nature because of the difficulties in splitting them up easily. Making video clickable and browsable is a research challenge, while making sound interactive leads to slow and clunky interactions like those with interactive telephone services.

The content of text is easy for computers to analyze, meaning that content can be indexed and searched; a computer will know if the word 'dog' appears in a piece of text, but it cannot tell if there is a dog in a piece of video. Textual content is easy to print out even on the most antiquated of printers and it is accessible to non-sighted users since it can be 'read out' by screen-reading technologies.

Sometimes text is all there is

The web is still struggling with bandwidth issues. Busy sites and slow internet connections mean that it is faster to download text-based information without pictures. To facilitate this companies sometimes design text-only or low-graphics sites for users with limited connection capabilities. Where this is not the case users themselves will sometimes take unilateral action and choose to download web sites with the graphics switched off in their browser, meaning that they just download the text bits of pages. It is faster for them but if the site is not designed to facilitate this, the end result can look a mess. Once again, accessibility comes into the picture since any site that is not designed for viewing without images will be rendered unusable for users that rely on screen-reading technology.

It will not be like this for long

The flexibility of text described above is temporary and it will only be a matter of time before graphics, sound and video reach a level of manipulation that similar functionality can be built into them – clicking on certain objects within a running video to switch to another chunk, seamless video joins where different threads are followed within an interaction, automated recognition and indexing of content and so on. Also, users are changing. Exposure to TV and other media means that users could become more literate in other media types than text.

WEBCODE
text to video

However, it should be stressed that text will always be a valid medium in its own right. Even when other media get a foothold in the world of information distribution, text will still occupy a sizable part of the communication of information. Consider the small inroads that media such as television and radio have made on the book and the newspaper, both of which are still very much alive. This book is predominantly text as well. Although new forms of media will make inroads into the world of information communication, there will always be a corner of new media that is forever text.

Designing text for consumption

There is an interesting pattern developing in modern-day eating habits. We in the western world are changing from eaters to grazers. What that means is that we used to sit down for a definite meal three times a day, but nowadays the average office worker 'grazes' throughout the day, snacking on things here, eating a few sandwiches there, grabbing a bite on the train on the way home. Food consumption has become a nebulous background task.

To some extent the same is true of information. We used to sit down and have big information sessions: a visit to the library, an hour-long documentary on the television, a day of courses at university. Today, with a web browser running in the background on our computer desktop, we can continually dip into information while we are working or waiting for the computer to do something or waiting for the meal to cook. This change in the consumption patterns of information (once referred to as 'gargling at the fountain of knowledge') is being reflected in the way that information is designed.

One of the leading banks conducted a research program concerning how customers read their leaflets. One interesting finding was that a reader will often pick a leaflet up and flick through it from the back to the front (this sounds strange until you give it a try yourself and realize how natural an action it is). As a result, the bank redesigned the leaflets to support this behavior as well as the conventional front-to-back reading behavior. Have a look at leaflet design next time you are standing in a queue in the bank. Novels and stories rely on a linear narrative and thus they must be read from front to back. Other, more functional information in printed form is very rarely read from start to finish in a linear fashion. I have a copy of Don Norman's *The Design of Everyday Things* that I have never actually read cover-to-cover, but I have dipped into it so frequently that I must have covered it all at least seven times.

WEBCODE
reading

In part, the structure on the web could just be reflecting this change in behavior and in part it could be helping it to happen. Whichever way around it is, the end result is that text content has to be designed to fit the reading habits of the users.

Goals, audience and scope (GAS) analysis

Despite these changes in our relationship to information there are many ideas relating to existing text that are still highly applicable. Especially the parallels between text production for new media and text production for marketing and communication purposes. Certainly for one screen-full or 'eye-full' of information the rules are much the same as classic advert text: succinct, crisp, catchy and to-the-point. There is already a large degree of good literature on this subject so I will not cover it in depth. One thing I will mention is GAS. GAS stands for goals, audience and scope. These are the three important factors when setting out to design any sort of communication, be it conventional or digital.

The *goals* are what you want to achieve with your communication. Do you just want to inform people about something? Do you want to inform them and have them remember it? Do you want to persuade them to do something? Do you want them to use a new information source within an organization instead of an old one?

The *audience* are the people you are communicating with or, more accurately, those that you want to communicate with.

The *scope* is the range of the communication. What media types are going to be included? What are the boundaries of the information? How up to date is it going to be?

This is how GAS applies to text content, but the same ideas can apply equally well to other types of media. The whole subject is covered in more depth in chapter 9.

Scannable text

Broadly speaking, the content of new media systems can be either informative or entertaining or a bit of both. Here, I am going to concentrate on informative text. The essence of informative text for new media is that it should be highly 'scannable'; readers should be able to review the text and get an idea about the content before they actually dive in and start reading properly. Indeed in some cases readers will get what they need just by scanning and will not have to read the content in detail. To assist in making the text easily scannable, there are a few guidelines.

Inverse pyramid structure

Basically you want to get the information to the user as clearly and as quickly as possible, so begin any lengthy text document with the conclusion. The user can read this and see if this is all the information they want. If they decide they want more then they can read more. If it is a large document you could even consider expanding this idea from 'summary and article' to 'summary, overview and article'.

You see a similar thing in large printed reports: busy middle management will not have time to read the whole thing, so any report author that is any good will include an 'executive summary' at the beginning. Another good parallel is the writing of press releases for distributing to the press. The opening sentence or two has to summarize what the press release is about and the press release in its entirety has to be as short and to the point as possible.

Bad examples

In the world of conventional media there are situations where this rule is turned around and the viewer/reader is deliberately not given an overview. The worst medium for this approach are the TV documentaries that revolve around one issue and spin them out for an hour or so. 'What sank the ancient British warship the *Mary Rose*?': instead of starting off with the findings of the latest research, the viewer is strung along for ages with different theories before the final conclusion is reached. Another example is that of the bill-boards used for selling newspapers. These are intended to sell newspapers, not to inform the public, so if the trial of Max Jones has just finished and he has been found guilty then the banners all say, 'Jones Trial: Final Verdict Reached' and leave the reader to buy the paper to get the actual news. In these examples the goal of efficient information communication is being sacrificed for the equally important goals of entertainment and commerce.

'Front loading'

'Front loading' is one of those macho, new media phrases that sound cool, which is good because you remember it and people like it when it is mentioned at meetings. The basic idea is pretty simple. Consider the list of links below in the form: explanation then link (the link is shown as underlined text):

> This part of the information deals with the design of textual content in new media systems. <u>Text design</u>.

> This part moves on to consider the functional role of layout and visual style in new media systems. <u>Layout design</u>.

It is generally better to reverse the layout so that you have the link then explanation:

> <u>Text design</u>. This part of the information deals with the design of textual content in new media systems.

> <u>Layout design</u>. This part moves on to consider the functional role of layout and visual style in new media systems.

WEBCODE
audio
browsers

Providing that the text of the link is well chosen (more about this later in the chapter) this arrangement will allow people scanning the text to read the link text and go on to read the explanation text only if they do not fully understand the link text. It also benefits visually impaired users relying upon an audio browser to read the text out. They can get to the links quickly without having to listen to loads of explanatory text first (although there are now audio browsers that allow the user to skip through the text and just listen to the link texts).

The idea can also be applied to paragraph structure since an important part of information extraction, which happens before extensive reading, is looking at the first few lines of the paragraph. To support this, one should ensure that the first lines are indicative of the content of the paragraph and not just a vague, nice bunch of sentences.

Short paragraphs

Huge paragraphs of text are completely unfathomable, even in conventional media. Keep paragraphs as short as possible, split large tracts of text up, be more extreme than in normal text for printed media.

Many headings

One thing that can be used to provide information about a tract of text before the reader reads it is to use plenty of headings to break the text up and give information about the coverage. Headings should be short and to the point, otherwise they simply add more text to the information.

Do not promote

Do not use promotional language, as it is a definite 'turn-off' for users. On a functional level it interferes with efficient information communication and on an emotional level it can make them feel patronized and silly. The majority of users know what they want and will react negatively if you are trying to present them with something that they do not want, especially if that presentation is phrased in verbose promotional terms. For example, I could have started this paragraph like this:

> **Another wonderful rule for writing text!**
>
> There is one more rule for text that is so useful it could empower your writers when they turn their attention to writing for new media. It is so simple and easy to apply that even after simply reading what it is, it will increase the efficiency of your web text by up to 72.4% . . .

Avoid 'fluffy' writing

What I am trying to get at here is that sometimes a document can have too much text or, to be more accurate, too much *superfluous* text – what I call 'fluff'. Cut this out.

Do not say 'If you want more information on our products then click on this button', accompanied by a button labeled 'click for more information'. Instead, just have one link with the text 'more product information'.

Writing consistent text

When writing one page of text it is easy to ensure consistency; often it happens automatically. With a collection of interlinked documents the issue of consistency becomes more important and needs to be dealt with explicitly, especially as a site starts growing with contributions from other people, contributions gathered over a period of time etc. In such a situation the consistency can be difficult to manage. Consistency is important in a number of different areas.

Consistent 'tone of voice'

Text can be written in many different styles, from formal and business-like ('executive summary of the key points to be actioned by the committee') to trendy and casual ('what's hot and what's not'). The key thing is getting it right and not overdoing it.

WEBCODE
tone of voice

Within a new media system the same 'tone of voice' needs to be used throughout the content to ensure a consistent communication to the reader. Exceptions include qualified references to other documents that do not use the same 'tone of voice' and separate sections of the site that are aimed at different target groups. For example, if you offer service to business managers and students (as a major bank does), then you will want to communicate with them in very different ways.

This point is especially true for some European languages where there are different ways of addressing someone: different ways of saying 'you' – a polite 'you' and a more formal 'you'. You need to decide which you are using and stick to it.

Consistent level of knowledge

A complex site involving much information and interactive services should have the textual part written on the basis of a very definite model of the user. Are they a first-time user of the internet or are they expected to be experienced users? Based on this model, text should be chosen to help the user with the site.

Getting this aspect wrong results in either experienced users feeling patronized by child-like explanations or new users getting confused. The worst example are sites that do both: the opening page explains in lengthy terms how to use the mouse to click on a button and then the second page assumes that the user knows about closed user groups and logins. Users with experience will find the mouse explanation frustrating while users will little experience will be thankful for the mouse training but will have problems when confronted with the complex stuff. The result is a system that is not satisfactory for either user group. (There is a good overview of different user backgrounds in chapter 10.)

Consistent direction of address

Occasionally the text will give instructions to the user. The more inter-active the site, and the more computer illiterate the audience, then the more instructions the site will contain. The direction of address must be consistent throughout; in other words the same entity must be emphas-ized in the instructions, you (the user), me (the system) or neither (neutral). Consider an instruction to the user to click on a button to delete a message:

> You can click on the button to delete the message

> I will delete the message when the button is clicked

> Clicking on the button will delete the message

Consistent pronouns

Another variation of the above is using different pronouns to talk about the user. Pronouns are words such as I, you, they, we. When designing user-related titles and buttons, should the text on them take the 'I' form or the 'You' form? Thus, should the label on the personal profile page be 'My profile' or 'Your profile'? A BBC web site once had a frame in the main site within which were several other 'mini' sites. The designers had not agreed a format for addressing the user and so while the outer frame had a button 'Where I live', the site within the frame had a button 'Where you live.'

As well as applying to the person using the system, this point should also be considered when writing about other entities, for example a company or a product. Consider the following three different ways of discussing a company in a promotional, new media system:

> We are the world leaders in our field

> They are the world leaders in their field

> Zobular are the world leaders in their field

Consistent terminology in links and titles

Throughout an interlinked new media system there are clickable texts and buttons pointing back and forth to all the different interconnected elements in the system. These texts should all be consistent in their naming of the separate elements. Thus if the start screen has a title 'Start screen' there should not be links that claim to point to 'Start page' or 'First screen' etc.

A classic example is the award-winning 'Muzzy' language package produced for children, which is a brilliant integrated mix of video, cd-rom and cassette tapes. In the Italian video the hero of the cartoon is a gardener called 'Toni'. Switch to the Italian cd-rom though and the same character suddenly becomes 'Bob'. It was obviously designed with different names for the hero in the different languages but the management of the terms was not rigorous enough between the different development groups and so it ended up with a clash.

Capitalization in titles and headings

In a large collection of textual elements there may be titles and headings of different depths (first-level headings, second-level headings, diagram captions etc.). Designing consistent graphic styles for these levels of headings is important. However, one important part of the graphic style that is often overlooked is the pattern of capitalization. Basically it does not really matter which scheme you choose as long as it is used consistently. Here are the main options:

Just the first letter capitalized

Just the Letters for Key Words are Capitalized

All Words Start With A Capital

WHOLE TEXT IS CAPITALIZED

WEBCODE
menu capitals

Setting headings in all capitals may seem visually appealing; all the letters are the same size and shape, but text set in all capitals is not as easy to read as small case letters. There is an interesting exception here and that is that setting text in all capitals can be slightly more efficient in menus, where the emphasis is less on reading large amounts of text and more on recognizing textual shapes.

This may seem like a rather nit-picking thing to concentrate on but it is easy to do it consistently so it might as well be done. Furthermore, by deciding it at the beginning you avoid subsequent people having to think about it each time they write additional text for the system.

Text length

With the move from text on the printed page to text on the screen, strange things have happened to the idea of a page. Information no longer needs to be presented on bits of dead tree chopped up in sizes based on archaic units of length. Information can now be chopped up according to the inherent structure and coverage of the content. Although at once liberating, this effect does bring up new problems and questions: How long should a page be? When should we chop the information up?

Keep it short

The first thing we can say is keep the length short no matter what; unnecessary content will only slow down the reader trying to get information out or the reader trying to evaluate if the document is worth reading.

What is short?

Having used the word 'short' several times so far the next question is, 'What is short?' As with many issues surrounding the length and structure of content, there are no 'golden rules'. It all depends upon the nature of the content. Text should be as short as possible but long enough to say what it is that you want to say. Not only should it not contain extraneous information but the information that it does contain could probably be rewritten or restated so that it is more concise.

Keep length consistent if possible

One big effect of the move from the printed page to the screen is the loss of the physical nature of the page. A page can be of a length to suit its content. If a page contains a contact address it could just be a few words long, but if it contains the text of a scientific publication it could be a lot longer. In this case the user would see nothing untoward in the difference in lengths. However, there are situations where a user expects pages to be of similar lengths, for example, if there is a collection of similar chunks of information, issues of an online magazine, comparisons of cars, descriptions of touristic cities etc. It would be problematic if the page on San Francisco was just one paragraph while the page on New York was a huge collection of text and photos. Users would not be able to build up a good idea of the coverage of the information and would be disappointed if they were expecting a lot of information on a particular subject. Nor would they be able to classify the collection of information. It would be neither a good in-depth comparison of cities, nor a quick overview of them, but a rag-bag mix of the two.

The general rule is to strive towards similar length for collections of similar sorts of information.

Scrolling

An issue closely related to text length is that of scrolling. If the page is longer than the window displaying it then it will have to be scrolled to read the lower parts. This is acceptable, to some extent, if the page just shows one long article. Where scrolling starts to cause problems is if there is some visual or textual element that is better if the user can see the whole thing at once. Think of large diagrams or tables. The worst thing to have to scroll for is the navigation. This is something where it is far better if the user has the overview in one go. In the same way, it is awkward to choose a meal when you are in a restaurant with a menu printed on lots of small pages – you have to keep flicking back and forth to get an overview and compare things – it is far easier to have the menu all on one or two pages.

The best approach is to write the text in a structured manner and split it up logically. There is no way that you can completely avoid scrolling since the window size can be varied by the user and thus can always be smaller than the page size. Instead of trying to ban scrolling, it is better just to minimize it, using it only when necessary.

Funnily enough, lots of things are helping to sort this issue out. The designers are starting to split information up more effectively, the users themselves are changing and becoming more used to scrolling in documents and the hardware is changing as well with the introduction of mice with scroll wheels. As these become more common the hand–eye coordination problems associated with scrolling become less of an issue.

Above or below 'the fold'

A useful concept is one borrowed from the world of newspaper design. There they have the distinction between 'above the fold' and 'below the fold', referring to the top-half and bottom-half of the front page. The distinction was introduced because of the way papers are displayed, folded in the middle with only the top-half of the front page showing.

The idea is that this part that was showing should contain enough eye-catching things to make a punter want to buy the whole thing. As a result the top-half usually contains banner headlines, large photos and tasters relating to the rest of the content. In contrast, below the fold (the bottom-half) is usually fairly text-rich, with the occasional small picture.

In the world of the web and the scroll-bar this concept translates into above and below the scroll: just as a reader's first view of a newspaper is the part 'above the fold', so their first glimpse of a web site is the part 'above the scroll' – the part that they can see without having to scroll. This is the part that has to grab their attention and provide all the key navigational functionality.

Structuring long texts

Sometimes a text has to be long. It may be a direct copy of a printed document or it just may not be possible to condense it further. A long text needs to be structured. It needs to have something done to it so that readers can quickly get an idea of the subject and progression of the text without having to begin reading at the beginning and read right through to the end. There are several approaches to this, and if necessary all the approaches can be used together. It is not a case of one or the other.

The main one to be dealt with here is structuring the text by means of the writing. This is another of the side-effects of using plenty of headings throughout a text. It provides structure to the text and, more importantly, that structure is tangible to the user without them having to read the text in detail. The textual content of the headings gives clues as to the structure. If numbering is used then that also provides information about how the content is structured. Finally, the style of the different levels of headings provides valuable feedback about how the sections and sub-sections relate to one another.

The other two approaches to communicating the structure will be dealt with in later chapters. Chapter 4 on layout will look at ways of emphasizing the structure of a body of text by utilizing more layout possibilities than just headings. A simple example is using indented paragraphs for citations. Chapter 13 will deal with presenting structure by breaking the document up into smaller chunks and linking these together.

Here in this chapter there is still much to say about the relationship between links and text.

Links and meta-information

WEBCODE
links

I think it is a Peter Sellers *Pink Panther* film where he shouts 'I am leaving for Africa!', opens the door to leave and walks straight into the broom cupboard! It is important to know what is behind doors before you go through them. Likewise with links in new media systems: it is helpful (indeed vital) for the user to know where the link leads to before they click on it.

Before discussing the writing of text for links I should say that links are examples of what in the jargon is called 'meta-information'. Meta-anything sounds strange but it is a fairly simple concept. Basically, meta-information is just descriptive information. Meta-information is information about information. If I were to hand you a book and say, 'This is a good book on design and it's got 50,000 words in it', then that would be meta-information. It is not information in the book but information about the book. The blurb on the book jacket also falls into this category.

In the world of selling books, the meta-information on the book jacket helps the reader make a decision about investment. They decide whether to invest money and buy it. In the world of new media, meta-information plays a similar role. The information is fragmented and interlinked and the user needs to know about a chunk of information before they invest time and effort in reading it or downloading it, especially if that information is slow to download or will interrupt their current flow of reading.

With this in mind it is important that readers are well aware of what information is behind the link before they actually click on it. Sometimes the content is clear from the context of the link, but if there is any doubt then the graphic or text that forms the link should indicate what the content is.

The classical bad example is clicking on a link and waiting ten minutes to download a stereo sound file which turns out to be a recording of the company director saying 'Welcome to our web site'! My favorite example is the page from an early Schiphol Airport web site, which described the fax facilities available at the airport. The text 'fax machines' was clearly a link but it was unclear what it linked to. What would you get when you clicked on it? Instructions on how to use the fax, a map of where they are perhaps? No, you got a huge and slow image of someone using a fax machine; no use whatsoever.

Phrasing of the link

If a piece of text is a link then what should you write in it? Should you just use your normal writing style and join a few words up to form the link or should you explicitly acknowledge the link. Research has shown that 8 to 20 words in a link is a good length, but this is by no means a rule; you cannot make a link a good one just by cramming a certain number of words into it. Here are a few approaches to link texts with the words underlined forming the link.

Gather links at the end of the page

One of the better approaches is to gather all the relevant links together and put them in a separate part of the page, top or bottom or in the margin somewhere. It is important that the links are self-explanatory as they have been taken away from the context that explains them.

> ... The company has a good financial grounding and is active in the export market ...

> More about the company:
> Financial background
> Management
> History

Link from ordinary text

Another good way is simply to link a well-worded part of the text to the appropriate information like this:

> The company has a good financial grounding and is active in the export market.

The drawback is, of course, that the text may not contain a suitable piece of text that can act as the link.

Include the link in brackets

The drawbacks with the above method can be solved by including a suitably worded link in brackets.

> The company has a good financial grounding (<u>financial informa-tion</u>) and is active in the export market.

This gives the author the freedom to add links easily and without too many constraints on the text that forms the link.

Add instructions to the link

Instructions could be added to the link:

> The company has a good financial grounding (<u>click here for financial information</u>) and is active in the export market.

Generally this is necessary only when dealing with a user group that has absolutely no exposure to the web, and even these users will quickly learn that text of a particular color and underlined can be clicked on. If you really think it is necessary to explain it then simply put a general statement at the top of the page that underlined text can be clicked on with the cursor for more information.

Just have a standard link in brackets

Although this looks like a good consistent approach it comes with the same drawbacks as the 'link from ordinary text' above, as the exact nature of what the link points to is only indicated by the text that it is near, and sometimes this will not be enough (consider its use in the fax example earlier).

> The company has a good financial grounding (<u>more information</u>) and is active in the export market.

A further drawback is that, when this approach is used on a web page, users with visual difficulties who rely on an audio browser can (with a suitable browser) just skip through and hear the link texts. In this case they would just hear, 'more information, more information, more information'. Not helpful at all.

Printing text

Occasionally readers will want to print information out, so bear this in mind when writing links. If the link style is a different color without underlining then it may not be clear that it is a link in a black and white print-out. Look back at the examples above and think about how clear they would be without the underlining showing what the link is.

Do not litter the text with links

As with any new technology there is always the temptation to overuse it; to think 'Gee! I can make a piece of text a link' and then to make every other word a link or cross-reference. The result of this is a text so littered with links that it can be difficult to see where one link ends and another one begins, while the chopping and changing of the colors degrades the legibility.

Adding links to text within a body of text should be done with restraint, and should follow a coherent strategy so that users have a good idea of what sort of links to expect. For example if your information relates to the stock-market then having a link to stock prices every time you mention a company means that the text is indeed riddled with links but, because these are all the same sort of information, it is less distracting. The user does not have to stop every few words to guess at what a link points to.

Telling the user what the link points to

Are they external or internal links?

For the user there is a great difference between a link that points to more information within your collection and a link that points to information elsewhere on the web. For this reason the difference between the two should be made clear. Often this difference will be clear from the wording and context of the link but other approaches include using a difference in appearance or grouping such links together in a well-defined part of the page layout (see chapter 4 on layout).

Is it a link to something big?

With bandwidth limitations or with things on a cd-rom that require a degree of loading or initiation the user needs to be forewarned of this. They need to know what they are getting and how long they will have to wait to get it.

Is it a link to a sound?

Avoid anything that includes an unexpected media type. Sounds especially can be off-putting to users if they start up unexpectedly. The classic bad scenario is a computer on a stand at an exhibition that includes unexpected sound – a sure way to frighten visitors away (more in chapter 6 on sound).

Does it require something that the user may not have?

It is pointless waiting ages for a well-publicized item of content only to discover, when it has downloaded, that you do not have the correct software to view it. This used to happen with the earlier versions of web browsers, but these days you experience problems only if you are viewing something out of the ordinary. Even so, this is no reason not to use novel software; it is simply a case of warning the user about the situation and providing them with links to download the software that they need.

You should think carefully about scaring users off, though. If they just want to order something with an order form that they print off from the web site then you do not want to make them have to download a piece of software in order to print out the order form. However, if the user wants to see some wonderful, whizz-bang examples of new media that you are offering, then they may be willing to spend a while downloading the latest software to view it.

Is it relevant to them?

Of course, the key thing users want to know is, is the information relevant to them? They want to be sure that the information is what they are looking for, that it will answer some question they have or that it will entertain them. If they are convinced of this then they will be willing to wait, fill in huge forms, update their software or whatever else is necessary in order to view it.

Other meta-information

We have had a good look at the idea of meta-information in links, telling the user about the information before they start looking through the information. Now let us look at a few other important examples of meta-information. The first is of relevance to cd-roms and the web, the home-page. To some extent this is just part of the content but to some extent it is the meta-information for the whole new media system.

The home-page

In chapter 15 on narrative I shall discuss the importance of the first five seconds of an interaction. This is a very general idea that plays a part in all aspects of design for people, but here I shall just look at the part text plays in this area.

The entrance to a physical building is the first contact that a visitor will have with a company. Architects designing offices for a particular company try to reflect the company image and ethos in the design of the entrance and the lobby; they try to make it imposing ('we are a big company'), yet hospitable ('welcome in if you have business with us'), efficient ('we know what we are doing') and solid ('we are going to be here for a long time').

Similarly the first five seconds of interaction with a new media system are important. If a user has paid for a cd-rom they are probably willing to get to grips with the information, but if it is a web site then if that user gets frustrated or bored with your pages in the first few seconds the chances are that they will whizz off somewhere else.

The two Qs

So what should the first page be? It should not just be inviting, it must also be informative. It must meet the initial question of users with fast and clear answers. The role of the first page with regard to functional textual information is the two Qs: Qualify and Quantify the information. Qualify it: What is this site? Who has put it together? What information is available here? Quantify it: How up to date is it? How much information is there here? What we are talking about is meta-information again, but meta-information about the whole site rather than just about one document.

Hidden meta-information

On the web, as well as the meta-information described above that accompanies or is directly part of the text, there is also meta-information that is not visible as part of the text but is associated with the page and presented or used elsewhere in the web browsing technology.

Titles

Web pages have a title. This is different from the headings that appear on the page; it is text that does not appear in the body of the page but appears at the top of the window in the title bar. Although it may not seem important and is easy to overlook, it is the text that is used when a user makes a bookmark to the page (or, in Internet Explorer parlance, adds the page to their list of 'favorites'). Usually titles make much use of their context for the interpretation. If I am reading the web site for a company called Zobular, and I click on 'products', then a page with the title 'what's new?' is clear. Take it out of context and after a period of time the text 'what's new?' in my list of bookmarks becomes meaningless. The key is to include some of the context in the title. 'New products at Zobular' for example.

A related approach is to record the sections that the user is in so that every time they click to another sub-section that choice is reflected in the title (this sort of information is often included in the page itself; see chapter 14 on navigation). Our example would thus be 'Zobular – Products – What's new?' The only danger here is that these sorts of titles can get long and if the user has a narrow window containing the bookmarks then the end part of the title will be cut off, and that happens to be the most important part!

Keywords to support searching

WEBCODE
meta-tags

A new copy-writing concept on the web is the meta-tag (once again that buzz-word crops up!). These are invisible bits of information added to the document. The reader does not see them, but the meta-tags are used by search engines and other automatic systems to help classify the information in the web page. Meta-tags come in various types, but the main one I want to consider here is the keyword. Keywords are the words that you want associated with that particular web page: if users are searching for those words then you want them to be directed to your page.

The skill lies in choosing the set of words that your target group is likely to use when searching for the information that you are supplying. Here are a few pointers.

Include misspellings

If the word is even slightly complex think about how people could misspell it. I was once showing the web to someone who was interested in osteopathy but had not used the web. When we searched for web pages on the subject there were only one or two, and they were not impressed. Later I realized that we had spelt the word wrongly and had found pages that also happened to have spelt it wrongly in the same way.

Try misspelling a word in a search engine and see how many pages there are that also misspell it. A good example is 'millennium'. The point here is that if the authors can misspell it then people searching can also make the same mistake. So if you did a web site about the millennium then it would be a good idea to put keywords in for 'millenium, milennium, milenium' etc.

Localize yourself
Add some words to pin-point the town and country that you operate in. Sometimes people are searching for information about their own town or for a provider of a particular service that is close to them, or at least in the same country.

Include associated and better-known terms
Include terms that the target audience may be familiar with and may search on. For example, some companies are less well known than their products: PhotoShop is from the company Adobe, the game 'The Sims' is from a company called Maxis etc. The product names are what the average user is going to be familiar with, and search on, so make sure these are in the keywords.

Think about different languages or spellings
If I am selling antique brass faucets and I can supply to both the UK and the US then I ought to have the keywords 'tap' and 'faucet' in my web site pages.

Identify good starting pages within the site and attach keywords to them
The idea behind keywords is not to attach them to every single page in a web site: users searching for something may be confused by suddenly entering a site at the 'lower levels'. Conversely if all the keywords are packed into the home-page then users will still have to do a lot of navigation and clicking about once they find your home-page in a search engine. Identify the best starting points for information that users are likely to be searching for and add keywords to them. Find a good balance between the two scenarios above.

Don't tell keyword lies
Do not include keywords that have nothing to do with your content. If you use popular terms such as 'MP3', 'sex' or the names of your competitors you may attract more users to your site, but they will not stay around for long when they discover that you have lied to them.

To draw a real-world analogy, if you owned a specialist bookshop on design you could increase the number of people visiting it by hanging a big sign outside saying 'RESTAURANT'. Although visitor numbers would increase, you probably would not sell more books and you would certainly get some irate visitors.

Breaking the rules

Having said all this about the importance of meta-information I ought to point out that there are instances where it is interesting for the user to discover what lies behind links themselves but these are instances usually connected with entertainment products and not with functional products.

Text and interaction

Earlier, I looked at what sorts of phrases to include in the text that forms a clickable link. Complex web sites can involve a high level of interaction and part of this interaction is usually built around text, so we need to have a look at the role of text in interaction.

Choice of terms for buttons

WEBCODE
bad word

Often links are extracted from the text and clustered in a separate part of the page. These links then form navigational buttons to browse the site and move from one page to another. The choice of text for these buttons has a big influence on the usability of the whole. Even one badly chosen word can introduce an element of ambiguity into the interface. The texts used in such navigational buttons should be:

Simple
Do not be funny or use jargon. Choose simple words, descriptions or concepts that the user is already familiar with.

Short
The width of a column of buttons is governed by the width of the longest text. Keep the text to a single word or as short a phrase as possible. Think about other ways of saying what you want to say; if it is shorter make sure that you have not sacrificed clarity for length.

A good example is the replacement of 'List in alphabetical order' with the simple 'A–Z'.

Unambiguous
If there are two or more similar concepts in the collection of buttons, the texts chosen should distinguish adequately between them.

Sometimes the choice of text can be confusing due to the nature of the content of the new media system. If any confusion can arise then a different term should be chosen.

For example a cd-rom-based annual report contains a section detailing how well the institute met its operational costings. This is accessed through the button termed 'Performance'. However, imagine that the report is for an arts center. In this context 'Performance' could be taken to mean something connected with performance art. A safer, less ambiguous term could be 'Figures' or 'Financial targets'.

Paired
In many new media environments user actions come in pairs: create/delete, show/hide etc. Make sure that buttons have pairs and that you are not missing key functions from the interface. Also, choose words for the pairs that go well together; that match in terms of what they are saying and meaning.

Further information on buttons is contained in the next chapter on the influence that layout has on lists and navigation buttons.

Legacy terminology

Watch out for terminology growing in the project and then making its way into the interface. This happens with technical terminology and shorthand terminology.

Technical terminology

Sometimes the technical language of the system developers makes it into the interface and we get buttons such as 'save this query' instead of 'save this search', or 'no records found for those parameters'. Users are starting to get used to more technical language in the interface but by keeping it non-technical you ensure that more users can understand it.

WEBCODE
hospital

The worst offenders for this in the real-world are the signs in hospitals. They are all phrased in technical, medical terms or three-letter acronyms. This means that the people who work there can understand them but probably do not need them as they already know their way around, while the people who *do* need them – the visitors or patients in the hospitals – have difficulty with them. One of the few research studies in this area found that terms such as 'cytology' and abbreviations such as 'OPD' were understood by less than 5% of the general public.

Shorthand terminology

When developing a new media system there are many discussions about the project and shorthand terms start appearing and being taken up by the staff. Eventually the terms can become so deep-seated that they end up getting built into the user interface without anybody thinking about whether they are appropriate.

Consider the cd-rom project that involved a large body of information with an accompanying short overview of it. In the meetings these two parts got abbreviated to 'fast section' and 'slow section'. These terms almost made it into the interface, where they would have been unclear, and certainly 'the slow section' would have had negative connotations. No one wants to choose to look at a 'slow section'. In the final design they were replaced with 'in a nutshell' and 'in depth'.

Different (English) languages

WEBCODE
english

The project mentioned above was aimed exclusively at the UK market. What if it had been aimed at the American market as well? In America does 'in a nutshell' mean 'in concise summary form' as it does in the UK, or does it just mean something inside the shell of a nut, which could be confusing if you are in the middle of a new media interaction? When we think of the differences between American English and UK English we usually think of the innocuous examples – 'sidewalk' instead of 'pavement', 'faucet' instead of 'tap' – but occasionally there are examples where the meanings are completely different.

Take the business and banking site that was offering a free pair of 'suspenders' to visitors who completed a questionnaire. In American English 'suspenders' means something businessmen use to hold their trousers up, and having a pair in a zappy color used to be a real fashion statement. In UK English 'suspenders' are the little elastic things that women use to hold silk stockings up and currently have erotic connotations. Not quite the thing for the business image of a leading bank.

This book is aimed at both the audience in America and the audience in the UK. Even here there are many items that have completely different names in the two languages. For example 'a sheet of A4' is a sheet of ordinary UK writing paper, but the paper size 'A4' is unfamiliar to many Americans; a cashpoint in the UK is an ATM (automatic teller machine) in America. What are the available methods to solve such problems?

Steer clear of problem words

Microsoft's Internet Explorer uses the term 'favorites' for web pages that users want to remember for later. Netscape calls them 'bookmarks'. The word 'bookmarks' steers clear of any problems with UK and US English since it is spelt the same in both languages. 'Favorites' is spelt differently. Although this is only a small point it is still worth considering properly: problems associated with it could be that non-US users associate it with the American market and there could be a perception that it is more geared up for browsing American pages than UK pages.

Choose one language and stick to it

Here again consistency is king. Early on in the design of any text-based new media system that uses English the decision should be made as to whether it is going to be addressing the UK or the American audience. The correct type of English should be chosen and this decision should then be stuck to throughout the whole project.

But be aware of the other language

However, there is always the chance that a user from the other language group will come into contact with the new media system. Even if you aim a system at one physical market there are still users in that place that may have emigrated, or are visiting or whatever. Thus it is still a good idea to stick to one style consistently but you must also be aware of the other and think about changing things if a key phrase is sensitive in the other language.

Use both languages and select as appropriate

If resources allow, the new media system could have the content realized in both languages. The decision about which version to use could be made automatically, for example on the web based on which web address the user uses (.com or .co.uk). Alternatively the decision could be made implicitly based upon user information such as 'please enter your postal address' or explicitly by asking the user if they want to read the content in US or UK English.

Other similarities

Of course there are many other flavors of English apart from those spoken in America and England and the same principles apply. Furthermore, many other continents have their own collections of languages and dialects, some vastly different and others surprisingly similar. Try to be aware of the words in your language that are similar to 'dangerous' words in other languages, especially if you expect people with a background in both to be reading your site.

Writing for changing content

With cd-rom-based new media the views of content can change. With the web the content itself can change.

A cd-rom-based system could offer the user the ability to search through information. The search results page that they see would then be a template that would always contain different content. Similarly a standard page layout could be used for large amounts of the same type of information. The textual content of the template, the framework that surrounds the content, has to be written to cope with different sorts of content. It is not good having the text 'your search found the following results' for all searches because many searches may return no results, and although the text is 'true' it is confusing for the user. The above is also the case with the web, although here even the content itself is capable of being updated every few minutes if necessary.

Time-neutral style

On the web we are used to information such as weather or stock prices changing dynamically, but other information also changes. Even information that seems to be quite neutral and fixed can still go out of date given enough time. Thus one should adopt a 'time-independent' style. Avoid writing things such as 'three years ago' and instead write 'in 2001'. Instead of 'we are planning to expand in this area next year', say 'it is expected that we will have expanded into this area in 2005'.

Other facts that are precise can be made more robust to the passage of time by deliberately making them imprecise. For example 'the company has 34 members of staff' will have to be updated every time someone joins or leaves, while 'the company numbers more than 30 members of staff' will not have to be updated as often and even when the company has 100 employees it will still be technically correct.

Cusp-related text

Many sites contain information that mirrors or shadows information in the real world as it changes. There are, however, some instances when a short passage of time can have enormous ramifications, especially around a 'cusp', a key transition or event in the passage of time. Very often such a cusp event is accompanied by a web site, for example the millennium, the launch of the Euro in Europe, a particular sports match, or a presidential election.

There will be much said both before and after the cusp event. The key thing is that it will be a different world after the event. This needs to be reflected in the content of the information.

Of course a cusp event does not have to be as earth shattering as a major person dying or an election being won. Even something as small-scale as a special offer on tickets has to be well orchestrated and managed on a site to ensure that it comes into force correctly on one day and disappears completely on another.

One classic example I came across was the site of a major political party that had on the home-page, 'What we would do if we won the election'. The day after the election the home-page was 'We have won', but there on the next page was 'What we would do if we won the election'.

Clearly the goal is to keep the site consistent with what is happening in the world. This does not necessarily mean that the information has to be removed from the site after a cusp event. It can be left there, but if so it must be *qualified*. In the case of our political party a link could have been given with a statement explaining that this was the information before the election was fought and won.

Exercises

Short terms
Imagine a new media system comprising a collection of examples of different styles of interaction - a cd-rom interaction scrapbook. Each example has a mini-demo, a title and they are roughly collected together into 10 or so categories such as 'tree structures', 'interacting with text' etc. A textual menu is needed to let the user choose between three ways of accessing the collection. They can either be ordered alphabetically on the titles, clustered together in categories or shown as a page of graphical 'thumbnails'.

WEBCODE
short terms

What would be good text to put in the menu to indicate these three choices as clearly as possible in as few words as possible?

Shorter headlines

Writing for limited screen space, and writing for the web in general, involves being terse and precise with your text. There are other media where this is also the case, for example the composition of banner headlines in newspapers.

Get hold of a newspaper and study the headlines used for the articles on the front page. Try to abbreviate them even more.

WEBCODE
headlines

A better term

In a particular search engine the results of a search for some terms that the user types in come back in a list. Each entry in the list (each hit) has a 'score'. The score is a value between 0 and 1 that indicates how good a correspondence there is between the user's search terms and the content of that thing that was found. It is automatically generated and depends on all sorts of things such as how often the user's search terms appear in the document, how close together they are etc.

WEBCODE
better term

Is the term 'score' a good one and is it a good idea to give it as 0 to 1? Discuss other ways of presenting the same information just by changing the terms and values, i.e. no bar charts, icons etc., just different text.

Replacing icons with text

Find a physical product or a new media system that employs icons in the interface. Design a set of textual alternatives to the icon set. Make sure that the texts are very short and clear in their meaning. Test out the icon version and your text version on different people to see which is the most effective.

WEBCODE
icons and text

Instruction game

This is a game for two people. One person tries to write clear instructions to achieve a simple task (brushing your teeth, making a cup of tea, ordering a book on a chosen web site etc.). The other person tries to come up with ways in which the instructions can be misinterpreted.

WEBCODE
instructions

Urban myths abound regarding the testing of user instructions for early computer systems. It really is an art to get them right.

Web addresses

There are many interesting examples of terminology and formats related to communication addresses such as e-mail addresses. If my name is Frank and I work at Zobular in the USA then my e-mail is probably something like frank@zobular.com, pronounced as 'Frank at Zobular dot com', easy to pronounce and the terminology possesses a certain logic to it; Frank really is 'at' Zobular! Far better than some internet providers who used to stick with the old telephone idea and issue people with e-mail numbers that were just as difficult to remember as phone numbers.

The early days of web sites saw other bad set-ups for the technology. A web address was called a URL (a universal resource locator – another bit of jargon) and always began with a bit of technical stuff: 'http://' followed by the longest letter in the alphabet to pronounce: 'w' repeated three times 'www' so that the first 11 characters you typed in were always the same and it took ages to pronounce them. Nowadays the browsers add them automatically and no one even bothers to quote them.

Imagine that you can overturn the entire system of web and e-mail addressing and replace it with a new one. What would be the priorities? What would be the first steps? How would you ensure that it was as simple/consistent as possible? Is it important to know which country the domain is registered in?

WEBCODE
new urls

Layout

WEBCODE
layout

Introduction

In the last chapter we looked at the content of text in a new media system. In this chapter we are not concerned with the content but with the layout; the position of the separate elements in relation to the screen and in relation to each other.

The positioning and grouping of interactive elements play a role in all sorts of digital products. With classical multimedia, designers and users have long been familiar with the idea of placing elements of information and elements of the interface at different points on the screen. With the web, that ability came gradually; the first versions of HTML (the web page layout language) were concerned just with the content and not with the layout, but things have changed, mainly because authors wanted the ability to put things where they wanted on the screen. These days even 'technical' programming languages such as C and C++ can be accompanied by a variety of visual programming environments which allow user interfaces (front ends) to be created from standard elements in a quick and relatively easy, 'drag and drop' manner. Although the current range of interface development tools and languages allows the designers and programmers to quickly fill the interface with all sorts of graphics, buttons and icons, they do not in themselves guarantee a good interface.

The emphasis in what follows is not on 'flashy' visual design, but on the functional positioning and grouping of information to make the user interface of a new media system simpler and easier to use.

Appropriate use of technology

To begin with I want to reiterate the mantra of appropriate use of technology. New media offers the designer so many layout possibilities that it is sometimes difficult to narrow the design down to just that which works. On the web the page layout languages (HTML and CSS) offer the author a good range of facilities, font sizes, styles and so forth. The fact that these are offered does not mean that they must all be used as often as possible.

A good starting point is to think about how layout is approached in conventional publishing. There are many fonts and effects available to the designers of magazines but if you look at well-designed magazines you see that they are put together with great restraint and that they benefit from this. I am not advocating that you copy layout styles from magazines, but am simply advocating that you consider their design philosophy of restraint and appropriate design and try to apply it to new media.

Plain text

Let us start with plain text; just blocks or paragraphs of text. During reading the eye does not slide smoothly along each line, it skips and jumps along them, reading them in 'bite-size snatches'. Anything that helps the eye to do this helps with the legibility of the text. There are many factors that affect legibility of text. Let us have a look at a few of the key ones.

Legible fonts

The most obvious factors that affect legibility are the size and style of the font. These are interrelated. Shrink any font down small enough and it will be difficult to read. However, the size at which it becomes completely illegible depends upon the style. Some fonts are especially designed to be recognizable in small sizes: the letters seem large because they make use of all the space that is available. Such fonts are thus ideally suited to large amounts of fairly small text. Other fonts are more decorative and have fancy elements at the expense of efficient use of space. The letters have twirls and shaded bits and are very individual, but sometimes less easy to read in large blocks of text. Such fonts should be used only for titles, headings and captions.

WEBCODE
legibility

For plain body text the font size will also have an influence on the legibility. Research has shown that as you increase the font size towards 12pt the text is easier to read, but that increasing the size beyond 12 points has little further improvement.

The size of the font also has an effect upon the number of words per line and the amount of text per page (physical printed page or a screenful of text), both factors that affect the readability of the text.

Text body width

Reading text is not just a case of getting the 'bite-size snatches' of text mentioned above. As you read text, your eye skips between groups of words and skips from one line to the next and this skipping from one line to the next is also highly influenced by the text layout parameters. If the lines of text are too long then you have to swing your head and eyes back a long way to get to the beginning of the next line. With such a long swing it is easy to get to the start of the lines and lose track of which line is the next line that you must read.

WEBCODE
news type

This problem can be minimized by keeping lines short, but if they are too short then there are so few words per line that the smooth reading of the text is interrupted by the continual moving down to the next line. The optimum number is 10 or 11 words per line; this is the usual count in book layout. Newspapers usually choose a count that is approaching the minimum acceptable by readers – 6 or 7 words per line.

Text alignment

Alignment also affects this shifting of the eyes to the start of the next line. If all the left-hand ends of the lines are aligned one above the other it is easier to jump to the beginning of the next line. If the text is aligned on the right margin then the left hand margin will be all over the place ('ragged left') and finding the start of the next line will be that little bit more difficult, thus hampering smooth reading.

Reading from the screen and reading from print

WEBCODE
screen
reading

Much research has been done on reading from print but this is not necessarily the same as reading from the screen. Reading from print is a much more subdued affair. Reading from the screen is a different experience: no one will settle down to read for a few hours from a conventional computer screen. Thus reading on the screen is a more interactive affair: clicking, evaluation, browsing sometimes with the express goal of collating information to be printed for reading. Fortunately some research is now being done on reading from the screen.

Legible colors

All the above points have dealt with text sizes and alignments. Another factor coming into its own with digital information is the use of color. More accurately, the difference between the color and intensity (brightness) of the text compared with that of the background that it is displayed against. Obviously the closer the text is to the shade and intensity of the background, the more difficult it is to read. In the extreme, text with the same color and intensity as the background is invisible.

Text on a background with a difference in intensity is easier to read than text with a difference in color only. The most legible color and intensity combinations are those with dark text on a lighter background: black on white, blue on white, black on gray, etc. In general the legibility of text declines with longer texts; the eye always gets tired reading and certain color combinations exacerbate this. (This is given deeper coverage in chapter 7 on color.)

Text with properties

As well as straight blocks of text, a new media system will also have text that is special in some way, text that fulfills a role other than just text in a block. Usually this will be as the interactive part of a new media system. Let us start with some of the most common text properties in interactive systems.

Highlighted

Text can be highlighted to attract attention to it by making it bold, coloring it a high visibility color or, as in the early days of the web, making it blink on and off. Blink is like shouting; I won't say 'never shout' but I will say 'only shout when you have a good reason to do so'.

Disabled

Text can be displayed to show that it as an unavailable option, in a collection of menu items for example. The usual way to do this is to 'un-highlight' it by displaying it in gray or some other low-key color. The option is said to be 'disabled'.

Selected

The converse to the above point is also a good example; when one option is selected from a collection of options it can be colored, highlighted or accompanied by some sort of mark to show that it is the one that is selected.

Choosing additive styles

Sometimes styles should be chosen that are 'additive'. This is best illustrated with a simple example. Imagine you have a page of text with the headings set in a large red font. In the text there are links and sometimes one of these headings is also a link. You need a style for links that can work in both contexts. Obviously having a link as red might work in the text but not in the headings because they are already in red. A better solution would be having links underlined or in italics or even adding a small icon in brackets after it. This would work wherever the link was, be it in the text or in the red heading. These two styles would then be independent and could be combined without interfering with one another. (A buzz-word for this ability to combine the effects is 'orthogonal' as in 'the styles are orthogonal', useful if you are trying to impress clients.)

Listing and grouping

When writing for new media, lists play a more important part than normal, owing to the short telegram nature of text for the web and to the inclusion of lists of links, either in the text or as part of the accompanying navigation. It is usually a good idea to extract links from the text and gather them together in another part of the page or screen. The usability of such a list or group can be influenced by choosing good terms (as discussed in the previous chapter on text) and also by the layout.

Grouping

WEBCODE
piles

Gathering links together is just one part of the story. The other part is how to organize them within that gathering. The approach is one of grouping things together. This act occurs a lot in personal information management. Just look at how you organize your desk or the drawers in your filing cabinet – piles of related material. Even something as simple as a shopping list can become easier to use when you group all the dairy things together and all the bread products together, so that when you get to the dairy section you can just concentrate on the appropriate section of your list.

When faced with large amounts of visual information the brain attempts to understand it by seeing patterns in it. If you can support the brain by building groups and patterns into the list then the brain can say, 'Right, I've done that group, seen this group, what next? . . .'

The process described above can be supported by the visual design of whatever it is that is being considered. In the world of new media, supporting this process is very important since there are often lists of options, menus and sub-menus, rows of buttons etc.

The clustering does not even have to be into definitely divided groups. It is enough to have a simple division in a list of options. Consider this list

<u>Products</u> <u>New products</u> <u>Online shopping</u> – <u>About us</u> <u>Contact us</u>

The division is there in terms of the conceptual difference of the two groups. The first contains options connected with what the company is selling and the second is about the company itself. Incorporating a visual hint of a division makes it even clearer and does not upset the visual continuity of the list too much.

What to group?

Grouping brings order, but what do you base your groupings on? There are a few approaches. First, you can group according to importance, or frequency of use. Two or three groups of buttons that are of different levels of importance can be grouped together. Consider the following buttons for an address book application:

<u>Find address</u> <u>Create new address</u> – <u>Delete address</u> <u>Edit address</u>

By grouping the most common actions together and grouping the less common actions together we can ensure that the user only has to concentrate on a regular basis on a few options.

Another way of grouping is according to the scope of the options. Options that are applicable across the whole new media system can be put in one group and options that are applicable to a sub-part of the content can be put in another group (when they appear). For example, options such as 'e-mail us', 'login' and 'exit' will be globally applicable, while options such as 'save this search' and 'next' will apply only in certain contexts within the content.

Grouping like this aids users in dealing with the options. They can read and understand the group of global commands and then they will not have to read them again each time they go to a new page (providing of course the global commands remain the same throughout the interaction in terms of layout and presentation).

How to group?

Grouping is useful, and we will now move on from 'what to group' to consider the question of how to group things together.

Proximity

The most obvious manner is bringing things into close, spatial proximity with each other. All things related in a group are gathered together. Classic examples are to be found in real-world technology such as the car dash-board. All the car-radio controls are clustered together, all the heating controls are together etc. Here in this chapter we have already seen how proximity grouping can play a role in a simple linear listing (either vertical or horizontal), where groups can be created by introducing gaps to split the list up into sub-lists.

Grouping by proximity may not always be possible since elements may be constrained by other factors to stay in certain positions on the screen. In such circumstances they need to be grouped by some other means.

Color

One way of grouping items that are not near to each other on the screen is to group them by color. It is a useful approach because it can be used in conjunction with the grouping by proximity discussed above. Consider warning lights on a dashboard or control panel. The lights can be grouped by proximity according to the system they relate to, but they are also grouped by color as to warning indication. Here again we can use the buzz-word 'orthogonal', meaning independent of each other.

Connectivity

Items can be related to one another by artificially introducing connect-ivity between elements, for example by joining them with lines. In the

WEBCODE
cooker

real world you can see this approach on some gas cookers where a raised line on the top surface shows which knob on the front panel is associated with which burner on the top.

This approach can be combined with color so that related items are present in different parts of the layout but are united by all being on some colored panel that snakes in and out of the elements on screen. One of the early Sun web sites used color coding and connecting lines in this way.

This is one technique that is often misused; designers introduce nice-looking colored areas into their web site design and by chance the colored areas group things together that are actually completely unrelated.

Indent

With items of a predominantly textual nature it is possible to set up grouped structures by using indented text layout. Related items are grouped together and then indents are used to show the groups and the relationship to other groups. A typical table of contents for a book is a good example of this approach.

Behavior

In the interactive world of new media the relationship between different elements can be emphasized by using behavioral factors to indicate that things belong to the same group. Examples are behaviors such as rollovers: as the user explores the interface with their mouse they get an indication of which items belong to a particular group by their behavior as the cursor passes over them.

How to split

As well as providing cues for the grouping of items, one can also give cues for the opposite: the *separation* of items. Consider the following.

Gaps/spaces

This is really just a restatement of grouping by proximity earlier – the idea of separating groups by introducing extra space between them. In a list of textual items you can simply add a few extra spaces to indicate the boundaries of groups within the list. Care should be taken with textual items consisting of more than one word, where the difference between the three types of gap should be clear: gaps between words in an item, gaps between items within a group and gaps between groups.

year 1   year 2   year 3   all students   old students

If all three types of spaces were the same it becomes ambiguous, although using underlined links would always clarify the situation (see 'link layout' below).

Dividing elements

Explicit dividing elements can also be added such as punctuation or lines, or some other symbol. Care should be taken to ensure that these dividing elements do not add confusion to the layout and that they do not make it look too busy.

year 1, year 2, year 3 – all students, old students

Gathering elements

As well as elements denoting separation between groups, a similar effect can be achieved by using elements that gather the items together. In terms of conventional punctuation dashes and commas separate things whereas different forms of brackets gather them.

[year 1 – year 2 – year 3] [all students – old students]

The illustrations I have used have been for horizontal rows of items, but the same principles apply equally well for vertical arrangements and for arrangements spread across two dimensions.

Link layout

When links are collected together, problems can arise if is it unclear where one link begins and the other ends. Links are usually distinguished from ordinary text by some graphical means. You have to be careful that this means of distinguishing them shows which collections of words are to do with which link. The style has to stretch across and include the spaces between words. If links are displayed without being underlined (possible, but not recommended) but as italic text and you had the following:

head start information

it would not be clear what the links were. Is it one big link to 'head start information', three separate, single word links, or what?

A graphical style that is used in the typewriter world is underlining. This is very rarely used in the conventional printed text world since it is possible to alter font sizes, styles and faces to achieve the same effect as underlining. With the typewriter underlining was one of the few ways to achieve some sort of distinction between font styles. As it degrades the legibility somewhat it is a pity that this hangover from the typewriter days is still with us. The only positive thing to say about underlining is that when it is used to show linked text the boundaries of the underlining gives the user important information about text links that are adjacent to each other so the user can tell the difference between:

<u>head start</u> <u>information</u>

and:

<u>head</u> <u>start</u> <u>information</u>

Another area where link boundaries are unclear, even when they are underlined, is when text is set in thin columns which forces some links to break into two lines. Consider the links:

<u>news headlines</u>
<u>home</u>
<u>page layout</u>
<u>listings</u>

If they were set in a thin column they could look like this:

<u>news</u>
<u>headlines</u>
<u>home</u>
<u>page</u>
<u>layout</u>
<u>listings</u>

Clues can be built in, such as leading capital letters, but this is quite subtle:

News
headlines
Home
Page
layout
Listings

The best solution is a graphical one: indentation or bullet points preceding each point. Thus our thin list becomes:

News
   headlines
Home
Page
   layout
Listings

Or using bullet points it looks like this.

- News
  headlines
- Home
- Page
  layout
- Listings

WEBCODE
bullet points

Both these effects could be used together but this can look a bit chaotic.

Layout for structure

The majority of documents, be they pure-text documents or true new media documents, have a definite structure, a way of dissembling the content into key groups and related units and sub-units. It is helpful for the user if this structure is tangible in some way. This makes them aware of the scope of the content and how the separate parts relate to one another. It makes it easier to work through the content in a linear manner as well as dipping in to read just a certain part of it.

In the world of new media there are different ways of making this structure tangible to the user. In the previous chapter on text we saw how adopting a concise writing style and the addition of extra text such as headings can give the user cues as to the underlying structure of the content. Later in the book in chapter 13 we shall see how to split the structure up into separate chunks and give the user an interactive means of navigating through the structure.

In this chapter we simply make the point that with new media there is still the opportunity to add cues to the structure using layout. Some examples occur in conventional media where there are layout possibilities; think of margin notes, footnotes or boxed texts that supplement the main body of text but are not part of the flow. In the world of new media one can utilize these (if appropriate) and add further layout cues such as colored areas, multi-column page layouts, even small, scrollable windows within a page that are windows onto larger blocks of content.

Screen positioning

Several times in the preceding discussions I have mentioned indentation, moving items around on the page to alter their perceived grouping and hierarchy, but how do we indicate hierarchy and importance simply by position on the page?

The answer lies in our information culture. Western reading goes left to right and top to bottom, i.e. first we read from left to right, then we repeat this gradually working our way from the top of the page to the bottom of the page. This means that we attach importance to items that are near the left or the top of the page. The most important area is the top left-hand corner, and the least important is the bottom right-hand corner; see Figure 4.1.

You can see examples of this in the positioning of company logos on headed paper and web pages, where the logo is usually in the top-left. Less important background information is consigned to the bottom right. Titles and key navigation elements are arranged at the top, and additional items such as footnotes and copyright statements are at the bottom. Similar effects can be observed on the layout of peripheral information in applications running on the computer. The Macintosh trash-can is bottom-right, the menus are top-left, with the most important menus on the left and the least important on the right.

Indenting text moves it to the right, thus decreasing its perceived importance: it is an aside, separate from the main body of text. The most extreme form is a small chunk of text aligned with the right of the page.

Most important

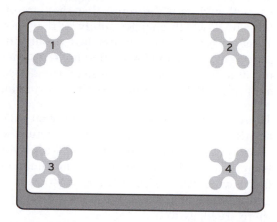

Least important

Figure 4.1: The order of importance of the four corners of the screen/page.

Other reading cultures

As a postscript to this subject I should point out that the arrangement of these hot spots is culture-dependent, relying on the geometry of reading direction. Chinese text, for example, is different in that it is read from top to bottom and then right to left. Occasionally Western words will be used in Chinese newspaper reporting, or scientific equations, and so one is faced with a clash of layouts: how do you fit horizontal Western text or equations into a vertical Chinese text? Some texts solve this by following the Western layout of left or right then top to bottom. This means they can easily slip horizontal things in, but the onus on interpreting the reading direction is then thrown on to the reader.

There is the illustrative (but probably mythical) story of the Arabian baby-food billboard. It showed, from left to right, a crying baby face, a jar of branded baby food and then the same baby face smiling. Designed by a Western ad-agency to be language independent, it had no text and was understood by Westerners, but unfortunately it had a completely different message in Arabia where they read from right to left.

Layout grids

Designing layout is not just about designing the layout for each page in isolation: as the user navigates their way through the system they will be constantly shifting from page to page. It is essential that key things do not appear and disappear and shift around in their position on the screen. As much as possible of the layout framework should be consistent, so that users should have the sense that they are operating with a fixed visual framework which changes subtly as they move around the information. Thus, designing layout is not just about individual pages, but is about aspects of design and layout that are the same throughout the site, resulting in a layout that is as consistent and logical as possible and can be applied to all different parts of the informational content of the site.

There are overlaps between designing an overall layout and other design activities such as designing the structure and navigation of the site. Obviously you cannot just start off with layout grids and say 'here's the bar with the primary navigation and the menu with key topics' without first having decided what the navigation is, what primary navigation is and whether or not you are having key topics and how many of them there are likely to be.

Forms and flow

In interactive new media systems there is a flow of text with regard to reading, but there is also the idea of a flow of text with regard to two-way interaction. This can be either instructions on how to carry out some process (how to download and install a program) or a fill-in form requiring the user to fill information in fields for the system to process.

In such situations use is made of the spatial layout to support the process. Spatial layout supplies its own cues to the order and sequence of the items displayed. Once again this is tied up with the reading culture and the placement of instructions follows the cultural reading pattern. For example consider the following instructions:

Fill the kettle, switch it on

Rinse the teapot, put tea into it

This layout can be modified to support more complex issues in filling information in. Sometimes there is an 'either/or' construct. You are filling in a form to do with finding housing. Are you looking to buy or to rent? If buy, then fill in part 12; if rent, then fill in part 13. It is possible to position these two parts next to each other so that when the process is followed from top to bottom they are clearly represented as parallel tracks either of which could be chosen.

Where would you like to live?

How many rooms are you looking for?

Would you like to buy or to rent?

Buying	**Renting**
What price range are you looking for?	What monthly rent do you intend to pay?
Do you have another property that you must sell first?	How long a contract are you looking for?

Such layout techniques are used in complex printed forms as well as digital versions, but with new media there is also the opportunity to do interactive things. You can ask the user which they are interested in at the bottom of one screen and then, when they click through to the next screen, you can begin that screen with the appropriate question, all irrelevant questions are hidden from the user.

Bad information location

As an example of bad spatial location of information consider the status line in the web browser. This is a single line of text, often with a little icon, that appears at the bottom of the web browser. Start up your web browser and have a look at it. It is used for communicating feedback about the status of the page being viewed: progress with loading, errors, security etc. It is also possible for the designer of a web page to put text into this area. However, there are good reasons not to do so. First, the browser is conceptually divided into two parts: the frame of the browser and the contents of the browser. The status line communication takes place in the frame of the browser while the user is used to looking for information from the web site in the content part of the browser.

Secondly, and more importantly, the location of the information is in a part of the browser that is very low priority, the bottom left-hand corner. Expecting users to notice and read this text is very irresponsible indeed. In the real-world it would be rather like talking to someone and putting part of the communication on a Post-it note on your left shoe. Once again it is a case of the designer doing it because the technology was there.

Graphic material

'Read all about it! Full story and pictures!' used to be the cry of boys selling newspapers on street corners. Text is important but so are the pictures – in particular, the content of a picture. However, there are times when a picture can fulfill a function irrespective of what the content of the picture is. I am thinking of the situation where long texts have pictures that help with the navigation of the text.

Once you have decided that the image is appropriate to the rest of the content then you have to ask how much of the image is appropriate and how large and detailed does it have to be. You must show what you want to show, and must not show what you do not want to show. This is basic common sense in conventional graphic design but the lesson is still being learnt in new media. Images in new media eat up resources. This is true for the web where images can be heavy going for users, although less true for cd-roms and other physical data carriers with size restrictions, since the size restrictions are just so huge in comparison with image sizes. Basically, when you have an image you want to make it as small as possible, but still retain enough detail to show what you want to show and still show enough of the whole picture to give the user an idea of the context.

'Killer web sites'

Killer web sites are web sites with the emphasis on large splash-pages involving complex technologies and huge images and file sizes. The result is sites that kill your patience, occasionally kill your web browser, kill the desire to stay with the site, kill the desire to come back to it and basically kill the site's chances of achieving anything at all apart from having its home-page occasionally featured in glossy coffee-table books.

Designing layout for change

One of the characteristics of new media is that the content is capable of change, either an existing pool of content that can change in the way it is presented or, as in a web site, a pool of content that is added to and edited with the course of time. Thus the design of the layout has to cope, gracefully, with all possible combinations of content.

Templates

A template is a piece of layout designed so that it can be used for several chunks of content. In effect it contains layout and 'gaps' that are filled in by some other bit of technology. So it would say something like: 'long red line and underneath that the title and underneath that another long red line', where the title is supplied by some other technology and could be anything from 'Bush wins' to 'Theresa LePore wins prestigious information presentation award'; indeed, it could even be empty.

It could be a single page showing the results of a search or a latest news report where the nature of that latest news report will be changing from day to day, or it could be a template defining a style of layout to be used for a collection of items of information that all have the same structure but different content, for example film reviews that all have a film title, a reviewer's name, a date and of course a review. The key issues in both situations are as follows.

The items

In essence what items of information are going to be shown here? If there is a collection of items, do we need to show them all or can we just show the key ones and link to the others? For example, if news items are being shown, do we show the whole thing, or just the title and date and link through to the rest?

The length

Text can vary in length, so we have to make sure that the layout can cope with short bits as well as long bits. If it is too long perhaps we want to have a cut-off point and show the whole thing, unless it is more than 300 words, in which case show the first 300 words and then have a link to the rest. (But what about if it is 302 words?)

A similar problem happens with the number of items, for example in a list of search results. If there are lots do we want to split them up into pages and how many do we want to show on a page?

Empty items/no items

Always think of the worst case scenario: what if the search returns no results, or the number of students following a course is zero, or the number of reviews of the film is zero, or the number of items of antique furniture under 300 dollars is zero etc.

Catching all possible results of actions

A template associated with an action must be able to cope with all possible results of that action. Consider the template that formats the results of some form of search command. The ideal case is that the search will return 20 or 30 items of information that will be of interest to the user. In reality the range of possible results is far broader and includes extreme cases such as no items being found or hundreds and hundreds being found. The design of the templates should incorporate appropriate layout and messages for all eventualities.

Changing languages

In the previous chapter we discussed different types of English. For multilingual sites the designers of templates have to be aware of the different languages that are going to be used in their templates. Consider the design of a standard page layout for a multilingual site that includes a left-hand column of options. When you call in a translator to translate the template into German, for example, all the left-hand options in German will be a significant amount longer (around 30% on average; the width of the column will in fact be governed by the longest translation that you have). This should be taken into account when designing templates for multilingual sites incorporating not just content in the other languages but also elements of the interface – buttons, menus and so on. Care should be taken to design a template where such interface elements can vary in length without excessively disrupting the layout.

Changing display parameters

Finally, it should be remembered that certain aspects of the display of the content are outside the designer's control, for example the display of things within windows on the computer's desktop where the user is in control of the size of the window. The designer should make reasonable assumptions to begin with and ensure that their design looks good and works well for a chosen minimum size but also looks and works to an acceptable level as the size shrinks beyond this. The buzz-phrase here is 'the design degrades gracefully'.

Changing medium

Despite the fact that so much information is available to us on the screen, people still find that there are situations where they would rather work with a printed copy of the information. Sometimes this is for functionally obvious reasons – they want a route description to take in the car to help them find a client's office – but sometimes it is simply that paper is sometimes a better medium for simple reading.

This requirement for printed material should be supported in new media systems. It is not necessary to make every page printable, but you should consider whether readers will want to print out certain information and, if so, that information should be designed to make it easy to read when printed. (To some extent technology is catching up with this problem as cascading style sheets allow the designer to say how text looks on screen and what it should look like when the page is printed out.)

An alternative is to include the printed information as a pre-formatted document in a printable format such as PDF or RTF (Rich Text Format). However, this will be difficult for information that the user can para-meterize, and do not forget to include meta-information in the link to such a download so that users can think before they click.

Any printable files such as this on a web site are also part of the site and their content should not be ignored; it should be treated in the same way as the rest of the content of the site.

Exercises

Choose a font

Consider the two font problems below. You are in charge of the layout. What sort of font would you choose and how would you adapt the layout to suit the target audience? Explain the reasons for your choice:

Blink magazine. *Blink* is a very specialist magazine for short-sighted hippies – ex flower-people whose eyesight is starting to play up.

Train destination. On a train that is part of an underground railway system (a metro) the destination of the train is displayed on the side of the train in black and white with the white parts illuminated from behind.

WEBCODE
choose font

Functional text

Everybody in a group brings in one or two examples of functional text. It can be a catalogue, a set of instructions, labeling on a device, whatever. The key thing is that the emphasis is on functional information. Discuss the layouts used and how they are appropriate to what they are used for.

WEBCODE
functional
text

Difficult to use text

Select a piece of text that is useful in some way (a list of phone numbers, train times, instructions on using a piece of software, etc.). Design a combination of layout and fonts that makes it as difficult to use as pos-sible. You should not render it *completely* unusable: it must still be pos-sible to use it, just very difficult.

WEBCODE
difficult text

Icons

Introduction

The world of new media seems inextricably linked to icon design. Every screen-full of information, be it a simple demo or a complex application, seems to be strewn with icons, of varying sizes and styles.

There are some who claim that this spate of icons is like a disease, that new media systems get covered in them just like children get covered in measles. Others cite the compactness and international clarity of replacing text with icons. And all the while the designers are just getting on with tweaking pixels on minute pictures of arrows, documents and smiling user faces.

Icon design is not just about drawing cool little pictures to illustrate words. It is about communication. It is about saying things with simple pictures rather than with text. It is about abstracting the key features you want to communicate about something and finding the best way to present those features.

There seems to be some consensus that the mere presence of icons in a piece of new media means that it is well designed, but looking around me at the use of icons in such systems I continually see terrible examples.

Examples of bad design

One example I was told of was an icon of a small pig, which on closer discussion with the designer turned out to be a piggy-bank. This piggy-bank symbolized the concept 'save'. By clicking on a little pig you saved your profile!

Figure 5.1: Bad icons for 'save' (left) and 'change' (right).

Here's another: an icon depicting a number of small circles. They turn out to be coins or change (as in 'loose change') and what the icon actually signifies is change (as in transform something); see Figure 5.1.

The problem with these two examples is that the icon is not a good depiction of the concept. The designer in both cases has started with the concept, taken a word that describes the concept and then illustrated an alternative meaning of that word. A very tenuous link indeed.

One of my favorite bad examples occurred in a Mac-look-alike file system I used once. There were some file icons that had a small pair of glasses next to them. Only a few of the files were accompanied by glasses so what was different about them? I tried viewing the files and viewing other files but there seemed to be no difference. Then I tried editing the files. The files with the spectacles could not be edited, they were read-only files. Read-only, reading glasses, Aha! A pair of glasses meant read-only!

Again the problem here stems from the involvement of spoken language. The designer had tried to illustrate the term 'read-only' with an icon instead of dealing with the concept. Using glasses to signify read-only seems OK, but most other text files can also be read. The fact that they could *only* be read got lost when the icon was designed. The important conceptual difference about read-only files, the thing that sets them apart from other files and that therefore needs to be emphasized, is that they cannot be written to or edited. Once you realize this, the illustration of the concept becomes easier: a pen with a red bar through it, or a padlock similar to the Mac's locked-disk icon. That is the key concept.

Icons and symbols and text

Let us now go straight from the concrete to the abstract and discuss icons and symbols. This is an area bordering on the philosophical and I should qualify my treatment of it by emphasizing that this is written by one new media designer for other new media designers. I shall start with symbols. Symbols are simple pictures with associated meaning where that meaning has to be learned. The user is shown or sees a graphical symbol and is told its meaning by someone else, or by reading a manual, or just by clicking on it and experimenting with it.

Text is related to symbols. Text is a more efficient way of representing concepts. Instead of having thousands of symbols that must be learned, it has a few that can be combined and it is these combinations that have meaning attached to them. At the end of the day it still has to be learned. (Although the meaning of composite words can be deduced from the meaning of the separate words – 'orange juice' as a single concept can be deduced by the meaning of the separate elements – that is what language is all about.)

The key thing about icons is that they are a link to the real-world (a 'mapping' to the real-world to use the jargon). The ideal icon is one where the image and the context make the meaning clear to the user without their having to learn it. It should be intuitive.

Obviously the situation is not as simple as this ideal. Users will experiment with icons that are obscure and they will be understood and learnt as though they are symbols. Thus there is a gray area between symbols and icons. Symbols usually make use of pieces of imagery to make them a bit clearer and icons are never 100% comprehensible all the time. There is usually a bit of symbol in an icon and usually a bit of icon in a symbol.

Advantages of icons

Let us have a look at some of the advantages and disadvantages often cited regarding incorporating icons into the interface of a new media system.

Faster to select

Written language is a relatively recent addition to the skill set of human beings. In contrast, the ability to distinguish different objects visually has been in use for millions of years ('Hmmm, is that a big stone or a saber-tooth tiger I can see over there?'). What this means is that choosing one item from a menu of textual options requires more brain processing and thus more time than recognizing and selecting one icon from a collection of icons. With repeated use the user can start to rely on visual recognition of the textual options as patterns rather than actually reading them and interpreting them. This is why textual menu options can be set in all-capitals: although it reduces legibility for long texts, it aids recognition in choosing from among short texts.

Good supplement to text

Many of the issues surrounding the use of icons tend to concern themselves with which are better, icons or text (see later in this chapter). However, combining icons with text in a new media interface means that you get the fast access that visual images provide, coupled with the clarity and precision that textual descriptions offer. The only drawbacks are that you have the double investment of designing text and icons and the combination of text with icons does make heavy use of screen space.

International

This is a tricky one. Many graphic representations of objects are indeed universal and international. However, it is all too easy to be lulled into a false sense of security on this point and think that everybody everywhere views icons in the same way that you do. In fact the cultural influence on how we interpret visual information is huge and most people are unaware of how large a part it plays because they cannot see around it. See chapter 10 for more on contexts.

Disadvantages of icons

Higher investment – many icons

Current computer screens are high resolution and in a new media system you often need different versions of the icon in different sizes (for tool-bars, pop-up dialogues etc.). In the end you are making several copies of each icon. For the really small ones, you are into the time-consuming area of playing with pixels.

Furthermore, icons must often be made in several flavors or states: normal icon, disabled icon, highlighted icon etc. This all combines to increase the amount of design and production time involved in a good icon set.

Consider an icon set with three different sizes and three different states for each icon. If there are 20 icons, then there are already $3 \times 3 \times 20 = 180$ separate images.

Higher investment – choosing concepts

Choosing good concepts for icons can also take much time and effort. Coming up with an idea for an icon is easy, but coming up with a good idea takes time – brainstorming, evaluating, making sure it is possible in a 20 pixel by 20 pixel square etc.

As an example, consider the system extensions icons on the Mac (the Macintosh computer can have its functionality extended with so-called system extensions). Defining the term 'system extensions' probably took a very short time, but designing a generic icon for system extensions took a lot longer. One of the candidate designs was a stylized Macintosh computer with a funnel on top, symbolizing pouring something extra into the Macintosh; however, in tests this was always seen as a champagne glass on top of the computer, leading to ideas of office parties. Eventually they came up with the now familiar (and elegant) jigsaw piece icons.

Bad design is easier

The big problem with icons is that they can be badly designed. Bad design is also possible when composing text options on a text-based menu; however, the worst choice of textual terminology can never be as bad as the worst icon design. If I am choosing the text for a button on a photocopier that makes copies lighter, I could choose a term such as 'lighter', 'whiter' or 'brighter' and it would still be clear. This is nothing compared with the terrible icons I could come up with.

Designing single icons

The designing of icons is split into two parts: those issues that play a part when designing single icons, in this section, and those issues that affect the design of a set of icons designed to function as a whole in the next section.

Abstraction and presentation

The key question in icon design is, 'What is the essence of the concept that you are trying to communicate?' This is quickly followed by, 'How can that essence be given a distinct visual form?'

Finding visible entities

Isolating the essence of a concept is difficult. Giving it a distinct visual form is no easier. Certain entities are physical objects themselves and as such can be depicted without too many problems. Think of the icon for a computer or car: no problem.

Sometimes the essential thing is hidden and the designer must then concentrate on the visual aspects of it that are not hidden. The icon for 'hard-disk' does not usually show a round magnetic disk with a reading head, since few people have seen that. Instead it depicts the tangible visual aspects of a hard-disk: the box that the disk sits in or (in the case of removable drives) the protective plastic case that the thing is housed in.

The thing to be represented may have a visual identity that is highly indistinct and unrecognizable. 'Caffeine' for example certainly exists, but no one knows what it looks like and even if they did it would probably look like countless other powdered chemicals. In such cases the designer must choose an associated aspect that can be given visual form. In this caffeine example we have a stylized face of someone getting a caffeine 'zap'. And the designer must then see if the context is enough to support the user in deducing the meaning. See Figure 5.2.

Finally there are some ideas that are abstract and have no physical form associated with them. In such cases a surrogate object must be found that suggests the idea and this must be portrayed. Consider the concept 'protection': a designer may choose to embody this as some object that is designed specifically to provide protection of one form or another, such as an umbrella or a shield.

Figure 5.2: Representing intangibles. Caffeine as a molecule, a pile of white powder and as the tangible effect it has.

Symbols from other times

As technology becomes more miniaturized, everything is gradually turning into little silver or black boxes the size of cigarette packets. Is that little gadget a compact camera, an electric shaver, a mobile phone or is it just a packet of cigarettes? Iconic depiction of current technology is sometimes difficult because of this, and occasionally designers resort to graphic representations of historical technology which, although not altogether accurate, are at least easily recognizable.

Examples that spring to mind are 'no photographs' being depicted as an old-fashioned bellows-type camera with a red line through it. A 'computer' can be pictured as a rectangular box with the twin tape spools on the front, as they used to look in the 1960s, and warnings of trains usually depict an old steam train.

Using symbols from other contexts

In today's developed, technical world people are familiar with icons from many different contexts. As such it is possible to borrow icons from one area and use them in another area in the assumption that many users will recognize them and understand them in the new context. A good example is the use of the 'no entry' symbol from the road sign to signify 'no entry' in supermarkets to people walking and pushing shopping trolleys. (The more pedantic readers will realize that this is an example of a symbol and not of an icon.)

Extraneous meaning

When designing icons, avoid adding objects and backgrounds to try to make the icon clearer. These extra things often obscure the interpretation or get interpreted as the key concept. I remember a design exercise where a student was trying to draw an icon for 'sausage'. In order to clarify it they added some general butcher's paraphernalia such as knives and boards around the sausage with the result that, in tests, the icon was interpreted as 'butcher'.

Powerful simple images

Some images are perfect for icon design, they are highly visual and distinct. Examples include such elemental, primitive things as fire, water, person, sun etc. These are useful because of their power, but if they are not the focus of the icon, their meaning can be more powerful than whatever else is meant to be the focus. If I am doing an icon for 'day' and I put a big sun in, it will probably be interpreted as 'sun' or 'sunshine' or something like that.

Be careful with arrows

Of all the graphic devices the arrow is probably the most powerful. It is something similar to pointing with your hand. As soon as someone points with their index finger your eye and mind are inexorably drawn away from them and toward whatever is being pointed to. In a similar way arrows impart a high degree of movement and direction to graphics and icons. The arrow should be connected with the key concept in the icon. Associating the arrow with a less important item in the icon can have the effect of promoting that item, imparting it with an importance beyond what was intended.

One web site I used had a bar with the letters A to Z above the text. The letters were clickable but did not look it, so the designers included an arrow at each end of the bar to try to emphasize the fact. The end result was that the arrows looked like the key clickable elements.

Even triangles, when they are drawn so that they point to the left or the right, can look enough like arrows that users get confused and instill them with more function than they actually have.

Legibility

Occasionally an icon will have several elements The design should be balanced so that all the elements are visible and comprehensible from a distance. It is no good having an icon where close examination is required in order to distinguish some parts of it. 'Reading' an icon is composed of two stages: first recognizing what the icon represents, and secondly understanding what the icon means in the context that it is in.

Cues from context

Icons are always seen in a context. That context gives the user information about how the icon should be interpreted. For example, a magnifying glass in the context of an image manipulation program such as PhotoShop means 'zoom in', while a magnifying glass in the context of a system dealing with large amounts of information means 'search'. Icons for giving directions in stations are always seen in and about stations. Icons connected with the operation of a new media system are always displayed on the screen when that system is running. The context is always apparent and the context is always used in interpreting the meaning of the icon.

This can make the designer's task easier since the context will provide many clues as to the meaning of the icon.

Context should also be taken into account when testing icons. Complex icons tested separately from their context or from the other icons in the set are far less likely to be recognized than if they are seen in their 'natural' context.

Designing icon sets

Icons are rarely designed in isolation from each other. An icon is usually part of a larger set of icons for a new media system. Designing a set of icons follows similar guidelines to designing a collection of sounds for a new media system as we shall see in chapter 6. To begin with you must ensure that certain aspects remain similar throughout the set. Separate icons must clearly be related to each other. This aids users in finding the icons among other visual information and gives panels containing several icons a consistent and smooth appearance.

To achieve a similarity in icon style the designer must first define an iconic house style. They must define the key elements of the style that will be used in all subsequent icons. This iconic house style must cover at least the following elements.

Color

For simplicity of presentation icons are usually designed with two colors, a foreground color and a background color. However, this is a hangover from the industrial design days of icons printed on plastic or metal. In the world of new media there are no costs involved with extra colors in icons. However this advantage can also have disadvantages in that care must be taken not to end up with an icon set looking like a page from a scrapbook. Here again the skill of restraint is important. Color schemes should consist of a few key large area colors coupled with a few key highlighting colors (see chapter 7 on color). The colors chosen should also bear some relation to any color scheme that has been chosen for the new media system as a whole.

Style and layout

The different images used in the icons must all be created following a similar style. Are the people to be represented as little stick people or are they more rounded characters? Are the pictograms made from simple geometric elements (circles, squares) or are they all styled in a more free-hand manner? Are they very precise with everything joining up exactly or are they more vague and sketchy? Whatever the decisions that are made at the outset, they should be followed consistently throughout the development of the icon set.

Weight

Icons should contain roughly the same balance of colors so that when a collection of icons is seen on a screen they look consistent. If some icons have a large area of blue while others have a large area of red a collection of such icons will look messy and jar on the eye.

Standard elements

Some icon sets make use of standard elements in the icon. Usually these standard elements are decorations to the frame of the icon, rounded corners, bars along the bottom. Some icon sets include the textual description for extra clarity for the native language speakers.

Vocabularies

Sets of icons are usually related in some way, for example they represent actions to do with common sets of objects. Care should be taken in ensuring that these commonly recurring objects are represented in a consistent way within the icons, e.g. arrows always look the same, or a document is always represented in the same way unless it is to be distinguished from other documents.

Clustering

Designing the interface to a new media system is not just about the icons, equally important is how the icons are laid out in the interface: where they are placed on the screen, how they are clustered together and in what order they are presented.

For more information about such issues the reader is referred to the previous chapter on layout.

Differences

Having stressed the importance of making groups of icons consistent and similar I should also warn designers not to go too far in this direction. Ultimately the key to selecting one icon from a group of icons is that the icons are *different*. The goal is to get the balance right so that the end product is a set of distinct icons that nonetheless relate to each other visually and are part of a set.

Icons or text?

The first vital part of icon design is to ensure that icons are the best means of representing the information, and that you (or the graphic designer) are not just designing icons for the sake of designing icons. How many of us have puzzled over the lighter/darker icons on a photocopier? Half-filled circles drawn in white on a black background. Which means lighter and which darker? One European-based photocopier company struggled with them for a long time before hitting on the idea of simply replacing them with text 'lighter' and 'darker'. Okay, it may be language dependent and thus not international, but it is better to use text that is confusing to users of some nationalities than to use bad icons that are confusing to users of all nationalities.

Use text when prototyping

A key difference between icons and text is that icons require a high level of investment of time to make them work as intended. Text is more flexible, it is easier to set up and change and use in sketches. Only when the interface functionality has settled down should you think about investing time in designing the icons. There is nothing worse than deciding to drop a function from an interface and hearing the graphic designer say, 'I think we should keep that function in because it took me five days to design that icon'.

Text should be high investment

Having stated the above point, it does not necessarily follow that text requires no time. Even with text for options, care should be taken to ensure that the set of words and concepts being used are clear, understandable to as many people as possible and as short and succinct as possible.

The size of chapter 3 on text for new media should give an indication of how important this is.

Icons are international

Icon enthusiasts continually emphasize that icons are better than text because they are international. There are two points to be made here. First there is a high degree of cultural influence in the interpretation of icons: icons are based on one's experience of the world and that is fundamentally shaped by the cultural context that we are brought up in.

Secondly, so what if icons are generally international? One can always build different versions of the new media system incorporating text in different languages. It is more investment than just using one language but it may be less investment than designing a hundred icons or so, in different sizes, with and without highlight/disabled color variations etc.

Give the user the choice

Sometimes investment is not a big issue, for example a highly funded, flagship new media system or a system with a small number of choices anyway. In that case one can apply one of the few rules of new media design, 'When faced with a difficult decision ask yourself if it is possible to do both options'.

It is always possible to incorporate both text and icons into a new media system. This could be done either both on screen together, with the text as a small addition to the icon itself, or as separate interfaces with the choice of text or icons given to the user (consider the button bar on some web-browsers which can be configured as text, icons or both).

Case study: pass the icon

Icon design is not just about having a 'how to develop good icons check-list'; no designer working on a real project relies purely on textbooks and guidelines. Design involves learning by doing and the designer must also be in touch with how the icons are being interpreted. A good method of practising and experiencing icon design within a group is the exercise 'pass the icon'.

The designers sit in a circle and each has a long strip of paper (say 10 cm wide and 2 m long), at the top of which is written some concept such as radioactivity, alcohol-free, read-only file or whatever. They illustrate this with a quick iconic sketch representing the key features. Each of them folds the paper down so that only the icon they have drawn is visible and not the text. Everyone hands their paper to the person on their left and they then look at the icon in front of them and write on the paper the concept that they think the icon illustrates. They fold the paper over the icon, just leaving the text showing and hand it on again and so on. Each of the resulting pieces of paper goes 'icon – text – icon – text' with each interpretative link being done entirely in isolation from the others. It is a sort of 'Chinese Whispers' game but with icons instead of the spoken word.

At the end of the exercise the strips are opened out to reveal the chain of associations and interpretations that have taken place. The results are both hilarious and fascinating and good illustrations can usually be found of all the points covered in this chapter. It is a good example of learning by designing.

WEBCODE
icons to try

Exercises

Icons to try

Here is a list of unusual concepts to try to represent in icons; they are all pretty unreal but it is good fun having a go at them. They could also be used in the 'pass the icon' game if you have a group of people.

Change language

Radioactive

Alcohol free

Read-only file

Caffeine free

Deep water

Send mail

Auto-pilot on

Self-destruct

Arrivals

Unbreakable glass

Disk full

No games allowed

WEBCODE
familiar icons

WEBCODE
icon
scrapbook

WEBCODE
icon context

Icons you are used to

Find a product or new media system that you use regularly and that has icons that you are familiar with. Test out the icons on people who probably do not use the system, and see what proportion they can interpret.

Icon scrapbook

Keep a collection of icons that you encounter in your day-to-day work. Those on packaging can be ripped out and stuck in a file, others can be photocopied, scanned into your computer or snapped with a digital camera. There are also large collections of new media icons on the web.

Icons in context

The context of an icon plays a great part in its interpretation. Once you have collected a few real-world icons, try showing them to people without their context and see if they can guess what they mean. If they cannot say, then show them or tell them what the context is and see if they can get it then.

6

Sound

Introduction

The world of multimedia is strangely paradoxical in that it is not as 'multi' as it should be. The area is dominated by visual design. The multimedia tool manufacturer Macromedia summed it up well with their observation that:

Sound is the forgotten child of multimedia.

Many new media designers come from the world of graphic design and, because of this, sound is often badly handled in new media systems. It is generally given only token acknowledgment with one feeble beep or click being used for all mouse actions, or it is over-used and the system exudes all sorts of strange, long noises that are cute and make you smile for the first 30 seconds but become annoying and excessive for the next two years of use.

Sound is a medium every bit as important as the visual medium. It can be used as a stand-alone medium without the visual channel, it can give subtle support to complex, visual interfaces or it can be used for the parallel presentation of information to the user. Although sound is as useful as graphics it is very different in nature. Let us compare graphics and sound in new media systems.

Sound versus graphics

Sound is active, graphics are passive

There is a big difference between the two media with respect to the behavior of the user interacting with them. Sound is an active medium and the user plays the passive role. Sound can cut in and interrupt the user's actions; it can be so active and intrusive that loud sound can easily be annoying or even frightening.

Removing intrusive sound from your perception is hard, and trying not to hear something is extremely difficult. The last line of defense is the childlike behavior of sticking your fingers in your ears and making loud beeping sounds yourself to mask the incoming sounds. This active nature of sound is reflected in the uses that sound is put to: alarms are nearly always audio, whether they are for fire warnings, telephones, lifts or reactor meltdowns.

In contrast graphics are the reverse: the medium is passive and the user is the active agent. The user must actively look around the visual space, seeing and recognizing the information presented as graphics. It is thus possible to overlook or miss elements presented as graphics unless they are given higher priority through size, animation, illumination or high saturation colors.

This is true in real-world situations where visual information is distributed all around us, but is slightly less true when dealing with new media. The fact that the visual field is narrowed to just the screen does tend to give new media graphics more of a directed, active nature. It is also tied up with the dynamic nature of the things being displayed. It is similar in some ways to television. Television is largely visual, but the small visual field, the dynamic nature and the orchestration of the programs on it makes it more of an active medium with passive users. The only reason you might fail to miss a visual element is if you are in the kitchen making the coffee. (For a discussion of who is in control of the interaction refer to chapter 15 on narrative.)

Sound is non-localized, graphics are localized

Graphics are context specific; they can be highly localized. Or, put simply, you can stick labels on things. Sound is difficult to localize; using advanced stereo reproduction one can achieve some degree of direction to it, but not with a high degree of accuracy. This is illustrated by the classic three-phone problem: there are three phones on your desk, one is ringing, you grab it and say 'hello' only to discover that one of the others is the one that is still ringing. The ringing sound cannot be accurately localized to the correct telephone.

Often you see combinations of the two media, each one fulfilling the role that it is best designed for: sound to attract the user's attention to the fact that something needs looking at (literally 'sounding the alarm'), coupled with a flashing light to localize the alarm to a particular object or system. This is often used with banks of elevators, where the 'ding-dong' sound alerts the user that an elevator has arrived and the illuminated arrow above the door shows them which elevator is about to arrive.

Sound is transient, graphics are permanent

Sound is transient. It plays once and then is gone. To give sound more of a permanent character it must either be repeated frequently or be broadcast as a constant background sound. Repetitions are used in platform announcements in the station and an example of constant background sound is the audio signal some countries use at pedestrian road-crossings to let poorly sighted users know that the lights are instructing them to cross. A less familiar example of background sound is the continual 'beep-boop' sound broadcast through the alarm systems at reactor plants that lets the workers know that there is no alarm and that the system is still functioning correctly.

Graphics are permanent. Hang a sign up and it stays there constantly for all to see; screw a plaque to the wall and it can hang there for decades. In the dynamic world of new media where graphics can appear and disappear quickly this statement should be modified to say that graphics *can* be permanent if required.

Sound is dynamic, graphics are static

Sound is dynamic. The physics of it is tied up with variations in pressure over time and so it must be spread out over time. Having said that, there are different ways of approaching this relationship with time.

First it can simply be used to transmit information or atmosphere with little or no relation to the actual time, for example spoken text or music. It is dynamic but no explicit use is being made of its dynamic nature.

Secondly we have the other extreme: sound that communicates very little information but is used for its dynamic attributes, such as a continual sound that changes to reflect the change in state of some system. Think of the old-fashioned kettles with whistles on them. Related to this is the use of simple sound to reflect events rather than the continual state of a system. This is the infamous 'beep' of the early computer world.

Conventional graphics are static, but, with the advent of the computer, graphics too have the ability to be dynamic. Dealing with and designing animated graphics requires a very different approach from static graphics (see chapter 8 on video and animation).

Notation

Sound is usually difficult and complex to notate. Simple amplitude diagrams can show you the duration and envelope of the sound but they do not tell you if it is a dog barking, a choir singing or a dustbin lid dropping on a concrete floor. In stark contrast graphics do not need a notation because they are their own notation. A picture can be simply represented as a small picture; no other notation is really necessary. This is the reason why graphical editors can be so intuitive while sound editors can never achieve the same flexibility.

Sound in the real-world

Before considering sound design for new media, let us look at sound around us in the real-world and how we relate to it. The real-world is positively overflowing with environmental sound. I do not just mean the natural sounds of birds and the bees; but also the sounds of traffic, bicycle bells and building work – noisy and brash though some of it is, it is still a part of the sound-scape we live in.

I shall begin with a look at how sound affects babies and then consider a range of sounds. I could start to talk about the range of sound according to measurable quantities such as volume or frequency. but these are fairly self-explanatory and not a vital part of design. What is more interesting is to consider a range of meaning, or impact, upon the human listener. Loud sound does not necessarily have the most impact upon the listener as sound can be empowered by associations, meaning and the context it occurs in. Consider a sneeze in a lecture theater: it is a loud sound, yet it is so neutral in terms of associations that most people hardly even notice it. Now consider the effect of other sounds at the same volume as the sneeze: a mobile telephone or someone saying 'Oh no!' The meaning and association attached to a sound are usually more important than any other physical properties it may have.

Babies and sound

Listening starts very early on in life. Young children are very sound aware (think again of the active nature of sound described above). As we get older we learn that the visual is usually closer and thus more important than the audio, which tends to be more distant. For babies these two media are sometimes given equal importance. I have heard babies say 'doggie doggie' when there is no doggie anywhere to be seen, and then

I become aware that there is a dog barking somewhere far off in the distance. My 'grown-up' brain screens it out as background noise while, for the child's brain, it is as important as seeing a dog at close range.

Even when children visually identify objects and start naming them, they still use the sound as part of the label: a moo-cow, baa-lamb, choo-choo train, bow-wow etc. As you get older this sound-oriented language is used less, but there still remains a certain degree of sound in language with the onomatopoeic sound of words that describe environmental sounds such as boing, thud, tinkle, groan etc.

Silence

Just as white is the absence of color or form, silence is the absence of sound, and just as white space plays a key part in graphic design, so too the power of silence should not be underestimated. Silence has just as important a part to play in new media design as the whole range of sounds that are available.

Noise

With the term 'noise' I am bundling together all those background sounds that have little impact on the human listener. They can be informative in certain contexts (listening to the level of gas while cooking for example), but in general they are just ongoing background sounds that carry little information.

Pleasant sounds

There is also a group of sounds that are pleasurable to listen to without having a high degree of meaning – natural sounds such as birdsong or water flowing and created sound such as music. They may not convey any concrete information or meaning, but they do communicate or instill certain emotions in the listener.

Physical effects

Some sounds can have pronounced effects not because of associations or meaning, but because of the physics of the sound itself. The obvious example is very loud sound. Beyond a certain threshold loud sound can bridge the more conscious levels of the brain and directly panic the underlying animal brain we still have. Very high-frequency sounds can also have an adverse effect on listeners, although the effects are less of panic and more of irritation.

Certain sounds can also have the dire effect of 'setting one's teeth on edge'. Although this varies somewhat from person to person, a fairly large proportion of people hate it when someone claws their fingernails down a blackboard to produce that terrible screech. Others get a shiver when they hear the noise of teeth grating against rough, unglazed pottery.

Emotive sound

The most powerful emotive sounds are those that play a part in human communication, usually because the sounds have very strong emotional associations: consider the sound of a child crying, or someone shouting angrily.

Interestingly enough it is possible for other non-human sounds also to have these effects. Certain animal sounds fall into this category because of their similarity to human-made sounds. Consider my friend who lived close to the local dog kennels. Every morning, the dogs were let out for exercises and then shut away again. When this happened they set up a howling choir which, although not loud, was of a certain timbre that really pulled at your heart-strings and distracted you totally from anything that you tried to do.

Sound with meaning

The sound with even more impact on the human listener is sound with explicit meaning associated with it. This could be a well-defined meaning such as a fire alarm or a car horn, or sound that has well-defined associations such as the hissing of a snake or the screech of a skidding car.

Speech

Speech is a special case: it is sound with meaning, but very definite meaning. In fact it is sound with almost no other purpose except meaning. This meaning, though, can be contained in speech in more ways than just in the words. Someone talking communicates far more information than just what they say. The subtle variations in pronunciation, word usage, speed and tonal qualities can sometimes impart more than the information content of the words. The listener can tell what the speaker's state of health is, how they feel emotionally, sometimes even if they are lying or not.

Consider the sound of a 5-year-old saying in a giggly voice: 'I am a doctor'. From the quality of the voice you can pick up the approximate age, the regional accent, the gender, the fact that the child is happy, and putting them all together makes you think that they are, in all probability, not a practising medical physician.

Sound technology

Now let us have a brief look at the technology for creating sound artificially. To begin with consider mechanical sounds. When I dealt with this above with natural sounds, what I was touching on were sounds made 'by accident', either in nature or as an undesigned byproduct of everyday life. In the designed part of everyday life there is also a great deal of mechanical sound, although it is usually sounds originating from metal things impacting each other as a result of some electrical or physical signal – things such as door bells rung by electricity or a rope, fire bells, clock bells, telephone bells. In all these cases, communication is taking place, but the message being communicated is very basic; in essence it is a simple 'Oi'. Depending on the nature of the bell and the context, that 'Oi' is interpreted in different ways, as: 'Oi, get out of the way', 'Oi, there's someone at the door', 'Oi, we are on fire' etc.

Electronic generation of sound was the first big breakthrough in sound generation. The use of electronically generated sounds has a surprisingly long history and the absence of any computers meant that the main focus of the electronic sound was in electronic music. One of the early high points was that wonderful instrument the Theremin, conceived in 1917 and later responsible for the eerie backing music for most of the science fiction films produced in the 1950s. Gradually, electronically produced sounds and music became more commercial and affordable and in the 1960s the electronic Moog synthesizer began to appear on the popular musical scene.

With the birth of commercial computing there was little initial attempt to combine the two threads of electronic sounds and computer technology in a wide-scale commercial approach, partly because of the limited disk space available in those days and partly because of the lack of a standard way of storing musical data (until MIDI came along). The result was that even up until the 1980s the most widespread computing sound was the beep, which was the electronic variant of the eternal 'Oi!': 'Oi, you've got mail', 'Oi, the program has finished running', 'Oi, there was a system error' etc.

Nowadays, increased storage and processing power have meant that it is possible to do a lot with sound on the computer. As well as highly interactive tools to generate sounds it is also possible to digitally record sounds and manipulate them in interesting ways. The computer also allows designers to combine sound with interactive technologies and produce multimedia and web pages incorporating sound in the interaction.

Sound design

Sound is a rich medium, as we have seen with the discussion of sound in the real-world. In technological terms the designer now has access to powerful sound-oriented tools and the audience has sufficiently advanced technology to make the inclusion of sound in new media an important option to the designer.

Sounds with meaning

The main result of the move from mechanical methods of sound production to digital, computer-based methods is that things have became a lot more flexible. The meaning of sound has moved away from just the simple 'Oi' that we saw earlier. Sound can now take on new and complex meanings. The designer can develop vocabularies of sounds and couple sounds with all sorts of actions within a new media system.

Sound, graphics and animation

There are two good sources of guidance in sound design. The first is looking to the real-world for the roles that sound fulfills there and using that as an inspiration. We had a look at this in earlier sections of this chapter. The second source is to look at graphic design, and in particular animation, in the world of new media.

When we compared sound and graphics at the beginning of this chapter we saw that sound is an active medium whereas graphics is passive. What this means is that sound is very good at conveying information about events while graphics is good at presenting large amounts of information for the user to peruse. In this respect it is difficult to replace graphics with sound since they fulfill different roles. Their roles start to overlap when we consider dynamic graphics in the form of animation.

The sorts of things that animation is called on to do are also the sorts of things that sound can be called on to do. Both are usually transient, temporal things that can be linked to events and are used to inform the user about what is going on in their interaction with the system.

Sound for changing states

Feedback is the system telling the user what is going on (more on this in chapter 12). If you want to provide feedback about the alteration of the state of something then graphics is more appropriate. When I throw something in my desk-top trash can, the trash can icon changes to show something in it. This is better than starting a background sound of flies buzzing that continues for as long as there is something in the trash can.

Sound for events

In the real world many actions and events are accompanied by a sound that confirms the completion of an action. The simplest example is putting a cup down on a hard surface; as well as the tactile feedback there is also the reassuring 'clunk' sound. If you want to provide information about an event in a new media system then sound is very useful, not necessarily as a replacement for animation but more as a confirmatory sound to support the animation. Once again when I throw something into the desk-top trash can there is a reassuring 'clung' when it happens.

WEBCODE
bill gaver

Although we are talking about sound in a supporting role to animation it is a very important role. Consider one of the earliest systems with sound, the television game of Pong. Sound was not functionally vital but it was nonetheless a key part of the interaction and playing it with the sound turned down was unthinkable. The work of Bill Gaver in the 1980s and 1990s is a good source of information on functional sound in our everyday life.

Sound for navigation

Sound can assist with navigation, and indeed in the real-world blind people rely to a high degree on sound to help them with navigation. When creating virtual, three-dimensional, navigable environments with stereo-sound facilities, sound can be used to enrich the navigation. This can be seen often in computer games where you are moving around in a three-dimensional world with sounds in it. Using sound to support navigation in non-three-dimensional worlds is an interesting challenge.

Metaphorical sounds

When incorporating sounds into a new media system it is sometimes a good idea to adopt metaphorical sounds: sounds that sound like things from the real-world. For example a system that records an image of the computer screen for later use could use the sound of a camera with motor-wind taking a photo, a system crash could be signified by the sound of something breaking and a request for text-based chat with someone could be represented by the sound of a phone ringing or a knocking on a door.

Sound for realism

Sound also plays a part in trying to recreate real-world aspects of something within a new media system. As well as assisting with the navigation, as we saw above, sound also adds a lot to the atmosphere within a computer game. Background sounds and music can achieve just as much as state-of-the-art graphics when it comes to building up a particular atmosphere.

WEBCODE
marketsound

Sound can also add realism to more functional contexts, especially if sound is a key factor in the user's task within that context. There is a software company called Marketsound that produces software for people trading on stocks. One of its products offers users the chance to hear a simulation of pit cries as they use it.

Physical aspects of sound design

As well as the higher-level points above, there are a few points to bear in mind on the lower levels of sound design.

Volume

Visual feedback is always confined to the screen and as such is local to the new media system. No matter what you show, users always know it is on the screen and thus part of the new media system. Sound, on the other hand, is not so easily localized and loud sounds can easily shock or confuse the user, possibly impairing the use of the system.

Lead-in

The shock factor of a sound depends on three factors. The first, the volume, has been dealt with above. The second is the nature of the sound itself: as we saw, a loud sound of a sneeze is less shocking than the sound of an angry dog barking. The third factor is the lead-in (or attack) of the sound. A sound that starts suddenly can give a greater shock than a sound that starts quietly and gradually builds up. Even a very fast build-up can still make a sound less of a shock to the user.

Length

Graphics are spread out in the spatial dimension and sound is spread out in the temporal dimension. As a result, sound as feedback can have a great impact on the duration of the interaction.

Sounds used as part of an interface should be designed to be as compact and short as possible. If they accompany visual feedback, it is usually the case that the sound feedback takes longer than the visual feedback. It should be possible for the user to react to the visual feedback and carry out follow-up actions before the sound part of the feedback has finished.

Designing sound sets

When designing a set of sounds to be used in a particular new media context it is important to design them so that they are coherent and consistent. It is interesting to note that there is a similarity between these guidelines and those for the design of sets of icons (see chapter 5).

Physical attributes

To begin with it is important to ensure that the sounds belong to the same set in terms of their physical attributes. In other words, irrespective of what the sounds are, they should have similarities when it comes to aspects such as volume, pitch, length and so on. If I have sound feedback for dragging and dropping an icon into two sorts of folders I may expect two different sounds to be used but I would not expect the sounds to vary very much in volume.

Obviously this consistency should be balanced against the need to vary these factors in the name of design. For example, a warning sound would be expected to be somewhat louder than a confirmation sound.

Associative attributes

The choices of the separate sounds that make up a sound set should also be considered. They should all be based upon some theme that draws them together as a well-defined set. One approach is the theme of sound production, i.e. using sets of sounds that are produced in similar physical ways, such as sounds involving water – dripping, splashing, running – or sounds involving metal – hitting, ringing etc.

Another approach to themes of sounds would be to collect sounds that are related not in the nature of the sound but in the context where the sound comes from. This might be, for example, a sound set where all the sounds have something to with a factory environment – hooters, machine noises, switches – or where the theme is a car – revving engines, indicator clicking, horns etc. These themes can either be directly related to the subject matter of the new media system or they can be chosen as an abstract metaphorical sound set.

How they combine

With a user interface that involves sounds there are often situations where sounds are playing at the same time. As such, the design of a suite of sounds should take this into consideration. Any sounds signaling important events should be discernible from background sounds. This is the visual equivalent of saying that the cursor shape should be different from the background pattern on the screen.

Using speech in new media

As I pointed out earlier, speech is a special case of sound. It has both advantages and disadvantages over other sound. The advent of digital recording means that it is easy to store and use speech fragments, and faster processing and streaming mean that it is easy to chop up the spoken word and combine chunks into new sentences with new meanings in real time.

Furthermore, the fact that many users are accustomed to receiving information in the spoken form means that a user interface that uses this has a very low threshold and learning curve.

Let us look at some of the issues involved in the use of speech in new media.

Parallel channels

Very often a new media system will need to communicate to the user using two channels. It will need to show the user something in one channel and then comment on that something that is being shown using another channel; for example, training systems may give an on-screen demonstration with associated instruction. Trying to put both the demo and the instructions on-screen together can result in confusion over which part is demo and which is instruction. Speech can play an important role here since it can function as the second channel without interfering at all with the visual channel.

Assumed intelligence

One drawback of speech-based communication from the system is that users can make the assumption that because the system is talking to them it is possessed of a human level of intelligence. Interactions could then go wrong or become frustrating to the user if they are interacting under this misconception.

User embarrassment

Any system that utilizes sound is going to attract attention of people other than the direct user, especially in public or semi-public contexts. Users may, of course, object to this attention and thus it could cause problems with the interaction. Imagine a job-seeker's web site where when you visited its home-page you got a sound file that said 'Welcome to job-seek, the site for those who are looking for another job!'

Slower interactions

The inclusion of speech elements in an interface can have the effect of slowing the interaction down, especially if users are unable to interrupt the speech. If they must wait until the end of every speech fragment before going further then the interaction will be drawn out. Users who appreciated the support of the long speech fragments when they first used a new media system will become frustrated with continued use of the system as they have to continually wait for the completion of spoken texts.

Interference

One of the differences we saw at the beginning of this chapter was that sound is dynamic and graphics are static. This dynamic quality of sound means that it is possible to miss parts of a sound-based presentation of information, for example, if there is interference from sounds external to the new media system. With graphics the message is always there for the user to see and problems like this happen only if the display uses animated information of some kind. The designer of the information should consider the effects of sound interference when designing the system.

Context

A key part of understanding any communication is the context that the communication occurs in. This is true for all aspects of human communication. Consider learning a foreign language. If you go into a shop to buy a loaf of bread there are only a handful of things that you expect the person serving to say: 'Can I help you', 'Anything else?', 'Thank you'. You already have a good idea of what you are listening out for. The same is true of interacting with new media. At any point in the interaction the user has a certain expectation of what the system is going to do or to say. This is vital in supporting the user's understanding of the system.

The importance of context should be borne in mind when testing new media systems. Speech fragments should be tested in the system context that the user is going to encounter them in and not tested independently of the rest of the system.

Sound and speech as primary interaction

Occasionally, the new media designer must work on a system where sound and speech are the most important, if not the only, input and output channels available. One can think of environments where the user's visual concentration is required elsewhere, or applications for visually impaired users. Also, shifting the focus from visual to sound means that the physical form of interactive devices can be substantially miniaturized by not using screens and keypads. The other key area of application is telephone-based, interactive systems.

Text rules apply

Speech does have a few overlaps with text since they are both concerned with words. As such, some of the points made in the chapter covering text for new media (chapter 3) are applicable here. It is most important to keep the amount of information as short as possible and to be attentive to the terminology that is being used.

Fewer choices

Speech-based interfaces put higher loads on the short-term memory of users. Instead of users browsing menus of choices in their own time, they must listen to them being recited and hold them all in their head while they make a choice. Multiple choices in the interaction should therefore be kept to a minimum and the number of choices should be limited. Also, keeping the actual spoken texts short allows the choices to be quickly listed for the user, making efficient use of their short-term memory.

Voice fragments

Often in a speech-based system information given to the user will be 'patched together' from a collection of building-block speech fragments. If we have speech fragments for the numbers 0 to 9 then we can create a speech-based system that returns phone numbers: 'The number you require is 028 3642'. If we want to do dates, we need a bigger pool of sound fragments.

Putting patchwork sentences together like this does make them sound awkward. They lack flow and intonation and pauses need to be well managed. Making the building blocks bigger takes away some of these effects but it then means you need a bigger pool of building blocks.

Time problems

Since all the interactions and choices have to be vocalized, there is a tendency for interactions to take a long time. The system must list all the possible options before the user makes a choice. Flicking through a list of names, for example, involves having them all read out and this takes time.

With screen-based interaction, the more experienced a user becomes, the faster they can interact with the system. They learn that the choice to save the file is about the middle of the first menu and can quickly swipe their cursor there to make the choice. With sound-based interfaces there is less opportunity for the experienced user to speed things up.

One way is to explicitly offer the user the choice of interaction styles: a first-time user's style with plenty of spoken help and explanation, and an experienced user's style with telegraphic or short sound-based interaction. Another way of speeding things up is to allow the user to pre-empt any choices that are being offered so instead of waiting for the system to complete its side of the interaction they can immediately interrupt with their response.

Conclusions

To conclude then, sound is a very different medium from graphics. It requires a very different set of skills in its use in design and care should be taken to use sound in contexts where it is appropriate.

Exercises

Digital Dictaphone
A good exercise involving a speech and sound-based interface is that used in chapter 18 dealing with the underlying system models: the digital Dictaphone, an interactive system that records and stores speech. It uses audio for all aspects of the interaction. Designing a system that is both comprehensible and usable is a real challenge with this rarefied medium. (See the exercises in chapter 18.)

The telephone game
The brain and ear have a wonderful way of screening out extraneous sound but suddenly getting alert when they hear something unusual or special.

If you are in a room with other people, try mentioning the name of someone close by who is engaged in a different conversation: they will often be oblivious to your conversation until their name crops up – then they will suddenly focus in on it.

WEBCODE
telephone
game

An even-numbered group of people can try playing the telephone conversation game. They all stand in a circle and are paired with the person opposite them. Then they turn to face outwards in the circle. One pair of people start talking to each other. After a minute or so another pair starts their own conversation, speaking over the conversation already in progress. This continues until all the pairs are having one-on-one chats. The amazing thing is that this is possible, that the brain and ear can isolate the voice of the person that they are talking to against the background of all the other voices.

WEBCODE
human sounds

Human sounds
Develop a quick bit of interactive new media or take apart an existing piece and replace the sounds with recordings of sounds that you simply make with your mouth. It is interesting to note the range of sounds that can be made. Also of interest is the observation that human-made sounds such as these can fit in acceptably with a piece of new media.

This is also a useful exercise to bear in mind for chapter 21 on prototypes and demos.

Designing a suite of sounds

WEBCODE
sound suite

Put together a new media interactive prototype that incorporates sounds, and keep the sounds external to the prototype and grouped together in a separate directory. A group of colleagues or students can then put their own custom directory of sounds together (taking care to use the correct sound file format and the same file naming as the original). By overwriting the original directory of sounds with one done by the other people, the sounds used in the interaction can be quickly changed and the entire interaction can take place with a new suite of sounds.

Collect sounds

WEBCODE
collect sounds

Get hold of a sound recording device and carry it around for a day collecting sounds from whatever context you are in. Feed them into the computer and try incorporating them into a simple new media system or a piece of animation.

Soundscapes

WEBCODE
soundscapes

This one is for larger groups with access to a space such as a hall or classroom cleared of desks. Divide into groups of five or six people. Each group must design a soundscape and then one of the group is blindfolded and must navigate through the soundscape.

The soundscape is achieved by the members of the group placing themselves at chosen points in the space and making chosen sounds and audio signals (whatever you want – but no talking) to assist the blindfold group member in their navigation.

This exercise can be further complicated by the addition of obstacles in the space and a goal to be reached.

Audio narratives

WEBCODE
audio
narratives

Record a sequence of noises that describe or are associated with carrying out a task that everyone is familiar with, for example brushing your teeth, doing the washing up or finding a TV program on a video tape. Somewhere in the sequence insert a 'rogue sound' from a different context and see how easy it is to spot it.

Color

07

Introduction

Color is everywhere in the world around us, both in the natural world, and in the world of artificial, designed objects. It plays a vital role in the design of interactive systems in general and new media systems in particular. If used well, it is a powerful and useful resource. If used badly, it can confuse, disgust and, in the worst cases, even have bad physiological effects on users.

In this chapter I am not going to cover the functioning of the eye in any great depth, nor will I get overly involved in the physics of color. The key point is to understand some of the basics and the effects that arise because of the way that the eye is built and to extract a few design guidelines for the use of color from a functional point of view.

Although the number of guidelines that will be established here is few, the subject is interesting because the rules that are established here are rooted in the physiology of the eye and as such are hard-and-fast and easy to verify.

Before we start looking at the uses and applications of color let us start by defining a few terms that we will be using.

Light

Color and frequency

Color depends upon frequency which is a property of light. You cannot have color on its own, you have to have light of a particular frequency

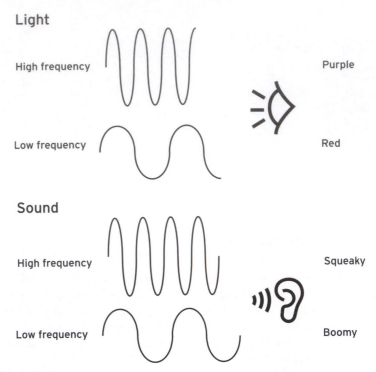

Figure 7.1: Color, like sound, is perceived differently at different frequencies.

and this is perceived, by the eye and the brain, as a particular color. This is similar to sound, where the frequency of sound is perceived as the pitch. Low-frequency sound is 'boomy' and high-frequency sound is 'squeaky'. With light, low-frequency light looks red and high-frequency light looks purple and in between we have the colors of the rainbow. See Figure 7.1.

Brightness and intensity

Another property of light is the intensity or brightness. This is independent of the frequency (color) discussed above, meaning that you can have dim red light or bright red light. Once again there is a similarity with sound. Sound too has intensity and this is perceived as loudness. So you can have loud squeaky sounds and quiet squeaky sounds just as you had different combinations for light. See Figure 7.2.

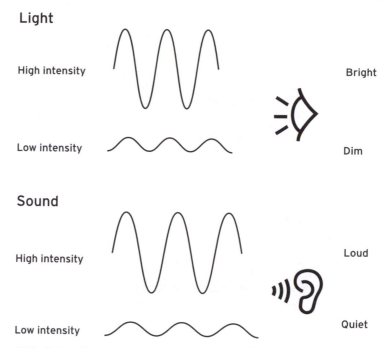

Figure 7.2: Color, like sound, is perceived differently at different intensities.

Perception of light

We have seen that light can have color and brightness (according to its frequency and intensity). Now let us move on to look at how the eye responds to color and intensity.

The eye's structure

The essentials of the eye's perception of light are that the light comes in through a lens at the front of the eye and this lens focuses the light into an image on the back of the eye (called the retina), in much the same way that a camera lens focuses an image onto the film in the back of the camera. The back of the eye is covered in little cells that then react to the light in different ways and send signals to the brain. See Figure 7.3.

These cells and the brain build up an image and meaning from these signals. Let us concentrate for the moment on the back of the eye where the lens projects the image. There are two different types of cells here, rods and cones, and they have very different properties. The rods react to the

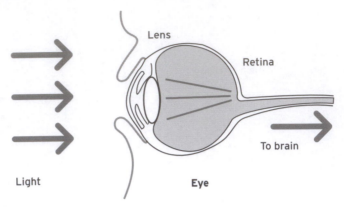

Figure 7.3: A much simplified diagram of the eye. The lens focuses light onto the retina and the signal goes to the brain.

intensity or brightness of the light and the cells react to the frequency or color of the light (remember that the two Cs go together – cones and color).

Rods and brightness

The rods are strewn throughout the retina and perceive differences in light and dark. Further from the retina are nerve cells that are connected to small groups of these rods. These cells gather information about what is happening in the collection of rods that they are connected to.

Much of the important information in vision is not to do with areas of light and shade but with the *boundaries* between one area and another. The rods do the basic work of vision, they are good at detecting boundaries precisely and they are also more sensitive to lower light levels than the cones.

Cones and color

As I stated at the beginning of the chapter, frequency is a property of light and color is the perception of that frequency by the eye. But this process of perception, this conversion of frequency to perception of color, is by no means a simple one. There are three different types of cone within the eye. Each type of cone reacts to a range of colors and that reaction peaks at a particular color. Thus as we run through the different colors and get closer to that peak color, the cone reacts more and more, and then once we are past that peak color, the cone reacts less and less.

The cones are sometimes referred to by the color at which their reaction peaks, thus the violet, the green and the yellow-green. However, our perception of color depends on a very complex interaction between the signals from these cones. It is not as simple as the brain saying 'Oh, we're getting a bit of a signal from the violet cones and a lot of signal from the green cones, so the color here must be a sort of blue'.

The green cones do not just react to green light – that is where their reaction peaks. They react to a spread of colors around that, even to blue and red light. Thus if the brain just got one signal from this one type of cone it would not actually be able to tell what color of light was falling on it. Yes, the cone is reacting to light but as it reacts to a spread of colors there is no way to tell from that one cone which color in the spread is hitting it. Furthermore the three spreads of colors for the three sorts of cones actually overlap a fair amount, so that all three sorts of cones react to turquoise blue light.

Thus, although I shall be talking about the violet cones, green cones and yellow-green cones, the perception of color is a much higher-order function of the nerves and brain. The creation of color in the eye and brain happens further from the eye as signals from neighboring cones are gathered and integrated in the mesh of nerve cells connected to the retina. When I see green it is not just the green light triggering loads of green cones in the retina (since the same effect could be achieved with really bright yellow light as well), it is how the three different sorts of cones react to the green light and how the mesh of nerve cells connected to them integrates these signals.

The whole story is very complex and fascinating once you start to get into it. However new media designers do not have the time to be experts in all the fields and a further investigation of color perception is only relevant for those who have a keen interest in this area or those that are involved in some new media project where color plays a key role.

As an interesting aside, the nerve cells in the eye are also sensitive to pressure. If they get squished they also trigger and send signals to the nerves and to the brain. They get squished like this if you get a blow to the head, and this is the origin of the 'seeing stars' effect. A less dramatic demonstration can be done by closing your eyes and pressing them carefully and gently against your arm or the palms of your hands. As the pressure rises and triggers the cells you half see swirling, strange patterns.

The difference in sensitivity to colors that defines the different types of cones is not, however, the only difference between the cones. There are other differences that are responsible for a variety of effects that actually take place in the perception of color and thus need to be considered when designing a new media system that uses color.

Color effects

Surrounding color alters perceived color

Above I have alluded several times to clustering; clusters of rods or cones are connected to single nerve cells and these in turn are clustered together and connected to other neighboring nerve cells. The end result is that signals from the 'top level' of these clustering nerve cells are signals not just from light falling on one small part of the retina but from the complex integration of signals from rods and cones and neighboring rods and cones. See Figure 7.4.

WEBCODE
color context

What this means is that the perception of any bit of light, its intensity and its color, is governed very much by the context that it is in, by the colors and intensities that surround it. There is a lot going on in the eye and the brain to give us a sense of 'color continuity' (grass is green, water is blue . . .) when in fact the color is constantly changing as the lighting conditions/viewing conditions are changing. It is difficult to choose colors in isolation or out of context; any color chosen is part of a larger collection and care must be taken regarding the color combinations that arise as a result of grouping colors. See Figure 7.5 (color plate).

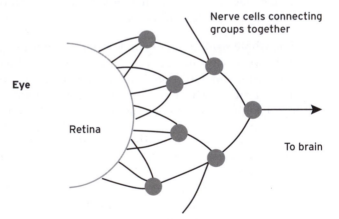

Figure 7.4: Rod and cone cells in the retina are clustered together into a network of nerve cells.

Orange on blue gives perceived depth

Many factors play a part in the perception of depth by the brain. As well as what is happening on the retina the brain is also aware of how much the eyes are moving together towards the nose (in effect how 'cross-eyed' you are going as you look at something close up). The more your eyes move together, the more the brain monitoring the muscles says, 'Aha, that must be something very close up'.

Another muscular thing that the brain takes into consideration is the amount that the lens of the eye is being pulled as the eye focuses on something far away. The lens at the front of the eye is quite thick when relaxed. Thick lenses are good for focussing on things near by. In order to focus on things far away the lens needs to be thinner. There are muscles around the lens that pull it to make it thinner in order to focus on things that are further away. The brain picks up on this and says, 'Aha, that must be something far away'.

This effect of the lens being pulled in order to focus can play a part even when things are not at different distances. It can come about due to the difference in frequency of light. If you have two things the same distance from the eye and of different colors, then the lens of the eye will have to be a slightly different shape to bring each of them into focus on the retina. (This is a bit of optics: different colors/frequencies focus at different lengths, which is a property of the light.) The brain interprets this slight variation in the muscles stretching the lens and says (incorrectly), 'Hey, these things are not the same distance away'. See Figure 7.6.

The best way to illustrate this is to have orange-colored objects against a dark blue background. The orange objects seems to 'float' a few centimeters in front of the blue background since the muscles controlling the lens of the eye have to do more work to bring the blue into focus.

Another factor that has some influence here is that blue things tend to be more distant anyway; the nature of the atmosphere affects the light passing through it and the light from things that are further away has passed through more air and so looks more blue than things that are close. Think of the 'distant blue hills'. As this is an expected arrangement of colors, there is a slight tendency to think that blue things are further away. Having said that I should add that this part of the effect is more of a 'brain effect' than something that takes place in the eye.

Jarring color combinations

Just like any other part of the body, rods and cones can get tired. When faced with intense stimulation they gradually become desensitized to the

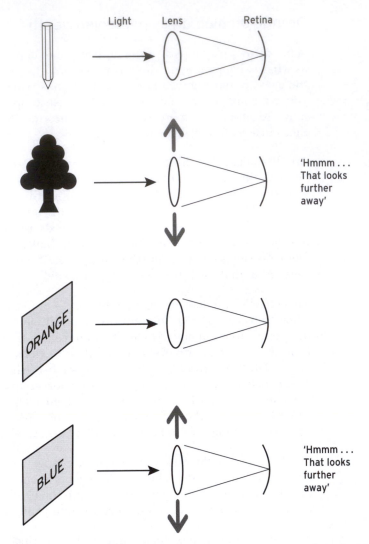

Figure 7.6: The lens of the eye is stretched more to focus on distant objects. It is also stretched more to focus on blue-colored things. In both cases the brain thinks they are more distant.

stimulation. A similar thing happens with smells and background hums: our senses and brain tend to screen them out. We really are geared up over years of evolution to be sensitive to change, so anything that does not change can, to a great extent, be ignored.

In general this is not a problem; indeed it is very difficult to be aware of it as the eye does a very good job of maintaining color constancy. When we look at something very red and stare at it, we do not see it gradually become less red. This tiring of the eye when stimulated by color is, however, apparent when we look at the boundary between two vivid and complementary colors.

Complementary colors are colors that are very distinct from one another. Consider red and green light. Green light has very little red in it and red light has very little green in it. Compare this with yellow and red, or red and purple. Yellow light has got quite a bit of red in it and purple light has got some red in it as well. (The actual definition is a bit more complex than is required here.)

So, if we take two complementary colors, red and green, and put them up against each other to create a sharp boundary, the cones receiving the green light become desensitized to green and those seeing red become desensitized to red. This is not a problem up to the point where the eye starts to move (and, contrary to what you may think, our eyes are moving quite a bit). What happens then is that the boundary shifts on the eye's retina and all sorts of things start happening.

The area that was exposed to green is tired of green and as a result extra-sensitive to red so when the boundary shifts and the red light hits that area the cones go, 'Wow! Red light, tons of it', and they really react to it. Normally when you see red light the red signal is created by some cones reinforcing the red signal while other cones in the area calm the red signal. When the cones have been tired by green light these calming signals are less and so the perception of red is really powerful. As the eyes move the boundary shifts the other way and the whole process is reversed as parts of the area exposed to red are now exposed to green. See Figure 7.7 (color plate).

The end result is that boundaries between complementary colors can play havoc with the eye and this effect should be avoided unless it is intentional.

WEBCODE
red green

Contrast for detail

The boundary effect described above is just one of many. The eye is specially set up to perceive boundaries as these are an important part of vision – they play a great part in extracting the detail of what we see. However, there is a difference between rods and cones in this area. Rods can detect different areas of light and dark and cones can detect different areas of color and absence of color. The key difference here is that rods are far better at detecting the boundaries between the different areas of light and dark than cones are at detecting the boundaries between areas of different colors. If small detail is shown as areas of the same color but of different brightness the eye can better discern the detail (because then the rods come into play) than if the small detail is shown as areas of the same intensity but different colors (because then the cones have to pick out the boundaries).

The exact details of why this is so are governed by the way in which the nerve cells between the rods and cones and the brain are connected to each other. The cells connected to the cones gather inputs from nearby groups of cones and compare them to get an idea of the color there. The cells connected to the rods also gather inputs from nearby groups of rods but they compare them to get an idea of where the light and dark boundaries are. (Once again, the wonderful complexities of the eye and the brain exceed the rather brief and glib descriptions I am giving here.)

Pale blue is bad for detail

There is an interesting situation here when we consider how the eye reacts to the color blue. Owing to the complexities of the way cones are connected, this sensitivity to blue is governed by the cones that are sensitive to violet light. They are quite different from the other two sorts of cones. To start with there are far fewer violet cones than the other cones (only about 5% of the cones are violet ones); however, this is compensated for by the fact that they are a lot more sensitive to lower light levels than the other cones.

The green and yellow-green cones are similar to the rods in the way that they are connected, so boundary detection in those colors is pretty good. The violet cones, however, do not have the same accuracy in terms of boundary. The effect of this is that if there is a boundary between two areas of color, both of which are rich in blue, and the two areas are similar in intensity (so that the rods cannot help) then the key player will be the violet cones, and these cones are bad at boundary detection.

The corollary to this is that pale blue is a very good color to use for background elements to information or for construction lines or other graphic elements that need to be seen but that are not a key part of the thing being displayed. Graph paper usually has a fine grid of pale blue lines, and construction lines in some CAD systems are pale blue in color.

Text and color

There is one very common visual task where boundaries and details are paramount and that is the reading of text.

Text should use contrast not color

In order to make text as legible as possible the text should be discerned from the background by means of a difference in contrast: dark text on a light background or vice versa. Studies have shown that black text on a white background is actually a little more readable that white text on black. However, care should be taken with large amounts of white space on computer screens as this results in a lot of glare and older users can find it difficult to cope with such high levels of glare.

Texts where the text differs from the background in terms of color are more difficult to read, with the worst case being blue, for the reasons described above. Blue-rich text should never be used against a blue-rich background with little difference in contrast. See Figure 7.8 (color plate). In fact, blue text should probably be avoided altogether unless there is a very high contrast in intensity between the text and the background when the rods can play a part. Such a combination of dark blue text against a white background is in fact pretty readable.

Yellow and legible text

WEBCODE
text colors

The eye reacts over time to color and this is also the case when reading text involving color. Certain color combinations are fine for reading text for short periods of time, but for longer time periods the eye tires and reading rate is affected. A good example of a color that has this effect is yellow: vibrant and highly saturated it is a very useful highlighting color but can be hard on the eyes when they have to look at it or work with it for long periods of time. Thus, color combinations for text that involve yellow as a foreground or background color tend to be very effective for short texts but to decrease in effectiveness as the text gets longer and the eye gets more fatigued. See Figure 7.9 (color plate).

Color associations

We have just looked at the effects that were closely tied up with the way that light and the eye itself behave. Now we can move on to color effects that are more concerned with associations of different colors.

'In-built' color associations

There are certain color associations that are deep-seated and basic in nature. Some people regard these as being 'in-built', while others say they are the result of early experience of our world and the world of nature. The true state of affairs is probably a mixture of the two.

There is a certain palate of colors that are regarded as 'cool' colors and that have a psychologically calming effect on people. Large institutional buildings such as hospitals and prisons make extensive use of these 'cool' colors such as light green and light blue for their effects on the residents. See Figure 7.10 (color plate).

More vivid colors have a negative effect on people when used in large areas, although they are useful as an attention-getting agent. Consider, for example, red whose deep saturated color demands attention from the viewer and is often used on signs and lights with functional messages. See Figure 7.11 (color plate).

Yellow is another highly saturated color, although more positive than red. It is a bright, happy color, the color of sunshine and smiley faces. Although combinations such as yellow and black have long been associated with warnings, the combination is used in nature in the coloring of wasps and bees and is carried over into the design of warning signs (black detail on a yellow triangular background) and markings for the boundaries of hazard areas.

There are other examples, although these deep-seated associations can be overlaid by other color associations connected with culture and work, and even personal color associations can be very strong. The end result is that it is very difficult to extract how much of our reaction to color is a result of some sort of hardwiring in our brain and how much is a result of being brought up in a culture that establishes and reinforces those associations. This debate, however, will not find a place here; the key thing is that these associations and effects are there and the designer must be aware of them, investigate them and take advantage of them in the design of new media interfaces.

Cultural associations

There are colors that have strong associations dependent upon the culture, though once again how much of this is 'in-built' and how much is learnt from the culture itself is always difficult to say. Suffice to say that they vary from one culture to another, often with surprising switches in the associations.

For example, the simple association of yellow with cowardice in many Western cultures contrasts with the association of yellow with grace and nobility in Japan and with prosperity in Egypt! Sometimes these associations are more apparent to the onlooker. One has only to visit Turkey to see that the color 'turquoise blue' is a very special religious color there, hence the origins of the name.

Any color associations can be influenced greatly by other factors. A particular color on its own may have a particular association, but when put in a certain shape, a different context or in combination it may have a completely different significance. To the average Japanese person red may symbolize danger and white death, but combine the two colors together in the Japanese national flag and you arrive at a completely different cultural association; symbology and text is a far more direct means of communication than color alone.

Sometimes these associations are used in a designed way, almost as a code when establishing color combinations for political movements or countries. In the nineteenth century, in Britain, women campaigned for the right to vote in national elections. The campaigners called themselves the 'suffragettes' and sported banners demanding the right to the vote. The banners were bordered in the three colors of the movement: purple, white and green. These particular colors were chosen because they carried associations linked to the spirit of the suffragette movement. The purple symbolized dignity, a color that occurs in state gowns of British royalty and in the apparel of top-ranking civil servants such as judges. The green symbolized fertility and hope for the future and the white represented purity.

In-depth knowledge of cultural color associations is not vital, but it is worthwhile testing colors against national perceptions to ensure that the design is not making any big color mistakes.

Work associations

Finally, we come to color associations connected with a particular area of work. These are less powerful and common-place than those dealt with above, but they are nonetheless worth a mention. There are certain fields of human activity that use color associations. Sometimes these color associations can be very rich and complex and sometimes the user groups that work with them on a daily basis can have them very firmly ingrained in their mind. Consider the color coding of electrical components and wires or the coloring of canisters of different sorts of pressurized gas.

If you are designing a new media system for a very specific, technical user group then it would be a good idea to inquire if they have a color coding scheme with which they are all familiar. This could yield a useful tool to use in the design of the interface. Remember though that just because they do have a set of color associations does not mean that you *have* to use it in the design; it simply means that it *can* be used if appropriate.

Color in design

Color uses

We have had a look at color effects and associations but let us now briefly look at things in a more functional way by considering the types of uses that color can serve in a new media interface.

Decorating

The simplest use is the pure decoration of aspects of an interface. A new media system does not have to look flat and functional all the time; there is room for decoration as long as the decoration does not directly interfere with, or distract from, the functionality.

Measuring

Color is a useful way of communicating information without having to resort to textual or digital means. Displaying information in this way may lack a degree of accuracy but it has several advantages including the fact that the user can 'read' the information and build up an overview of a complex situation more efficiently when it is displayed using colors. Consider the use of color on maps to show height; it is quicker to interpret and get the overview than having to interpret lots of figures and spot heights. See Figure 7.12 (color plate).

Collections of items with different priorities can also be color coded, giving the user a rapid means of getting an overview of the overall status of the collection. Physical control panels with many status lights are often implemented in red and green, enabling the user to quickly get an overview of the general status of the system: 'all systems green'.

Grouping

WEBCODE
color grouping

There are different ways of visually grouping on-screen elements (more on this in chapter 4 on layout). One way is through the use of color. This is a powerful way of grouping things since it is independent of position and thus elements that are grouped by color can be placed anywhere on the interface. This means that color can either be used to reinforce a spatial grouping, or it can be used orthogonally (independently!) as a separate grouping method. We could, for example, have an interface where all the buttons are spatially grouped according to function and when the user is logged in they get access to extra functionality. These extra buttons are placed in the appropriate part of the screen according to their function, but the fact that they are all associated with being logged in could be communicated by giving them all a common color. See Figure 7.13 (color plate).

Highlighting

As well as grouping, color can also be used to highlight an item, to distinguish it from a group (again chapter 4 deals with this in a more general way). The best highlighting colors are lively, high-saturation colors such as yellow or pink. See Figure 7.14 (color plate).

Realism

There are sometimes situations where the interface to a new media system will need to imitate some aspect of the real world. In such cases the addition of color can greatly increase the realism of the depiction. I am thinking here of interfaces where the clickable on-screen buttons are designed to look like metal equivalents, or showing feedback on the screen to look as if it is rendered on a small LCD screen with the right combination of black and grayish-green. See Figure 7.15 (color plate).

Color vocabularies

A color vocabulary is a collection of colors with functional associations, which are used within the design of a new media system. (There are similarities here with the discussion of design vocabularies in chapter 2.) There are many examples in the real-world if you keep your eyes open. I once had an alarm clock where all the bits to do with the alarm were color coded green; the alarm hand on the dial, the knob on the back of the clock to set the alarm hand and the alarm on/off switch on the top all matched in color, making it clear that they were all related in function.

The web convention of blue links for new links and purple links for visited links is also a very well recognized and practised color vocabulary, albeit a small one. Think also of the color vocabularies that are used in pull-down menus to indicate which option is selected, which options are not available etc.

Color vocabularies are complex things, involving input from the house style of the organization, the color vocabularies of any visual metaphors being used, the color vocabularies of the technology (such as the blue/purple links above) and new color vocabulary elements designed for the new media system itself.

Establishing the vocabulary

The vocabulary should not go against the normal color associations that we discussed above; for example do not use 'red' to mean water. Interaction should not be wholly dependent upon the color vocabulary. The information should be encoded in other ways as well so that someone who does not grasp the color vocabulary, or is not able to see it, is still able to use the system. The color vocabulary should play only a *supporting* role, albeit an important one.

WEBCODE
angry fruit
salad

When choosing different color schemes care should be taken to avoid the final screen design looking like the infamous 'angry fruit salad'. Try to select colors that are part of a larger palette or scheme and that work together harmoniously.

Such a color vocabulary can either be implicitly shown to the user during the interaction with the system, as with my alarm clock example above, or it can be communicated explicitly either in accompanying text (online help, manuals etc.) or in simpler terms in the interface itself.

Color blindness

Finally, when thinking about the user group, it should be borne in mind that not everybody can see color in the same way. Color blindness affects 8% of the male population (but less than 1% of the female population). The precise evolutionary reasons for its widespread occurrence will not be discussed here, but the end result is that when color is being used the designer should ensure that color is not the only means of communicating the information. This is also the case if the system being designed is to be used in an environment that involves colored light – in a submarine, a photographic darkroom, or under sodium-based street lighting. There should always be some means other than color to convey the information.

WEBCODE
color blind

This requirement may sound a bit abstract but the classic example is hyperlinks in text. Some designers think that the underlining of links looks ugly (and they are right) and they opt for a house style where links are distinguished by being a different color from the text. A color-blind user may then look at the page and be totally unaware of the links in the text. Communicating the information in a non-color-oriented manner, for example by underlining them, avoids this problem, so be aware.

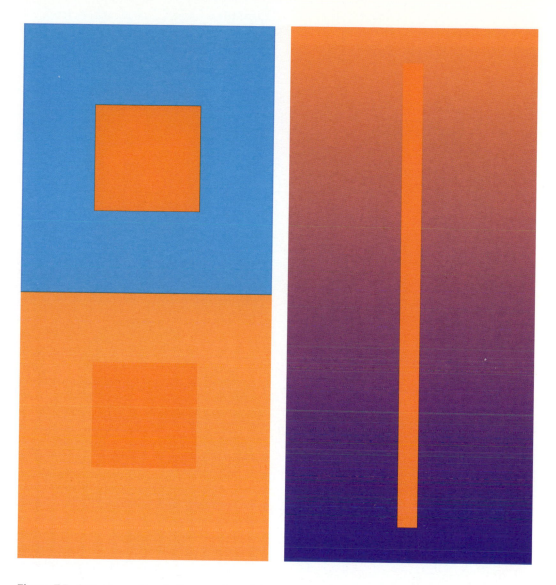

Figure 7.5 Color perception in the eye doesn't just depend on individual cones getting hit by a bit of light and reporting to the brain 'Hey, I can see a bit of red'. The cones are heavily interconnected with their neighbors and do complex integration of all these signals before sending anything to the brain.

The result is that the appearance of an area of color is greatly influenced by the color around it.

In the example above see how the color of the vertical bar appears to change as the background changes down the page and the two small squares appear to be different in color when placed against different colored backgrounds.

Figure 7.7 Colors that complement each other can have pronounced effects on the cones in the retina. Especially where the colors are very rich and intense, and where they border directly on one another.

Figure 7.8 When two areas of color are combined that have very similar brightness but differ in color the perception of the boundaries has to be done by the cones. The cones that are used in seeing blue are very bad at discerning boundaries and so text and background that are based on blue are very difficult to read. *Source:* extract from *Romeo and Juliet* by William Shakespeare.

I am too bold, 'tis not to me she speaks.
Two of the fairest stars in all the heaven,
Having some business do entreat her eyes
To twinkle in their spheres till they return.
What if her eyes were there, they in her head?
The brightness of her cheek would shame those stars
As daylight doth a lamp; her eyes in heaven
Would through the airy region stream so bright
That birds would sing and think it were not night.
See how she leans her cheek upon her hand!
Oh that I might be a glove upon that hand,
That I might touch that cheek!

Figure 7.9 Although black text on a yellow background is very clear and vivid, the combination leads to weariness of vision especially with long tracts of text and especially with older readers. Yellow is best reserved as a highlighting color. *Source:* extract from *Romeo and Juliet* by William Shakespeare.

Figure 7.10 Environments that make use of cool, pastel colors tend to have a relaxing effect on the occupants. For this reason they are often used in institutions such as schools, hospitals and prisons.

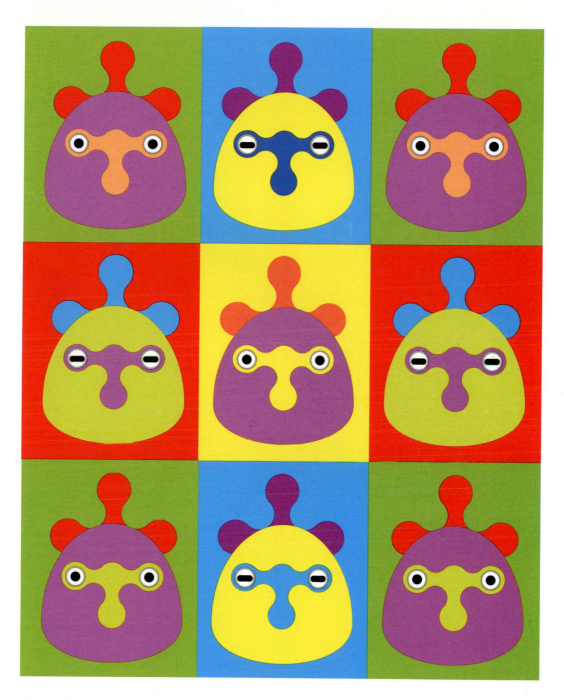

Figure 7.11 Vivid colors have a more stimulating effect on occupants, you would expect to see these colors in such contexts as restaurants or cinemas. Early asylums used to make use of different colored rooms in the treatment of patients.

Figure 7.12 Color coding can be used to show how some value varies in space. Here simple contours show how the height above sea level and the depth below sea level are often shown on topographical maps as differing intensities of blue and green/brown respectively.

The design of the range of colors is an interesting exercise in its own right depending on color associations in the particular context and upon whether certain bands need to be highlighted in some way.

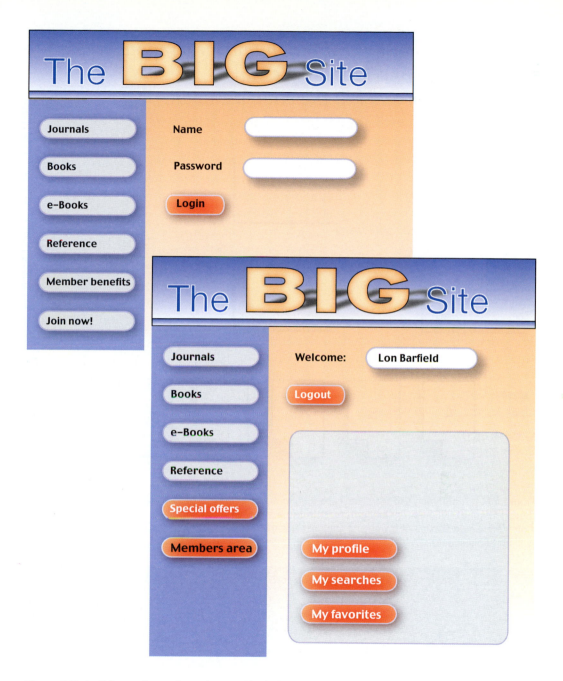

Figure 7.13 In this mock-up of a web page the buttons are organized and grouped according to functional area. When a user logs in they get extra functionality that is distributed throughout the interface. To highlight these extra functions, and to indicate that they are all connected to the login they are all given a different color.

But, soft! What light through yonder window breaks?
It is the east, and Juliet is the sun.
Arise fair sun and kill the envious moon,

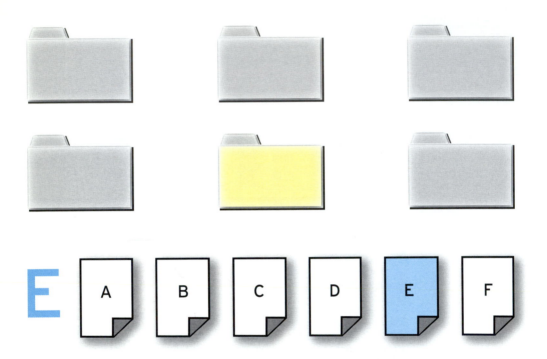

Figure 7.14 A common use for color is to highlight something; to pick it out from a group of similar things. Think of yellow text highlighters, showing a selected folder within a group of other folders or indicating which section of a web site the user has gone to. *Source:* extract from *Romeo and Juliet* by William Shakespeare.

Figure 7.15 Black text on a gray-green background is not the height of legibility, especially if done with LCD style bitty letters. However if you want to promote a user experience of up-to-the-minute news or stock prices then adopting an LCD read-out as a visual metaphor could be worth the decrease in legibility.

Exercises

Black and white photocopiers

A few weeks ago I was using a black and white photocopier to enlarge a map. The map was in black and white with one important route marked in a sort of beige color. When the copy emerged from the machine I discovered that it had copied the black parts of the map but that the beige area had not been picked up at all. There was not even a hint of gray on the copy. The machine had not responded to it at all.

The black and white photocopier reacts differently to different colors in a similar way to the eye. It does not have the same sensitivity to all colors. Obviously if the intensity of the color is darker then it will come out as a darker shade of gray, but colors of the same intensity will not necessarily result in the same shade of gray.

Bearing this in mind, think if there are any useful applications of this information. Get hold of colored paper and pens and experiment with a photocopier. What useful role would there be for graphics that disappear or appear when photocopied?

WEBCODE
photocopier

Color experiment

Try this simple experiment. Place a vivid red or green (or other pure color) shape on a white background and stare at the center of it for a minute or so. Keep your eyes fixed on one point on it and do not let them wander. Quickly remove the shape and now just stare at the white background. What do you see? Explain what is happening in terms of the coverage of this chapter. How could this effect play a role in the design of interfaces to new media systems?

WEBCODE
color
experiment

Maps for submarines

The parts of the eye that are sensitive to blue light (based on signals from the violet cones) are very sensitive to low light levels, far more sensitive than the other cones. This blue light sensitivity is what you want to rely on when you are straining your eyes in the dark to see things. So you do not want to tire the blue light sensitivity of your eyes out before you need them; you want to starve them of blue light so that they are in tip-top condition and readiness. One way would be to sit in the dark, but this is not always possible. Another way is to use red light for local illumination. Red light contains no blue light and so the blue sensitivity will not be affected and will be ready for when it is needed. This is the reasoning behind the red lights used in submarine control rooms when sailors are cruising at conning tower depth and need to go top side to have a look around in the dark.

Consider such a command room of a submarine when it has gone to red light before surfacing. The charts and signs used would still need to be

WEBCODE
sub maps

legible. What steps would you have to take to ensure they were all still usable?

How should the design of on-screen information be dealt with?

WEBCODE
color coding

Color codes in everyday life
Think of everyday examples of color coding and color vocabularies. Try to avoid very specialized examples; think instead of types of color coding that most people would know and that could be incorporated in some way into the design of a new media system.

Video and animation

08

● Introduction – movement and users

We are all very sensitive to change. By that I mean change in the tangible world around us. Consider that indescribable feeling when a low-level background noise suddenly stops. We did not notice it when it was there, and we certainly do not notice it when it is not there, but the change of the noise suddenly stopping is very noticeable. On the visual side, too, we are highly sensitive to change, more so than with sound. Catching sight of a slight movement out of the corner of our eye makes us immediately swing our head round to look at it. The reasons are rooted in our distant past. Food moves, and things that regard us as food move, so it helps to be very, very aware of movement – otherwise you get very thin or get eaten.

Such considerations are less important these days. However, we still have this sensitivity to movement hardwired into our brains. Sometimes it still has its uses and sometimes we can take advantage of it when we are designing new media systems that the user interacts with.

Terms

Before we move on, let us start by defining a few terms:

- *Change* is when a tangible property becomes different over time, usually in a gradual continuous manner. In this context the tangible property is visual and could be color, size etc.
- *Motion*, or *movement*, is when the position of something changes, either in nature or in animation. (For the rest of this chapter I shall concentrate primarily on movement, although certain other visual things that change will be mentioned in the process.)

■ *Animation* is change that is designed and created artificially using a technological platform (such as film, a computer, a flick book etc.)

Let us also bring interaction into the picture. Interaction relies on time, so anything interactive has a relationship with time; the user interacts in time, things change in time as the user interacts with them and things move in time.

Video and animation

In real-world terms the two main topics that I am bringing together are video and animation. Both of these subjects are wide in scope; one could write books about animation and video, but I am restricting myself to the aspects that have a point of contact with interaction and new media. The common feature is the introduction of movement into the user interface.

Change and narrative

When we consider time and the interface there are other subjects that play a role apart from video and animation. One that we shall be looking at later is narrative (chapter 15). The chapter on narrative is in the next part where I shall treat the development of the interaction with respect to time in more of a general and abstract manner. Here, I am mainly concerned with the rather lower-level detail of change and motion – not general principles, but basic ideas to do with the use of video and animation as elements within a new media system.

Video

Let us start then with video. Video is a media type that is being used more and more as bandwidth increases. Technical support for its use becomes more sophisticated and everything becomes more affordable. On the web it will be the next 'big thing', just like sound was a while back.

When to use video?

Of course, the fact that it is possible to use video clips within a new media system is not in itself a justification for using them. There are situations where it would be a good idea to use video and situations where it would be bad, or just not beneficial, to use video. Consider the following examples.

Good use of video

- A web-cam set up overlooking the site of a grand construction project and streaming real-time images over the web, as happened with the British Airways London Eye project.
- A cd-rom supplied with a printer showing how to carry out actions such as installing it and changing the printer drum etc. (As well as appropriate use of video this is also an example of good user group definition; only people with a computer will buy the printer and so you are pretty much guaranteed that nearly everyone will be able to view the video clips.)
- Video clips of cookery techniques. These are more direct and useful than textual descriptions as is evidenced by the strange terminology that sometimes appears in cookbooks.

WEBCODE
thank you

Bad use of video

- A corporate web site with a downloadable video of the CEO sitting behind a big desk saying, 'Welcome to our web site' in high-quality stereo. Great!
- A streaming web-cam set up in the office of a typical internet company showing typical people sitting behind typical computers just as they are in your own office.

WEBCODE
office

Appropriate use

The basic principle is to use video when the video can say something that would be impossible or difficult to say with a lighter-weight medium such as graphics, photos or text. This idea of 'saying something' does not just mean 'action'. Videos can also add something very personal to words. Just as an audio interview with someone is more telling than the text of an interview, so too a video interview is more than just the spoken words. You can see which points the speaker is passionate about, what they are doubtful about etc. No wonder one of the key events in a presidential election is the televised debate.

Where to place the video?

The limits on bandwidth for the internet and on storage and playback speed for cd-roms mean that playing a video is a trade-off between size and quality; it is either big and grainy or it is small and clear. Choosing small and clear means that there is then the question of how to introduce the video to the user.

Figure 8.1: Reserving a space on the page in which to show video.

In the page

The first approach is simply to reserve a space within the page for the video, in effect a small 'screen' on which to present the video. See Figure 8.1.

In a separate context

Alternatively, there could be a link to the video within the page and when the user clicks it a separate context is created. Either a space is opened up on the page and the existing content moves aside to create the space to show the video, or the user jumps to a special video-playing context, in a separate window that is popped up by the system or in a completely new page within the same window. This separate video-playing context can then contain the space to play the video as well as any controls and captioning that are required. See Figure 8.2 for these three options.

User interaction with videos

Appropriate placement of video is only half of the story. The other half is helping the user to interact with the video. The first building block of

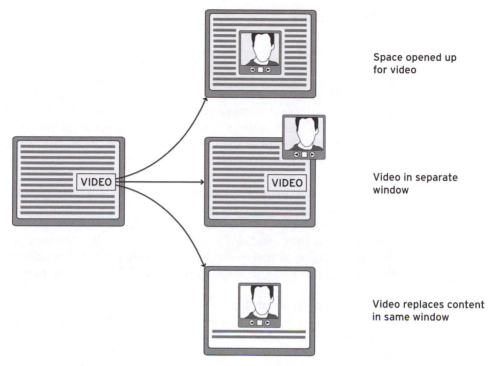

Space opened up
for video

Video in separate
window

Video replaces content
in same window

Figure 8.2: A link on a page leading to a separate context for the video. There are three options.

this interaction is making sure that the user knows that the video is there. There is nothing worse than building a link to a video clip into a new media system only to have no one click on it when you do the user testing. The counter example is also true; it is awful to click on a link in a mostly textual web site, to suddenly discover that you have just started to download a huge video file. It is the equivalent of sending off for a brochure and suddenly finding a salesperson on your doorstep two days later.

Videos have their own pace

In a new media system without video (or audio) the user is very much in control of the pace of the interaction. The moment video is introduced (or even just audio) the user loses that control over the pace (there is more about control in chapter 15 on narrative). Even in normal use, video clips can have a negative effect on the interaction if the user is not in control of them and they are long or inappropriate.

Video controls

An important first question with video controls is, 'Why are users watching the video?' What task are they busy with, and what do they hope to get out of watching the video? The easy, non-thinking approach is to include an array of buttons with the video clip that is similar to that found on a real-world video recorder. (The really non-thinking approach will include an 'eject' button as well!) The designer must concentrate on the context, the length of the video, the message of the video, the user's task, and decide what controls are appropriate.

If it is a video clip to do with spotting key events in a piece of action such as a sporting event then the user will be interested in minute detail and timing and will want to run backwards and forwards and freeze certain frames. At the other end of the scale, where the clips are very short and the user is expected just to run them through once, it is possible to bring the controls down to the absolute minimum. Consider the following.

Play immediately in context

If space is reserved on a page for a video then playing the video as soon as the page is presented to the user is not a good idea, Figure 8.3. The user has not yet had time to appreciate the context and there is a strong feeling of being out of control, further emphasized if there are no controls for the video.

If there is a separate context for the video then it would be more acceptable to start playing it as soon as the separate context is presented, Figure 8.4. The link that the user clicks on to go to the separate context should make it clear to the user that the video is going to be played straight away. Even then there is still the problem that the user is having to cope with two different things happening simultaneously: interpreting the new context (possibly involving a new window being popped up) and watching and listening to the video.

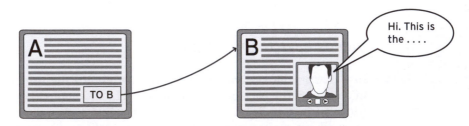

Figure 8.3: Starting a video playing as soon as the user clicks through to the page containing it.

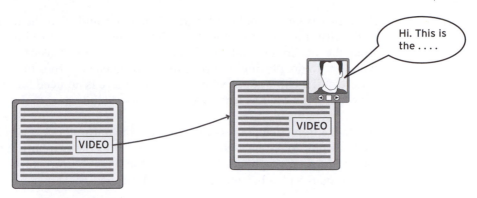

Figure 8.4: Starting a video playing as soon as the separate context for it is opened.

Incorporating a 'Play' button

This problem can be alleviated by including a separate 'Play' button in the video context. The user is then in control of the pace of the interaction. They choose when they are ready to see the video.

Incorporating a 'Stop' button

Expecting the user to sit through a chunk of video that they may or may not find relevant is not a good assumption to make. Incorporating a 'Stop' button to accompany the video allows them to cancel the playing of the video without having to resort to more system-oriented 'techy' methods (shutting down windows, going to the task manager etc.).

Completeness

Having two buttons for 'Play' and 'Stop' means that the user can start and stop the video clip as they want. However, this is still not a complete solution in that it may not cover all the operations that the user wants to perform. The user is limited by the functions available to simply being able to control whether the video is running or not. They cannot alter their position within the video quickly and there is no way of going backwards within what is being shown.

These limitations are not much of a problem when dealing with short clips of video, but in larger contexts the user is more likely to want to navigate their way around within the video clip, and to make this easier for them a more complex suite of functions is needed, mimicking the suite of video controls available on a conventional video recorder. There is more discussion about this idea of what functions are embodied in the controls when we deal with the underlying system model in chapter 18.

So think carefully about the length of the video and what the user is going to do with it. One option for short clips is just to have two buttons: 'play from the beginning' and 'stop'. This covers all the tasks that the user will want to do: playing, stopping and getting back to the start. The short nature of the clip will probably mean that there is no need for more complex functions such as fast forwarding and rewinding.

Another interesting point is that the flexible nature of new media means that buttons do not have to be permanent. Thus the two-button approach can be further simplified. Clicking on the 'Play' button starts the video and turns the play button into a 'Stop' button.

Keep things simple

Copying the icons from a video recorder is not always the best approach. Simple text is always clearer, or use a combination of both if you really must have icons. Also, just because the software supporting video playback on the computer allows you to perform functions such as fast forward, set marker etc., that does not mean that you have to pass all this functionality on to the user.

Exploration and forgiveness

The issue of allowing the user to interrupt video clips is an important one and is coupled with the issues of letting them know what they are getting into. The ideal situation is of course to provide the user with very clear labeling of links and also to allow them to interrupt.

However, there are some contexts where you do not want to distract the user with long explanatory links; you want them to explore and enjoy and get lost in something. This is especially true for more narrative-style and exploitative new media systems. Creating an immersive story line is difficult if you have links that say 'Love (this is a link pointing to a video clip that is 5 minutes 39 seconds long, it is 5.2 Megabytes in size and describes how Betty and Barker fall in love . . .)'. In such contexts it would be acceptable to provide less informative links but allow the user to interrupt easily and quickly and go back to where they were.

The opposite situation, having clear labeling and no interrupts, is less acceptable as there is still the issue of the user being out of control of the interaction. Finally, the big one to avoid is to have bad link labeling and no interrupts. This pretty much guarantees that the user is going to end up watching something that they do not want to see and they will not be able to do anything about it! (More about interrupting in chapter 15 on narrative.)

Minimizing video usage

Having decided that video is appropriate and having designed suitable controls, the designer is still faced with the fact that videos are big, heavyweight chunks of media in comparison with other media. Efforts should be made to decrease the size of the video files and minimize their use.

Size can be decreased by using mono-sound instead of stereo-sound. The size of the video picture will also have an influence on the file size. Another approach is simply to edit the video down to the most important points, thus making it shorter, and the resulting file smaller.

There are of course many technical ways of increasing the compression and thus lowering the size of the video file but I am concentrating here on design solutions, not technical solutions. A few more design solutions to minimizing video use follow; see also Figure 8.5.

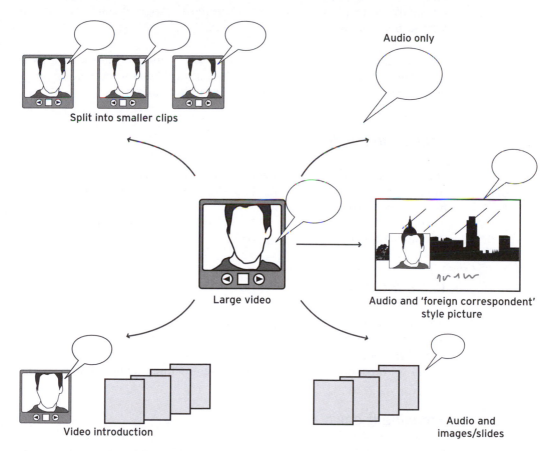

Figure 8.5: Five options to having one large video.

Audio only

Think carefully about the video you are using. How much extra information does the visual image add? If it is an interview perhaps it could be just as informative with sound only. This point is illustrated often on the television news where the reporter is outside the building where the conference/presidential meeting is taking place. All the information is in his spoken report while the picture just shows the lit windows of the building within which everything is happening.

'Foreign correspondent' model

Another approach that is familiar from the news on television is the 'foreign correspondent model'. When the reporter is unable to file a video report, the news program will broadcast the audio report and supplement it visually with a picture of the town where the report is coming from and a small inset photo of the reporter's face.

This is a good supplement to an audio-only chunk of information as it gives clues as to the person talking (it is always nice to be able to put a face to a voice) and the context they are talking about.

Images and audio

Often in a context where someone is talking, such as a lecture, the key thing is what they are saying. The video image of them just standing next to an overhead projector could be replaced by something far more instructive (and lighter in weight) such as animation or images or even the slides they are showing supporting their lecture.

Video introductions

It is possible to use video clips to set the scene and then continue with one of the other media combinations described above. You could have a clip of someone introducing themselves and then switch to some other media (photos, diagrams, animation) accompanied by an audio track.

Breaking it down

Even if you decide that a large amount of video is necessary, there are still ways to minimize the downloading if the video is being delivered over the web. The simplest is to slice the video up so that instead of one monolithic chunk of media it becomes a collection of units that the user can download as required.

A smaller-scale variation on this is to provide little 'tasters' of large chunks of video so that the user can quickly download and evaluate whether the video is relevant or interesting (and check if they can view the video on their particular computer configuration). This is a similar process to watching a trailer for a film and deciding whether to watch the whole film or not.

The bottom line is that video is like dynamite: it is powerful stuff but you have to use it appropriately and be very careful when using large amounts of it.

Animation

Representing movement

I made the point in the opening part of this chapter that we, as humans, are very geared up to being aware of motion. It is no wonder then that artists, and later photographers, have always been interested in the idea of capturing animation. Early paintings did their best to incorporate 'hints' at the movement that was taking place in a particular scene. Think of classic oil paintings of running horses where the horses are caught with their forelegs stretched out in front and their hind legs stretched out behind.

Even now that we have technologies to capture animation there are still low-tech contexts where such 'hints' are used. I am thinking in particular of comic strips: the dog's wagging tail is shown as a tail with 'wag lines' next to it, indicating multiple images of the tail in different positions; fast-moving things have 'whizz lines' shooting out behind them etc. See Figure 8.6.

Animation

Technology has now reached a point where the capture and replay of movement are easy. Furthermore, movement does not have to be captured from real life, but can be created using specialized tools.

Figure 8.6: 'Swoosh' lines on a falling brick and movement lines on a dog's tail.

In the world of new media, animation is a useful tool. It makes things easier to comprehend, since users are accustomed to trying to work out what is going on when things are moving (is it food, or does it think I am food?). It helps to fit abstract technological things into our model of the world. It can tell us about things that are going to happen (flashing 'battery-low' indicator on a laptop), things that are happening (progress bar when you are doing a download) and things that have happened (an animated 'you've got mail' icon).

Behavior and animation

Anything moving is likely to be interpreted in some sort of behavioral way. Things do not just happen, they happen suddenly, smoothly, aggressively, reluctantly, chunkily etc. It is a good indication of the power of animation that even the slightest effects related to change can have a big impact on the user.

The classic example of this is the 'standby' light that Apple introduced into their clear G4s around the turn of the millennium. It did not just blink on and off to show that the system was in standby mode, it *pulsed* on and off. What it was saying was not 'I have a supply of electricity and I am in standby mode' but 'I have the power of a tiger and I am lying ready like a coiled spring, waiting for your command'.

When we first had these computers installed in the lab I pointed this out to my students. This was the 'MTV' generation – fast, multi-medial,

12-second attention span, WAP enabled, and here they were voicing hushed 'Wows' at a small light pulsing on and off.

Simple animation, if it is well managed, can be a powerful communicator.

As a counter example illustrating the user's desire to read interpretation into animation, consider the animation used for file downloading in Microsoft Windows. As the process progresses the user is given rich feedback about what is happening. An animation runs with a spinning world on the left from which little pieces of paper appear and fly across to the right. Here they flip into an open yellow folder, and then just as they are nestling down into the folder there is a red star-shaped flash and the piece of paper has vanished!

The problems lie in two aspects of the animation. First, the sudden appearance of the red star-shaped flash. Red is the color normally associated with warning, so the red star-shaped flash looks like an explosion which also has negative associations. Secondly, there is a problem with the continuity: the page that flew across has suddenly disappeared, and there is nothing to show that it is in the folder. The whole animation seems to suggest that downloading is taking place but the second stage has not worked because of some serious problem, resulting in the loss of the downloaded data.

A more reassuring animation could have shown a green tick appearing when the page arrived and then the shape of the folder changing in some way to indicate that it has content, in a similar way to the trash can when it has content.

Naive physics

The science of physics is familiar to most people, if not in great detail. It is the study of physical properties and processes in the world around us. One particular branch of it studies how things interact with each other – what happens if you drop a book on a plank of wood, how far do you have to tilt a board before a brick on it begins to slide down, etc.?

What then is 'naive physics'? Well, if physics is about how the world works, then naive physics is about how we *think* it works. Take a classic example: the physics of dropping bombs or supplies from planes. Planes never release their payload directly above the target; they have to release them miles before they get to the target. Things dropped from an aircraft do not fall straight down; they match the speed of the airplane and so follow a curve as far as an observer on the ground is concerned, Figure 8.7.

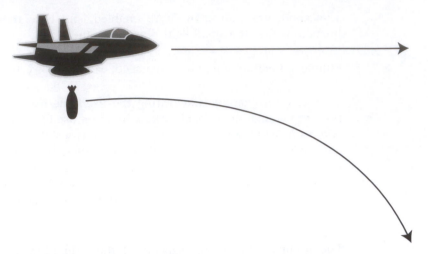

Figure 8.7: Real physics: a bomber needs to drop its bombs well before it reaches its target.

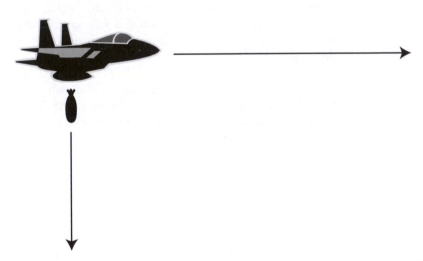

Figure 8.8: Naive physics: a bomber needs to drop its bombs directly over the target.

This is true and fits in with real physics (conservation of momentum and all that) but it seems 'strange' to us ordinary people, many of whom think that the payload is dropped directly above the target and falls straight down, while the airplane flies away, Figure 8.8. This later idea of what happens is naive physics. It sounds like a pretty erudite pursuit, but it plays a great part in something that is familiar to us all – animated cartoons. As we shall see later it is also relevant to animation in the user interface.

Animated cartoons are usually made to fit in with our ideas of naive physics. The cartoons take this naive physics and then exaggerate it. Consider the following:

- The running dog who runs over the edge of a cliff and hangs suspended, legs whirling, until he looks down and notices the drop; only then does he fall.
- The road runner getting ready to run; standing still he revs up his legs, leans back and then suddenly whizzes away.
- Getting hit on the head and seeing stars (see chapter 7 on color for the truth behind this).
- Falling in love and having your heart practically jumping out of your chest.
- Being awe-struck and your jaw dropping until it hits the ground.

(Incidentally, this list of animation effects is difficult to describe in purely textual terms and is a wonderful example of the point at which video would be an appropriate medium to use.)

The approach of basing designs on the expectations embodied in naive physics is also appropriate for movement in the interface to systems. Things should behave as the user expects them to behave, even if this is not how things really behave in the physical world. The designer is not trying to recreate an accurate model of physics in the real world, but to communicate with the user, and if better communication with the user means breaking a few laws of physics then that is perfectly acceptable.

Animation contains many visual clues about what is happening and what is going to happen. Exaggerating these visual clues is a good device to get the message across. The question that arises then is, when we reach the end point of interface development and have achieved the ultimate new media interface, will it be a cartoon interface?

Aqua interfaces

WEBCODE
aqua

In actual fact this is starting to happen. The term 'aqua' is starting to crop up more and more in discussions and articles about interfaces. 'Aqua design' is about cartoon-type things. It is about providing continuity of existence, continuity of motion, it is about breaking the rules of physics if breaking them will help the user follow what is happening. It is about a virtual world where things flow and shift and expand and contract fluidly, as required. In short it is about good design of new media.

Exercises

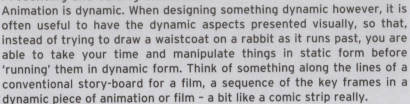

Presenting and editing animation

Animation is dynamic. When designing something dynamic however, it is often useful to have the dynamic aspects presented visually, so that, instead of trying to draw a waistcoat on a rabbit as it runs past, you are able to take your time and manipulate things in static form before 'running' them in dynamic form. Think of something along the lines of a conventional story-board for a film, a sequence of the key frames in a dynamic piece of animation or film – a bit like a comic strip really.

Imagine an interface for simple two-dimensional animation where you have to create and build it in dynamic form as with the rabbit's waistcoat above. Would it work? Would there be any advantages in taking this approach?

Now think of the more conventional approach, designing animation using some sort of visual annotation for the time-based elements, something along the lines of a script or musical notation. Think of a simple way of doing this. What tools would the user need? What would they need to see on the screen? How could everything be packed into such a small screen area? Come up with the basics of a design.

WEBCODE
editing
animation

If you are familiar with how it is done in tools such as Macromedia Director or Flash, then try to avoid reproducing these ideas in your design.

Musical terms

Music is all about something changing with time. The notation for music involves specifying which musical notes are to be played when and how. There are also many other elements in the notation such as 'repeat this part'. Find out as many elements of musical notation as possible. Can they be applied to animation in any way?

WEBCODE
musical
terms

Small video images in good contexts

Early cd-rom-based games were able to use only very limited video clips. They had to be short and occupy only a small space on the screen. Nevertheless the games endeavored to use video clips very effectively by building them into interesting contexts. One example was a static image of a hut with a closed door on the front. Part of the door was a sort of flap and when you clicked on the door a short video clip was played, occupying the space where the flap was and showing the flap opening, a face peeping out and then the flap closing again. Short in duration and small in screen space, it still managed to add action and atmosphere without the user being made aware of the limitations involved.

WEBCODE
small video

Can you think of any other ways of designing small format video clips like this?

WEBCODE
video endings

Seamless video choice

Imagine you were to record a short bit of video with alternative endings and you then built them into a new media system such that the system chose randomly which ending to use. The main part of the video A would be followed by either ending B or ending C. If there was a natural break in scene between A and B or C then it would be easy to play either B or C after A without any problem.

Imagine, though, that there is no break – you simply want the action and movement to continue and flow either as it does in B or as in C. How could you approach managing the switch from A to B or C without it looking as though a switch has been made?

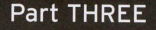

Part THREE

Interaction

■ **How this part relates to the other three parts**

The previous part covered the building blocks of new media, the underlying elements that make up a new media system. In this part we will be looking at *interaction*. Although inter-action could be considered as one of the elements, it is in fact more fundamental than that. Interaction is a framework and structure, part of all interactive technology. It surrounds us and includes us. It binds all the separate elements together.

Far too often it is regarded as something smeared on the surface at the end of a project, but it is far more fundamental than this. It is also about going deeper and designing all aspects of a system from the surface downwards so that the entire system matches the expectations of the user as closely as possible.

The first step is establishing the basis of the interaction. Ultimately any interaction is a form of communication between the system and the user. This basis is the 'GAS' analysis, standing for 'Goals, Audience and Scope' - three key factors in the initial stages of interaction design.

An extension of the GAS analysis is the idea of contexts. Contexts are the different aspects of the environment that have an influence upon the interaction; in effect they are the different contexts within which the interaction takes place.

Then come two important issues in the design of the interaction: the user model and designing the feedback to support the user model.

The next three chapters are the focus of this interaction section. They explain the framework that holds everything together. This framework is composed of the *structure*, the underlying relationships between the content; *the narrative*, which is the underlying thread of interaction and dialogue that the user and the system follow; and finally the *navigation*, the ways of supporting the user as they follow tracks through the content.

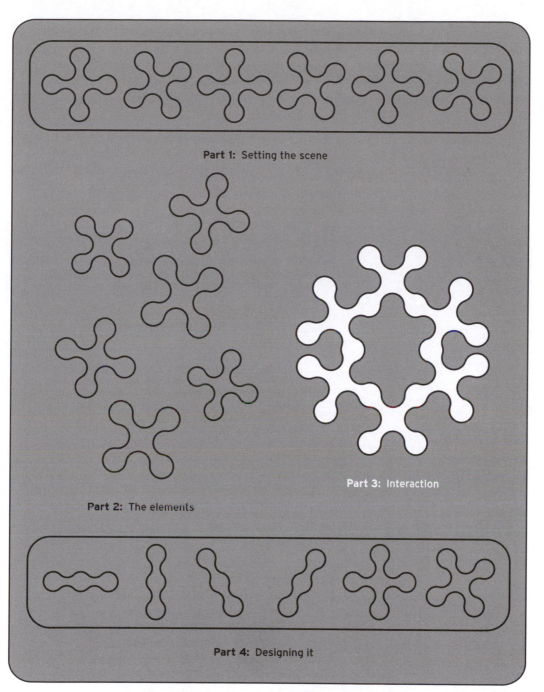

Part 1: Setting the scene

Part 3: Interaction

Part 2: The elements

Part 4: Designing it

Figure Part 3: How this part relates to the other three parts.

Goals, audience and scope (GAS)

09

Introduction

Interaction is a multifaceted discipline bringing together ideas and methods from many different worlds. The first steps, however, are relatively simple. Relatively simple to define, that is; putting them into action is not so simple. They revolve around the key concepts of goals, audience and scope: three basics that underpin any communication exercise in any medium.

Goals

Goals are the answer to the 'Why?' of the whole project. Goals are the reasons why the new media system is being created in the first place. The developers of the system have definite goals in mind when they embark upon the idea and these should be integrated with the goals of the users of that system.

In the light of practice in the real-world I should probably restate that as: 'the developers of the system *should* have goals'. There is still a high degree of 'me-too' in new media design – companies investing in new media technology simply because their competitors are. Without well-defined goals it is difficult to evaluate the investment being made – you cannot achieve a goal if you do not have one.

Developer goals

To some extent all goals of the developers in a commercial context are connected with making a profit in some form or another. Having said that, there is more than one way to make a profit and the sub-goals along the way can be many and varied.

Branding a company identity

One possible goal of a new media system is to assist in the branding of a company image. By providing information that the user wants, or by providing entertainment, the system can build up an audience and can then be used as advertising to reinforce the identity of the company or product in the user's mind.

Increasing traffic to a web site

Another common goal with web sites is to increase the number of visitors to the site. Again this can be achieved through providing a service to the users or providing entertainment.

Real advertising

Often the new media system is part of a wider sales and marketing exercise, either brand building as mentioned above or informing users of products or offers.

Accompanying service

A functional goal of some new media systems is to provide a service that supplements an existing product or service. One can think of a cd-rom with technical information and cool examples accompanying an authoring product.

Entertainment

Entertainment is not really a goal in itself, it is usually a means to an end such as commercial selling of the entertainment, or entertainment to attract visitors. There are also plenty of web sites that offer interesting entertainment purely with the goal of pushing their own brand.

Mixing it up

Sometimes there is an interesting overlap between the two, a situation where the goals of the developer are actually to make the user change their own goals! The developers want to turn brief visitors to a web site into regular visitors, or to turn browsing visitors into buying visitors.

User goals

Just as one can glibly say that the developer's goal is to make a profit, one can just as glibly say that the user is out to get something, but again there are many variations on what that 'something' is.

Getting entertainment

Many new media systems are just that – entertainment. They are amusements supplying games, music, movies etc.

Physically getting something

This is still a minor user goal although the proportion of sales taking place in the e-commerce world is on the up and up all the time as new services mature and existing companies migrate their operations onto the web.

Getting information

Getting information is a very broad, catch-all goal. It includes getting product information, factual information about a certain subject, real-time information, news, share prices etc. plus all the things that are done to that information – printing it off, comparing information, compiling it, reading it etc.

Communicating

Often the web is used as a communication medium to 'chat' or exchange images or music. To some extent the above points are also communication between a company and a customer but here I am referring to more personal one-to-one communication.

Win-win designs, umbrella marketing

The ideal way of combining these two sets of goals is to develop a new media system that lets the developer get what they want while at the same time giving the user what they want: a so-called 'win–win' situation. A good example of this is umbrella marketing.

I have written another book based on my regular *SIGCHI* column on real-world design. As this is the modern age I have an accompanying web site, www.DesigningTheRealWorld.com. The idea is that this promotes the book and gets people to buy it. Nice idea, but who is going to go to that site? Who is going to go to a web site that just tries to talk them into buying one particular book? It might work if the person is already thinking of buying it and wants more information about it, but the site is going to attract very few visitors who are just browsing for books.

A better approach would be a web site www.idhub.com, which took a broader approach and provided the user with an overview of books in this particular niche area – design for use. As well as providing an overview of books on the market it could supplement this with other subject-related information.

Admittedly this does require a larger investment in work and content than a 'buy this book' site, but it is probably better to invest more for something that works than invest less for something that does not.

Audience

If you are writing a book, putting a web-portal together, compiling a cd-rom, or even just penning an office memo it is vital that you know *who* you are communicating with. By that I do not mean that you know their name (although this helps a lot in one-to-one communication), but that you know what their profile is in terms of *their* goals, how they think, what their background is, what things they know and don't know etc. This is a clear case of the old adage, 'Know your user'.

In days gone by, a lot of products would have been crafted to match the user's exact size or needs. The cobbler, tailor etc. would have been serving the customer for years, would have a good idea of their size, likes and dislikes and would be able to tweak his work should it later turn out to be not exactly what the customer wanted.

With mass production and mass audiences it seems as if this idea is gone for ever. Everything in the Western consumer society is mass-produced, leaving only a handful of craftspeople operating in niche markets. This mass production for user groups is true for much of the new media world as well; cd-roms and web sites are designed on the whole to cater for groups of users. The low investment levels possible on the web mean that it is possible to set up very niche-oriented sites but although they cater for very specialized subject areas they still cater for a user group, albeit a user group of a more specialized nature.

Personalized web services

The concept of personal, one-to-one service is not completely dead, it is only sleeping. The increasing sophistication of web technology means that it is possible to tailor information to the precise needs of the user. More and more sites are offering this service, often using clever techniques to nudge the user into setting up a profile. Again it is a 'win–win' situation. The user gets personalized services and the developers get personal profiles and user behavior data. Despite these advances in the field of personalization, the majority of the content on the web is still designed for a wide user group.

Defining the user group

For multimedia distributed on a physical carrier, like a cd-rom, defining an audience is similar to any other product. For the web it is a bit different because it does not depend on a one-time purchase, it depends on continued use during which the audience can shift and change. However, the basics are the same.

You have to align your goals from the previous section with the person you are aiming those goals at. You have to define the user in general terms and in terms of the content of your product. Much of the general definition of audience is related to the existing study of marketing. It covers such things as monthly disposable income (how much they have to spend), area of work, area of interests, educational background etc. Those marketing factors are general enough to get good coverage in texts on marketing and market research. Here I simply want to emphasize the importance of this exercise, and to look at one key factor more unique to new media design: the technological background of the user.

Technological experience

The technological abilities of the user fall into three main areas:

- First, there is the area of general computer skills: can they switch the computer on and put a cd-rom in it? More to the point, do they actually have access to a computer?
- Secondly, the area of interactive skills: are they used to clicking and exploring new media systems, interrogating screen areas to see if they are interactive, able to interact their way out of a variety of different non-intuitive interfaces?
- Thirdly, do they have experience of the web? Although this is merely a combination of the above two points there is a fairly large body of

extra knowledge that is also necessary, such things as downloading times, caches, URLs, browser use, search engines etc.

In each of these areas the designer has to pitch the design of their instructions and tone of voice to the level of the user group. Pitch it too high and they will lose a certain percentage of users along the way. Pitch it too low and they will annoy and bore the more experienced users. Do it inconsistently and they are in danger of losing both sets of users. One solution is to have multiple instructions, a slimmed-down interface for the experienced users, supplemented by more detailed information for the less experienced users.

Scope

What is the subject?

As well as deciding what the goal of the system is and who the audience is, you also have to sort out what the content is going to be. In effect you know *why* you want to say it and *who* you want to say it to, now you have to sort out *what* you are going to say.

Sometimes, defining the boundaries to what is in and what is out is easy, but sometimes it can be more complex. And as well as defining the boundaries you must also decide on the depth of coverage and the manner in which things are dealt with or presented. (This definition of the content is tied up with the structure as well; have a look at chapter 13 on structure.)

Once you have decided upon the core subject and the structure you are then free to shift the boundaries about and set them either smaller or larger than the core subject area.

Setting the boundaries smaller

Why would the designer want to set the boundaries of the content of the new media system smaller than required? The answer lies in the resources; there are not always enough resources to realize the goals. However, it is always important to have large goals since smaller goals can then be steps on the road towards these larger goals.

Failure to plan in this way can result in wasted investment. A small amount of work is invested in a system, and when a bigger budget comes along a larger scope is set. Now the initial project does not fit into the larger picture and has to be scrapped or redone.

Setting the boundaries larger

Sometimes the designer sets the boundaries wider – the umbrella marketing example earlier is a good illustration of this. Any collection of information on a particular subject can be elegantly supplemented by extra services that users may find attractive, such as discussion areas, overviews of current web sites and search tools.

The drawback, of course, is in the level of investment, the best approach being to set up a framework that the users fill with content themselves.

Choosing a logic

You must find a logic for what is in and what is out; the choice cannot be arbitrary. At a certain point the user must say, 'Aha! I understand what the scope of the content is. I see how it all fits together. I understand what's in and what's out'. This appreciation of the scope and content should happen as quickly as possible while they are accessing the content. It should not be a comment at the end when they have been all through the site and seen what is in and what is out. The content and scope should follow a well-defined pattern, a narrative, an argument or a vision.

Communicating that logic to the user

Above I stated that the user should build up an idea of the scope and content as quickly as possible. One way of aiding this process is to choose a good scope. The other is to make sure that it is communicated well to the user.

In the world of conventional publishing, the classic example is the user building up an idea of the scope of a book before buying it. They have access to a number of communication channels to help them make the decision. Use of these channels needs to be well handled; they need to be promotional in nature to some extent but they must also be highly accurate. A book that claims to have information on all major web servers available may be bought by lots of readers, but if it does not actually contain the information that it claims to contain then sales are going to flatten off quite dramatically.

Exercises

Sales pitch

It is a global financial web site, the pay-off is 'financial information around the globe around the clock' and here is a neat idea for the home-page: we link the web site to a clock and when it is between 5 and 12 the home-page banner says 'Good Morning', when it is between 12 and 6 it says 'Good Afternoon' and between 6 and 5 it says 'Good Evening'. That means that the first contact anyone has with the site has a really personal feel to it. Good idea, don't you think?

What do you think?

Clues to user group

At a station I once saw a group of deaf people communicating in sign language. Several of them were carrying mobile phones. Phones for deaf people? The use of SMS text messages and the fact that some phones can be set to vibrate instead of ringing means that all of sudden this technology is accessible to a whole new group of users.

What assumptions can you make about the user groups that buy the following items of technology, in terms of any accessibility problems that they may have, any products that they may already have, and activities that they may do: a television, a Walkman, a personal cd player, a violin, a computer printer, a cd labeling machine, a braille keyboard for inputting text.

Think of other good examples of products, the ownership of which tells you something about the user.

Business and personal

Consider a site selling some product that is applicable to both private and business use (such as office stationery). What are the differences in people buying for the business and people buying for themselves? What do you think would be the main differences between their behavior when purchasing things via a web site and how could you support/encourage the two different user groups through the web design?

New media examples

Look at a few web sites or cd-rom products and ask yourself what the GAS analysis was for them. What audience were the designers trying to reach? What were they trying to say to them? Are the designs good? Do you think that they succeeded?

Contexts

10

WEBCODE
contexts

Introduction

Part of the GAS (goals, audience and scope) analysis used in the last chapter was the profile of the audience of users. Part of the profile of the users also involves the context within which those users will be using the system. The interaction between the user and the system takes place in a particular environment, a combination of factors that define the context. Perhaps the most obvious example is the physical context: where is the interaction taking place? In a quiet library or on someone's lap on a noisy airplane? However, there are other more abstract aspects to the context, such things as cultural contexts and software contexts, and they will be discussed in this chapter.

The consideration of contexts is a useful exercise, not only in the analysis of design, but also in the act of design itself since any design has to be suited to the context that it is going to be used in if it is going to succeed. Darwin proposed that the genetic traits in animals that survived were those that made them most fit for their niche in the ecological framework. This can be echoed in the statement that the systems that will survive and be used and taken up in the real-world are those that are designed to be most fitting to the context within which they are used.

To begin with, let us split the idea of context up into several different sections, starting with the physical context (where the system is), and moving on to the users' context (what their background is), and the technological context (what the system itself has to fit in with).

The opening sections dealing with the system's physical context may seem irrelevant in a digital world, but there are many examples of usability problems associated with the physical environment that could have been solved by the digital designers taking more account of the real context of use during the design phase.

The physical context

Placement

The first and most tangible part of the context is the physical placement of the system. Assuming that the system is not portable or mobile (and this is an important assumption), the placement of the system will govern the physical environment that the interaction takes place in. Indeed even mobile systems are used in the same immediate context when they are used; a lap is a lap, is a lap no matter where the laptop is actually being used.

Public areas

Sometimes a system will be designed specifically for use in a public area: a point of information in a large building such as a hospital or a shopping mall; a ticketing system or tourist-information system in a crowded station. Sometimes a system may be intended for personal use but may occasionally be used in a public space, such as a program running on someone's organizer or a web site displayed on a mobile device or on the screen in an internet café.

If the former is the case, then the public context should play a major part in the design. If it is the latter then the possible public context should have some influence on the design.

Other information sources available

Part of the context of an interactive system is the presence of other associated sources of information. The presence and nature of these sources should be taken into account during the design. Indeed these other sources of information should be an integral part of the system being designed. As an example, the existence of an accompanying web site to this book has influenced the design of the text structure and coverage.

Environment

One obvious influence that the immediate environment exerts upon a system is dirt. Not mud, but indoor dirt: dust and fluff. First, dust can wreak havoc with high technology, causing failures of electrical systems, overheating, obscuring displays, jamming buttons etc.

Any system in the public arena that works with a touch screen (and indeed any that do not) are going to get very greasy screens, especially spatial displays, maps etc. There seems to be an inherent human desire to point to a map and say 'this is where we are'. Just look at the metro maps next time you are in a station and you will see the station that you are in is all worn away from countless thousands of pointing fingers.

As well as environmental dirt there is dirt brought to the system by the users, even larger things such as cigarette ash and smoke and bits of food and drink. How many parents have had to stop their children jamming sandwiches into video machines?

Lastly, any system that is popular and useful will suffer the drawback of being heavily used. This in turn leads to its own problems: breakdown of buttons, burning-in of the screen etc.

All these factors are related to the physical design of systems rather than new media design. However, they are still important and the new media designer should be aware of them as they are factors that can affect the more digital aspects of the design. For example, button use can be minimized by ensuring that the user gets good feedback when a button is pressed. This will avoid the situation where the user thinks, 'Did it notice when I pressed the button? I'd better press it a few more times just in case', resulting in a button lifetime a quarter of what it could be if the user pressed it once and knew that the system had registered the press.

Audio context

The other way in which the location of a system can influence its use is in the effect of sound: 'sound pollution' to be precise. In busy public areas levels of noise can be high enough to cause problems with sound-based interaction, and can be distracting from other forms of interaction.

Furthermore, even in quiet environments sound can cause problems. Any interactive system that uses sound and that is used in a public context can have a negative effect on the user's interaction. It demands too much attention from other people in the vicinity and people do not like this, especially if they are unsure of the interaction with the system. Having a trade stand with a noisy stand-alone presentation is a sure way of attracting attention in the vicinity but it will also create an appreciable threshold for people actually interacting with the presentation.

Sound can also have an impact on the privacy of the user's interaction. There are certain tasks where users desire privacy, especially in the public arena. ATMs could have their interaction augmented with audio, but in the Western world money (and especially the lack of it) is a very touchy subject. Imagine an ATM loudly declaring, 'Sorry, you cannot make a withdrawal; insufficient funds'. Or alternatively, 'You have just withdrawn three thousand dollars'!

If you have a system that relies on sound as a vital part of the feedback, there may be problems if several units are installed together in the same area – something that often happens with interactive systems. The audio feedback from one unit will be heard by the user of another unit and may be misinterpreted as a part of their own interaction. A good illustration is that of supermarket checkouts that use barcode scanning. The system gives a beep to the user to indicate that the barcode has been correctly scanned. However, such units are usually installed in rows at the supermarket checkout, well within hearing distance of each other. The result is that cashiers (the users) may be uncertain about whether the confirmation beep is coming from their unit or the one next to them. Some manufacturers overcome the problem by giving each unit a different beep as feedback so that users can distinguish if the feedback they hear comes from their own unit or from their neighbor's.

A similar example in the area of audio contexts is the temperature alarm that alerts users by means of a high-pitched tweeting sound: fine, unless you are using it to monitor the temperature in a tropical-bird house.

Visual context

As well as sound impinging upon the interaction with the system the lighting can also have an effect. Consider the following.

Too dark or too sunny

There are many environments where the levels of light are less than those in a well-lit development lab. Not only are there dim and dusky places of use but the system could also be used at times when the daylight is fading or non-existent. Conversely, too much direct sunlight can make display screens and signal lights very difficult to see clearly.

Dealing with both these problems is a mixture of designing the externals of the system to offer shade or light and designing the digital parts of the system to be visually appropriate to the light level that they are to be used in. Use can also be made of sound in such situations, although refer back to the points on privacy above.

Colored light

Less obvious are the situations where a system is used in a context where the ambient light source is a colored light. When a light is a very pure light of one particular color all colors seen will just reflect different amounts of that light and thus look like different shades of that color. There will not be any other colors. The most widespread single-color environment are the yellow/orange sodium-based street lights that are used to light roads in many countries. Everything under their light looks different shades of yellow and black. A more interesting example is the red light used on submarine control decks prior to surfacing to aid night-vision: once again this will flatten the colors reflected to different shades of red and in such a critical environment the design of visual information should take account of this (see the exercises in chapter 7 on color).

A slightly less critical single-color environment is the photographic darkroom. As well as being lit by pure orange light, this has the added disadvantage that the lighting used is very dim. Visual communication designed for this environment has to be very clear indeed.

User 'baggage'

A part of the physical environment often overlooked is user baggage. Often users do not come to a system empty-handed; they bring baggage. This baggage can be the conventional luggage and briefcases if they are interacting with a system in an airport or on a station platform, but baggage can also be more casual – a stack of papers, a cup of coffee, a pen, a cigarette or a sandwich. Don Norman points out that there are precious few places in a modern crowded airplane cockpit to put a cup of coffee, but pilots still drink the stuff so where do they put their cups? The BBC, a broadcasting company in the UK, has had huge problems with people putting cups of tea and coffee down on expensive equipment not designed to function as a coffee table, with predictable and costly results.

WEBCODE
faucets

Often, when hands are full, feet are a viable interaction channel. This is the case in the kitchen and there are devices such as pedal-operated bins and pedal-operated fridge doors to assist users with their hands full. Another thing that users can 'carry' are substances on their hands. Classic examples are soapy hands in the washroom: 'pretty obvious' you might say, but I have come across numerous faucets that are so smooth and well rounded that operating them with slippery hands is very difficult indeed.

The user's context

The coverage of the physical context is not vital for a new media designer but it does serve to illustrate the idea behind contexts of use. Now I will move on to aspects of the context that do play more of a role in new media design. We start with the user's context: the sum total of all the things and influences that affect the user's understanding and behavior.

Cultural context

All users exist and interact within a cultural context. This is a tricky and interesting context, and very often it is difficult to take into consideration. Differing contexts due to different work environments we can understand because usually we have had experience of different work situations, but different cultures are more difficult to get the hang of because our own culture is so deeply ingrained in us, it is often difficult to take a step back and see its effects.

The Japanese spreadsheet

WEBCODE
japan
spreadsheet

A good illustration is the Japanese spreadsheet. A company decided to rewrite some software for the Japanese market. A Japanese focus group assisted in the design of the interface. Many things change when you switch from Western culture to the Japanese culture: some are ephemeral to do with general perceptions of the design, others are more concrete. For example the date is different in Japan: the year is given in terms of the reign of the emperor, so many years into the reign of such and such an emperor. The programmers were working on the date conversions when one of them voiced the question of what to do when there was a new emperor: the year count would all start from the beginning again with a new emperor name. They solved it by having an option where the user could restart the numbering of the years and type in the name of the new emperor: pretty simple solution, pretty elegant? 'Most definitely not!' was the opinion of the focus group when they were shown the addition. The Japanese emperor is supposed to be immortal, and no one should ever allude to his death or speak as though he is a mere mortal who will die soon – imagine their consternation when the assumption of his death was built into a piece of mass-marketed software!

This cultural context plays a part in all sorts of different areas of design; we saw how it affected color earlier in chapter 7. It even plays a part in the design of beefburgers. A large American burger retailer coined the term 'auto-condimentation' to describe the British love of adding their own salt and pepper to burgers while American citizens prefer it to be included in the burger mix.

Designing for different cultures is really only possible if there are different cultures present on the design team or, failing that, if there are focus groups from the different cultures. However, as a last resort you should at least try to grab an employee from that culture for an afternoon's evaluation.

The danger lies in saying, 'Oh, our system is so basic and simple there can't possibly be any difference in its use in different cultures . . .'. You would be surprised!

The user group context

An important part of the context as far as the system is concerned are the users; more precisely, the fact that there may be different sorts of users using the system. One immediately thinks of users and 'super-users' for complex computer administration systems, but even the lowly photocopier or drinks dispenser knows several sorts of users, all of whom should be considered in the design process and all of whose tasks should be made as easy and as efficient as possible by the design of the system.

Different levels of expertise

To begin with, among the everyday end-users there are different levels of expertise and styles of use. There are the casual users, using the system once in a while, forgetting everything they did last time and having to rely heavily on system cues and instructions. Then there are the regular users, using it daily for repetitive tasks that need to be completed as quickly and as free of errors as possible.

Super-users are those who are familiar with all the details of the system and frequently use it (or help others to use it) for more demanding tasks: the keen photographer who uses the aperture override on their automatic camera; the musician who uses both the keyboard and the foot pedals of the church organ; the Adobe PhotoShop whizz who can switch palettes or quickly rustle up a graduated border to a photo; the secretary who can intervene when the copier stops midway through a complex bit of double-sided copying and get you back to a point in the proceedings where you know what is going on.

Different user groups

However, when we move into more complex systems in the digital arena there are all sorts of different user groups characterized not just by different levels of expertise but also by different jobs or tasks related to the system.

Consider an online system for the publishing of scientific journals. There could be front-ends for the people who read the journals online, the authors that write the material, the editorial board that reviews the material and chooses what is published, the librarians who decide on what content they subscribe to and how they manage it, the society board that arranges subscriptions and access for the members, the maintenance staff who keep the whole web service running behind the scenes, the marketing people who need access to the contact information of all the end-users to inform them of new services, and so on. Each group should have its own dedicated interface. Many elements will be the same but each user group should always be confined to their own collection of information and not slip from one set of information to another.

Users with accessibility requirements

Another important consideration when we are dealing with user groups are those groups of users who encounter accessibility problems with conventional new media – users with hearing or vision difficulties.

Although a comparatively small group there is nonetheless an important point to be made in that the internet is a wonderful leveler. It is possible to run the internet in such a way that everybody can use it regardless of any sensory difficulties they may have. As such, it is the designer's responsibility to give some attention to these user groups. Furthermore it makes good economic sense; as the internet is such an empowering tool for these users they tend to be more likely to use it for activities such as shopping and searching than other users. Catering for them in the design can have a disproportionate increase in returns.

Existing users

An unfortunate context for new media designers involved on large commercial projects is that any redesign work of a system already in use has to be carried out within the context of the design of the original system. If you have a large number of users already using the current system then you are not going to want to scare them all off by reinventing the entire user interface when you do a redesign. Skillful methods have to be found to support the working practices of the existing user base while at the same time innovating with new interaction designs for new users.

This effect is called 'cognitive lock-in' and basically it means the user gets used to doing something one way and does not like being made to do it a different way. It plays an important part in the layout of supermarkets. As a user, there is nothing worse than popping in to buy some milk and bread and discovering that everything has been shifted around and you have to spend ages wandering around looking for the things.

Other contexts

As well as those broad classifications of contexts there are a number of others that are also important but that are somewhat less relevant to the focus of this book. Nevertheless they deserve a mention.

The technological context

A vital issue of context for cross-platform software and especially for the web is the technological context that the new media system is being used in. Cd-roms and other media carriers have to be made to run on different types of computers, the main ones being PCs and Apple. The range for interactive games is larger with several different games consoles on the market.

Even on a PC or an Apple computer there is great variety in the actual hardware: screen sizes (how big the screen is), screen resolution (how detailed/grainy the screen is), support for sound, speed of the internet connection or cd-rom drive, speed of the computer itself etc. This hardware impact becomes even greater as we consider presenting web information on other sorts of devices such as personal organizers, mobile telephones and internet-enabled televisions.

One of the main reasons for the introduction of games consoles was the ability to standardize these sorts of factors so that games designers did not have to take all the different variations into consideration.

On the software front the suite of programs that the user has on their machine can also affect their experience of the interaction. Certain programs are necessary to view information in certain formats: Adobe Acrobat to view PDF files (documents that can be printed out on the printer), QuickTime for viewing digital video clips etc. With web-based information there is also the question of which web browser the user is using as different web browsers have different capabilities.

A detailed investigation of these issues is not relevant here. The information changes rapidly and there is much coverage on the web itself.

Standards

A final note here is that there are an increasing number of standards that apply to the interaction between users and systems. Many of these are voluntary at the moment, but there is more and more pressure to make them obligatory. The designer should be aware of them, not so much because they are a tool for designing but because they can be useful for justifying a design to clients. If you say, 'this is the best way of designing it' then the clients usually want to get involved and say, 'well, couldn't we do it this way . . .'. If you say, 'this way conforms to ISO 8763', then such a discussion is less likely.

WEBCODE
standards

An area where standards are becoming more important is accessibility (use of new media systems by users with disabilities). Here existing legislation for disabled users is having to be interpreted in the light of the new emerging media and the lobby groups are so strong that test cases are being brought against online information providers regarding accessibility of information.

Exercises

Supermarket
Imagine you have the chance to redesign the layout of a supermarket to make it more user friendly. What should be your goals and motivations in the redesign? What sorts of things would you do regarding layout and signs? How would this affect the marketing and sales?

WEBCODE
supermarket

WEBCODE
exhibition
stand

Exhibition stand system
You have to design a stand-alone new media system to sit on a table at a stand at an exhibition. Sometimes there will be someone on the stand but often your system will be there on its own. What could go wrong and how could you prevent it? What factors should you take into account in the design of the interaction?

WEBCODE
train info

Train information point

Imagine you are designing a new media system extolling the benefits of train travel. It will be sited at the buffet car in long-distance trains. What factors in the physical context will influence the design?

WEBCODE
culture
context

Work and cultural context

If you have access to a group of people who come from different cultures ask them what things they find disturbing or annoying about new media systems in general. What factors are the same across different cultures and what things are more culturally dependent?

WEBCODE
jargon

Jargon

Consider the people in your immediate personal context: your friends and family etc. Try to write any words or terms that are used among them that probably would not be understood by people outside the group. Do the same for jargon connected with the context that you work in.

Are there any words or phrases used in the area where you live that are not used elsewhere?

11

User models

Introduction

WEBCODE
user models

When it comes to interaction always bear the following in mind:

The user doesn't know what you know, they only know what you tell them.

There is a school of thought that says that the user of an interactive thing (new media or otherwise) builds up a mental model of it in their head. During their interaction they base their actions on this model that they have in their head. This is the user's model, and there will be more about what it is later, but let us start with a few examples to clarify what we are talking about.

Cockerel alarm clock

The first example is the cockerel alarm clock that I introduced in chapter 1. This was an alarm clock in the shape of a big chicken and on top of his head was the alarm set/cancel button. You could tell whether it was on 'set alarm' by the cockerel's eyes which changed as you pressed the button and were either open or shut, but which was which? Did 'eyes open' mean the alarm was set or did 'eyes closed' mean that? Audiences to which I have put the question are usually split down the middle with the 'eyes closed = alarm set' group reasoning that the chicken goes to sleep at night just as the user goes to sleep at night: 'I close my eyes so I must make the chicken close his eyes'. The 'eyes open = alarm set' group counter this with the chicken must stay awake in order to wake me up in the morning: 'I go to sleep, the chicken stays awake to wake me up'.

Both groups have a user model, an understanding of what is going on. Both user models are equally valid since they are both supported by good reasoning. However, only one of the models is 'correct' in that it corresponds to the actual behavior of the clock. So half the people would have the incorrect user model and not be woken up in the morning!

This is a classic example of bad design. The system offers, or supports, two possible models for its use but only one is correct. We will deal with other problems of this nature later in the chapter, but first let us look at a few more examples.

WEBCODE
alarm clock

Dried scorpion

The nature of user models is such a key concept that I am going to give several examples to help the ideas sink in. This is a simpler example. The dried scorpion in question is a small parcel of folded paper covered in information about dried scorpions and how to handle them. The user slowly unwraps the parcel and at the last fold there is suddenly a loud buzzing and rattling from inside, causing no end of screaming and jumping. Inside the last fold is a simple rattler made from wire and a tightly wound elastic band. A wonderful creation.

WEBCODE
scorpion

This system (even a fake, dried scorpion can be classed as a system) supports a clear mental model and when the user gets to the rattling noise they interpret this in terms of the model that they have built up so far, and draw the conclusion that the dried scorpion is anything but dead. This is a case of supporting a false mental model for entertainment purposes.

Pressure dial

Here is an example from the history books. Just as internet technology is all the rage now, there was a time in the industrial revolution when steam was all the rage. Everyone was trying to make their fortune with new ideas harnessing this incredible new technology.

WEBCODE
boiler

One firm made boilers to supply high-pressure steam for engines. They spent some time testing new designs for efficiency and safety. During one such testing session there was a terrible disaster. Basically a boiler was a sealed container with water inside and a fire underneath. There was a pressure meter and a safety valve that let off steam if the pressure got too high. Standard practice for stoking up a boiler was not to put a bit of coal on and check the pressure, then a bit more coal and check the pressure, because that would take ages. The way they did it was to shovel away and stoke the fire up until the safety valve blew and then stop. Well, the two stokers started doing this but after a while they got concerned that the valve had not blown so they stopped and looked at the pressure meter; it was still on zero. They went back to their coal shoveling and ten minutes later checked the dial again. Still on zero. Either there was a leak in the boiler and it was not building up pressure or it was taking a long time to build up pressure. They carried on stoking and a few minutes later the whole thing was ripped apart by an enormous explosion as the incredible pressure of the steam burst out of the boiler.

It turned out that there were two problems. One a system error – the safety valve was blocked; in the event of dangerously high pressure it would not blow. The second was a user model problem. The pressure dial had a pin to keep the pointer resting against the zero when there was no pressure. What had happened was that the boiler was in fact very efficient. It had built up pressure rapidly and the pointer on the dial had quickly gone higher and higher until it had gone all the way around and was pressed up against the zero pin on the other side! The pressure was enormous but the dial still looked like it was on zero, so the two stokers were trying to stoke up a boiler that was already at bursting point.

If such problems and disasters can occur with the representation of a single value such as that, imagine how much can go wrong when you are designing complex multivalued systems packed with information on a computer.

Automatic sun blinds

Kieren, a colleague of mine, worked in a room in the research institute that had been divided into two from a much larger room. The dividing wall even split the window in two; half was in his room and half next door. Unfortunately, next door had the winder to put the window's sun-blind up and down. Whenever it got too sunny the person in that room would put the sun-blind down and it would shield both halves of the window. Kieren was unaware of the activities of his next-door neighbor and was only aware that the sun-blind went up and down in a perfect reaction to the weather. He thought that the blinds were being automatically controlled by some highly adaptive and intelligent sensor system.

Humans are always trying to build up models of what is going on around them; there is an inbuilt need to understand behavior around us. In this example Kieren built up a model based on evidence around him: although the model seemed unlikely, the evidence for it seemed insurmountable.

User models

In each of the examples above we have talked about mental models. These are models in our head about things around us. How things work, how they behave and (very important for this book) how they react as the user interacts with them. I shall stick to 'mental model' as a general term and 'user model' to describe the mental model of an interactive system that people use in some way.

What are user models?

User models have been the subject of some debate in psychological circles. Some people say that they really exist and the user really does have a model in their head of what is going on. If the interactive system is well designed then it helps the user build up a good user model in their mind and they can use the system better.

The opposing group say that nothing is in the user's head, the user just reacts to what they see in the world around them. If the interactive system is well designed then it tells the user what to do and the user reacts in the correct way and they can use the system better.

For the designer of new media it does not really matter which is the true state of affairs; indeed, it may be impossible to prove one way or the other. Basically, either one of the two approaches is a good basis for good design. We will continue here on the assumption that there are user models in the head.

User models and new media

Why all this talk about funny alarm clocks and sun-blinds at the start of this chapter? Isn't this meant to be a book about new media design? Well, user models are a vital part of interaction design in general and new media design in particular. It is vital that the user of a new media system knows what is going on at all times. New media is both complex and novel, and as such there is no precedence for presenting this complexity. The bottom line is that good new media design needs good usability and the basis of good usability is a good grip on user models. Let us have a look at some of the different types of user models that the user has of a new media system.

User model of the system's behavior

As the user interacts they build up a user model of the system, what it is capable of doing, how to get certain things done with it, what it can and cannot do, what functions are associated with the menu entries and so forth. This is their user model of the system. If their user model is true to the system's behavior and the user model is simple and fast to build up then they will not have problems using the system. If, however, it is difficult to build up, or it takes a long time to build up, it can lead to frustration and errors.

User model of the scope of the content

When it comes to web sites and information systems there are other user models. There is the user model of the organization of the content of web documents: the limits of what is in there, how it is covered and how it is structured and how the user can navigate through it.

User model of the content

Finally, there is the user model of the actual contents of the web documents. The goal of a good user interface design in this context is to minimize the mental load of the first two user models above and to let the user quickly get to grips with this user model – the true content of the system.

Building user models up

Communication theory

The idea of building a user model up in the head of the user has much to do with communication; a person has an idea, a concept in their head and they want to transfer that concept to the head of someone else. They do this by communication, making the idea in their head concrete and tangible in some shared language, written or spoken. The other person sees or hears this and builds up the idea in their own head, Figure 11.1. Simply put, it is the transfer of mental models from one person to another.

The communication in this example could have taken a variety of forms; it could have been text, pictures, icons, sign language etc.

Communicating via the new media system
What I want to do now is to move this model into the world of new media design. The person having the idea is the new media designer and their

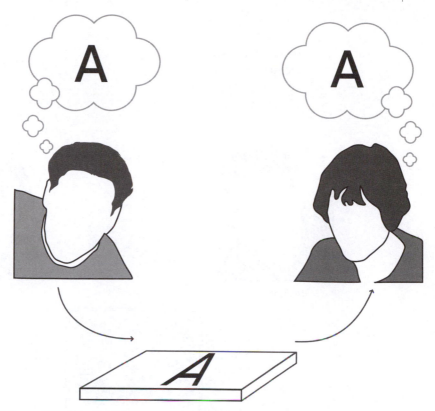

Figure 11.1: Communication: a person has an idea, represents it externally and another person interprets it to build up an idea.

idea is the user model that they want to communicate. They must communicate that idea to a second person: the user. If the designer is a student of new media design they do the communication by standing next to the user as they look at a demo saying, 'No, don't click on that, click here, this is the information bit, here, let me show you how to set it going . . .'.

A good new media designer will know that they will not be around every time someone interacts with the system, so the only way they can communicate with the user is through the system itself. The user is on the receiving end of the communication; they use the system and, based on the feedback that the system gives to them, they build up an idea of what the designer was trying to 'say' about the way the system works, Figure 11.2.

Figure 11.2: Communication: a designer has an ideal user model, represents it externally in the system and a user interprets it to build up their user model.

What the designer knows

**WEBCODE
designer's
model**

The designer actually has several mental models in their head. One of them is their own model of how the new media system works. Usually they will be so involved in the project that their model of the system will be far too detailed for an end-user. So the designer also has a 'designer's model', which is an ideal user model. That is the user model that they would like the user to build up; that is the model that they want to communicate to the user.

What the user knows

The designer communicates this 'designer's model' to the user through the system and if the communication is good then the user will build up their user model and this will be the same as the designer's model. Just as in a normal conversation, the person on the receiving end of the communication builds up an idea of what they think the person is saying, which ideally is the same as what the person doing the communication thinks they are saying.

When does the user build up user models?

Building up a user model does not happen in one go; it is a gradual process, not just confined to sitting in front of the new media system.

Before they interact

Even before having anything to do with a new media system the user may already have elements of the user model present. Parts of the user model may come from things that the user is already familiar with in the real-world that are being used as metaphors in the system. For example, a user of a typical computer desktop will already have bits of the user model simply because they are used to dealing with things on their real-world desk at home. Similarly with any digital audio or video system that uses the conventional buttons to control the playback, the user already has elements of the user model through their experience of video and audio players in the real world. (There is more on metaphors in chapter 19.)

When they see the system and context

The context that a new media system is in will tell a user a great deal about the interaction and thus assist them in their user model before they actually start interacting with the system. Just seeing an interactive kiosk-type system in a railway station, for example, immediately tells the user that it is probably something to do with buying tickets. To some extent the context can also include system elements external to the actual interactive part of the system, things such as packaging, manuals, etc.

Another aspect of seeing a system in context is that the user may actually see other users interacting with it and from this build up elements of their user model. This is more common with simple systems in the public arena such as doors and turnstiles; new media systems even when in the public arena tend to be more private when it comes to interaction. Other users will not see what is happening on the screen unless they are standing right behind the person using the system.

When they interact with the system

The main part of the creation of the user model happens when the user is actually interacting with the system. That is the point at which most of the communication is happening, the system is showing things to the user, and the user is reacting to them and trying things out.

This process is similar to the way in which children learn about the world around them: continual exploration and experimentation. The new media system should support such experimentation, it should give the user the chance to undo things that they have done, it should warn them of anything that cannot be undone (sending messages, ordering things etc.) and it should not react to experiments with rude error messages or system crashes.

Designing the communication and the user model

The designers then must design the way that the user model is communicated. Before they do that they must also design the user model itself.

The communication between the new media system and the user is usually referred to as feedback and it is such an important area that chapter 12 is devoted to it. The design of the user model also has its own chapter (chapter 18), which deals with the underlying aspects of user model design. That chapter is not so much about designing the user model but about designing the building blocks of the system that will be the foundations of the user model.

When it goes wrong

When things run smoothly one is usually unaware of what is going on; you really get to grips with understanding something when it starts going wrong. A quick look at where user models can cause problems is thus useful for understanding and avoiding errors in this aspect of new media and design. Apart from all that, it is simply more interesting to hear about things that go wrong than to hear about things that go right.

Fundamentally, user model problems arise from the user building up an incorrect user model and then making an action based on their user model. There are several different ways in which that incorrect user model can be built up. See Figure 11.3.

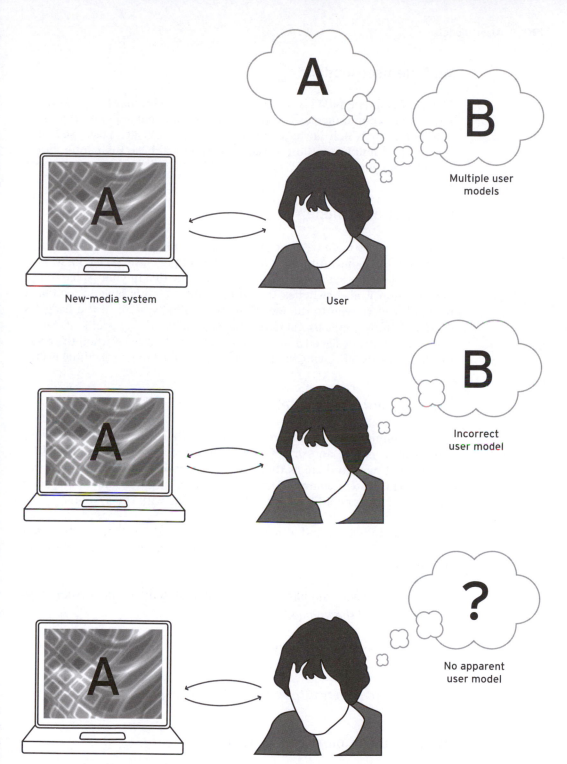

Figure 11.3: Three examples of where users' models can go wrong.

Multiple user models

This is of course typified by the cockerel alarm clock that I opened with. The system communicates two (or more) possible behaviors to the user. It is not clear which is the correct one since both are possessed of a certain logic and users run the risk that they will base their interaction on the wrong one.

Incorrect user model

Again, one of the opening examples, the apparently automatic sun-blinds, illustrates this point. Another real-world example is the fridge light. It is standard design practice that when you turn the dial in your fridge to the 'off' position it also switches the fridge light off. This is good feedback because it alerts you to the fact that the cooling system in the fridge is switched off, which is useful if you have set it to 'off' by accident. Some fridges are badly designed and the light stays working even when the cooling dial is set to 'off', giving the incorrect user model that everything is OK.

No apparent user model

This is common with interactive systems where the interface is very technical in nature and the effects of interactions have to be gaged by experimenting with them as there is no indication beforehand of what to expect. The system communicates no useful user model and so the user must build the model up by actually interacting with the system.

Imagine a technician and a new media designer describing the function of the gas pedal (accelerator in UK English) to a new user. The technician would say:

> *'The gas pedal supplies a richer mix of fuel to the combustion chamber of the engine.'*

whereas the new media designer would state the effect in the user's terms:

> *'The more you press the gas pedal the more power the car will have.'*

Many and complex user models

Some systems are fine tuned to offer all sorts of benefits to the user and in doing so they become incredibly complex and have a complicated user model. In the world of new media there are many authoring packages that have so many features added on that using them requires an in-depth knowledge of lots of different unrelated aspects.

Color codes in HTML

A classic example of such complexity is the early way that web-page builders specified color in the web-page layout language HTML. The color codes looked like this:

```
#0000ff
#ffcc00
#0ea57f
```

In order to specify a color in HTML using this encoding you had to know four things:

- First, you needed to know about the physics of additive color mixing, how to achieve the color you wanted by mixing the three additive color primaries: red, green and blue. For example, which two would you mix to get yellow? Mixing light color like this is very different from mixing paint.
- Secondly, you needed to know about the binary representations of these color triplets and the fact that 255 is the maximum intensity you could set each of the three channels at.
- Thirdly, you needed to know how to convert these binary intensity values to a technical numbering system used in computers called hexadecimal.
- And, finally, you needed to know what the color was that you wanted in the first place.

Confused? It was a color specification system that required a knowledge of physics, computing and math just to say 'yellow'. Needless to say things have been made a bit simpler since then.

Wrong on purpose

A user model can also be designed to be wrong on purpose. Strange though this may sound, this is the case with the majority of computer systems. The interface is a lie! It is not a true indication of what is going on underneath; however, it is a convenient and consistent lie and as such it is very useful indeed.

'Move' does not actually move data around inside the computer and 'delete' doesn't usually delete anything properly; the computer just says 'these bits of the hard-disk are not needed and can be used later' – in the meantime all the data are still there. A master drugs-dealer once found this out to his horror. As the police were raiding his home he dashed to his computer and deleted his complete contact database from his hard-disk just as they burst through the door. However, the police took the computer away and from the hard-disk they were able to piece the contact database together again and round up the entire network.

Another example was the 'search all content' function offered by a web site containing many different sources of information (articles, reviews, databases, image banks etc.). The user specified a search, clicked 'search all content' and then was given buttons to view the results that had been returned from the different content areas: 'show me the results that were found in reviews' etc. In fact, the system just did one little search in the beginning and then did the other searches one at a time when the user clicked on 'show me the results that were found in . . .'. The actions were not 'do one huge search and then click through the results'; it was more a case of 'do fairly ordinary searches on request in different areas of content'.

Real-world examples

Very occasionally this happens in the real-world. I once encountered a hand-dryer which had a button that you pressed to get a flow of warm air and the label beside the button said 'press-on, dry, press-off'. I tried this and it worked. Then I tried being a 'badly behaved' user and didn't do the 'press-off' part. The device had a time-out after about 30 seconds, so the user model it was presenting in its instructions was not the whole truth.

When it goes right

After that litany of what can go wrong I should add a positive note and state that when it goes right (which is often) the end results are very efficient. Users quickly understand what is going on, they can see how things work and what they have to do to achieve their goals and, if it is very well designed, they can even understand what to do before they start interacting with it. Furthermore the user also has a good feeling about the whole thing. They can just get on with the real task they are busy with rather than have to mess around trying to understand the interface to the system.

User models are vital, so try to be aware of them all the time you are designing new media.

Exercises

Elicit a user model

Choose an interactive system or service and talk to someone who uses it, preferably someone with limited understanding of the thing. Ask them questions to try to elicit their user model of the thing. Do not explain it to them: you are not training them and you want to get hold of their user model, not change it.

WEBCODE
elicit

Consider the following examples: the central heating timer, the video recorder, the internet, the insides of a computer.

Something you did wrong

Think back to a time when you made a mistake using an interactive system. Not a time when the system went wrong (e.g. my e-mail system crashed just before I sent it) but a time when you did something wrong because the system was not doing what you thought it was (e.g. when I put the washing powder in the washing machine I put it straight in with the clothes because the little drawer you were meant to put it in was so well fitted that I did not notice it).

WEBCODE
mistake

Explain the mistake you made in terms of user models. How could the design be changed to avoid your mistake happening again?

Pollux and Castor

There used to be a French animated children's series on the television called 'Pollux and Castor'. The series shifted to Britain and was re-dubbed in English. However, the team working on it did not translate the stories from French, but just watched what was happening on the screen and made up their own stories. So what happened on the screen fitted in with both the French story-line and the English story-line. They also gave it a different name, 'The Magic Roundabout'.

WEBCODE
pollux

Have a go at explaining what was going on here in terms of user models and feedback.

False mental models

When I discussed the dried scorpion earlier in the chapter I stated that it was a case of supporting a false user model for entertainment purposes. Can you think of any other situations where a system (a person, a show, a film, another dried insect) might deliberately support a user model that was not true to reality?

WEBCODE
false user
models

12

Feedback

Four-week feedback

WEBCODE
feedback

In the early days of the internet there was an internationally known beer brewery that used to offer guided tours of their main brewery, culminating in a very tasty beer-tasting session. When they got their web site up and running they offered the ability to book a place on a tour over the internet. Brilliant! The user could click and get a fill-in form, fill in their details, select a date and time and click the 'OK' button, whereupon they suddenly found themselves back at the home-page. Had it worked? Had it somehow bombed out? What was going on?

It all became clear four weeks later when a letter of confirmation arrived through the post. Only then did the user think, 'Aha! That click I did four weeks ago was OK then! Great!' This communication telling the user what was going on needs to be a lot sooner in arriving than four weeks. This is feedback and it needs to happen straight away.

Feedback

Feedback is communication from the system to the user about what the system is doing or about the user's interaction with the system. In the case of a new media system supporting communication between two users (think of ICQ, MS Messenger or other chat programs), feedback can be the information about what the users are doing.

Good feedback

When the system exhibits good feedback (i.e. well-designed feedback), the user is quickly and appropriately informed about what is going on and can understand what is happening in their interaction with the system.

No feedback

If there is no feedback then the user is unsure about what is happening in their interaction with the system. They have to guess at what is going on. Sometimes they will guess wrong.

Bad feedback

This is feedback that has been badly designed. The system tries to tell the user what is going on but the communication is ambiguous or, worse still, communicates the wrong things to the user.

Feedback and user models

In the previous chapter we dealt with user models. The designer has a designer's model: an ideal user model that they want the user to have, so they attempt to communicate it to the user through the design of the system. As the user interacts with the system they build up their user model, which, if it is well designed, is the same as the designer's model (have a look back to chapter 11 if you are not sure about this).

The system's role in the interaction is to provide the user with information about the interaction. This information, this communication between the system and the user, is feedback and it is what helps the user build up the model that the designer wants them to build up.

I opened chapter 11 on user models with the quotation:

> *The user doesn't know what you know, they only know* what you tell them.

The last four words are key. That process of telling things to the user is the feedback that the system provides.

There many definitions of 'feedback', ranging from its use in electronics to its conventional meaning of 'give me some information back about something'. In this chapter I take it to mean all communication from the system to the user, everything from the physical form of the system to the media it embodies, including the paper-based manuals provided with it and even the telephone help systems that support it.

Feedback in new media

Feedback in new media means keeping the user informed about what is going on. When I click the mouse on a button to place an order on a web site it is important that I know what I have done and that the system knows what I have done, and that I know that the system knows. I should never be left thinking, 'Did it register my order? Is it busy doing something now or should I try again? If I click again will it process two orders from me? Has it finished the action and is it now waiting? Has my computer crashed?' Feedback about the user's interaction with a new media system can be given to the user at different times in relation to the interaction.

Feedback after

This is the usual case of feedback, and means telling the user that they have done something, and telling them what they have done. The user should know that the system 'heard' their request and is doing it. When the request is done the user should be made aware of this and of the results of their request. A request can be anything from executing a complex search to clicking on the 'next page' button.

For example, a user goes to a web site and logs on by entering their name and password. When they have done this they want to get feedback that they are actually logged on to the site. If the page just looks the same they will be left asking, 'Am I logged on? Didn't it work?' It is better to make a clear visual difference in the before and after appearance of the page, or to take them to a different, 'personal' page.

Feedback before

As well as telling the user what is going on, the new media system should also tell the user *what will be going on* if they take a particular action. The user must be told what actions they can initiate and it should be clear how they can initiate them. The button to check the order should make it clear to the user that, by clicking on it they will not actually be placing their order, they will just be able to review their order prior to placing it.

Feedback during

In between these two is feedback that the system is actually doing something for the user. It should make it clear what is happening, when it has started happening, how it is progressing and when it is expected to finish. Examples of this include the many progress bars and loading messages that users will no doubt be familiar with.

This sort of feedback is good at keeping the user in the picture about what is going on but a better approach is to design the interaction so that this processing/pre-loading either happens without the user being aware of it or that it happens in some sort of entertaining manner (the former is of course preferable).

To hide the pre-loading from the user, the user could be shown something simple while the pre-loading is happening, for example a disclaimer or the instructions. Some systems use this time as an opportunity to advertise the features of the thing they are downloading.

Designing feedback

Interfaces that include the designer

Whenever I attend a demo of a system, be it one given by students, salespeople or the technicians who built the thing, they are always standing there in the background, nervously jumping from one foot to the other and continually interjecting with comments like: 'Whoops! No, don't press that, it's the other one you want. No! not that way. Errr, it's in edit mode now, here let me show you' and so on. It seems impossible for them to stand quietly and watch what is going on. In a strange way the person is actually becoming a part of the interface, a sort of accompanying semi-intelligent agent. The danger is that they are becoming a vital part of the interface and the interface will not function correctly without them.

It seems obvious to them what to do because they have been working on the system for the past few months. They have been eating, breathing and dreaming this interface, so much so that it seems unbelievable to them that someone sitting in front of it will not know everything that they know about it.

Unfortunately, that is exactly the case. The user of a system will receive only the information contained in the interface, not the information in the designer's brain unless the designer is standing next to them. The user will get only the manuals, the visual display and the on-screen tools available. The skill is for the designer to encapsulate what they know and build it into the interface in such a way that the user will be able to extract it and understand it themselves without the designer standing next to them wincing and tutting at every click.

Innocence of vision

A good interaction designer must not only be aware of this need to build everything into the interface but must also be aware of what sort of information they need to build in. They must be able to sit in front of the system and, even though they have been eating, breathing and dreaming this interface, they must imagine what it would be like to use it without knowing everything that they know. What is called for is a sort of empathy, an assumed naivety, an ability to temporarily suspend your knowledge of the system and place yourself in the shoes of someone who has never seen it before.

This skill is similar to the 'innocence of vision' preached by artists: the ability to switch off some part of yourself and to draw or paint only what you *see* to be there and not what you *know* to be there.

Tell them what they need to know

Communicating with someone is not about telling them as much as possible as fast as possible. It is about telling them what they need to know. If someone asks you the time you do not start telling them about where you bought your watch. You tell them the time. Furthermore you do not tell them the exact time, you usually approximate it: 'it's just coming up to five' instead of 'it's three minutes and twelve seconds to five, in the afternoon'. Usually they do not need such an exact readout.

It is the same with feedback for the user. In a new media system there is so much going on that you certainly do not want to tell the user all of it. You must be selective and continually try to put yourself in the position of the user to assess what they want to know from the system and when.

A good example of this is given by the e-mail headers that are part of e-mail messages. In early e-mail systems the whole header used to be shown with the message. This header was a mix of useful things (who had sent the message, when they had sent it) and useless things (what route the e-mail had taken, which computer system it had originated from). It took a surprising length of time for e-mail systems to be designed that screened the user from all the useless information.

To sum up, ask yourself not 'what can I tell the user' but 'what does the user need to know from me?'

Positive feedback

Feedback is not just about functional communication. It is not just about telling the user what is going on. Any communication with people involves an emotional element. If that emotional element is not part of the design then the user will pick up on the fact that the feedback is very unemotional and people do not like this. I am not advocating that you simply add emotive words to your text-based feedback, 'File not found. I can really share your pain about this'. I am saying that the designer should think about how the user feels about the interaction.

For example, if they are accessing information and do not have the privileges to access certain parts of the content then the message should not just be negative feedback: 'Access not allowed to you', but should be more positive. Not 'There is a problem' but 'Here is how you can get access'. Thus the message should include methods for the user to gain access to the information: 'Sorry, in order to access this information you first need to create an account (this will take about 20 seconds of your time)'.

Things to tell the user

After all that rather abstract discussion of feedback it may be useful to include a somewhat more concrete list of things that you might want to communicate to the user. This list is not exhaustive; it is very general and its inclusion by no means implies that you should attempt to communicate all of these things to the user at once!

You should be aware of all these points and by thinking about them you should build up a general awareness of the sorts of things you should or should not be communicating to the user.

Tell the *user* . . .

- What the system does
- And maybe what the system doesn't do
- If it is active or not
- Where they are in the structure or in the dialogue

- What options are available
- What the options will do
- That they have done something and what they have done
- If the system is doing it or not
- If they will have to wait and for how long
- If it has worked or not
- What the results are if it has worked
- If it hasn't worked why hasn't it worked, and what they can do to make it work

and for *information systems*

- What information is contained in the system and what information is not there
- Where users are in the information structure
- How the content is distributed through the rest of the information structure
- How the user can get to different parts of the structure
- When they have reached another part of the structure
- What information they have access to and what information they don't have access to
- If they cannot access information then what do they have to do to be able to access it

Problems with feedback

It is a good idea at this point to highlight some of the problems that are often encountered in designing feedback. This is what I meant by bad feedback at the beginning. It is not just a question of putting feedback into the design; it has to be good feedback. Any communication is open to misinterpretation, so you have to make sure that the communication you design does not fall into this trap.

Feedback that is hidden

Just as things in the real-world can obscure feedback, so too in the world of new media important things can go unnoticed if they are hidden from view. Working with multiple windows can sometimes result in important information being displayed in a window that the user has inadvertently closed or iconized. This happens in some web-based systems where a particular window is a dedicated help window and whenever the user clicks on help, the information is displayed in that window even if the window has been iconized or shrunk down into the task bar.

Another nasty one is the search screen that has so much clutter that the results of the search are below the boundary of the window ('below the fold' as described in chapter 3). The user fills in their search terms, hits the search button and then waits, unaware that the search is complete and that the results are listed in the lower half of the page where they need to be scrolled to be visible, the visible part of the screen remaining unchanged.

Feedback that is too late

The brewery example that I opened with is perhaps a little extreme. In some cases even a delay of a fraction of a second can have adverse effects on the smoothness of the interaction.

In the new media world this is typified on the web by checkboxes with a slight delay on them, for example with a very full inbox in the e-mail system Hotmail. Clicking on a checkbox sometimes has a delay of a second or more before it is checked. This leads to confusion and even double clicking (resulting in the box being checked then unchecked before any feedback is given).

Too much feedback

It may seem like a good idea to make sure that the system provides as much feedback as possible, feedback about every single action at every point in the interaction. This would make sure that the user can never say, 'I didn't know that was going to happen, I didn't have enough feedback'. However, this has drawbacks for the users who do know what is going on, and if you are overdoing the feedback this will be most of the user group. Try to choose the appropriate level of feedback (this ties in with the definition of user groups in chapter 9 on GAS analysis). If necessary, have more feedback designed in but in such a way that users see it only if they ask for it.

The classic real-world example was the near meltdown of a reactor at Three-mile Island, Harrisburg, in America when a domino effect in the failure of one sub-system after another meant that at one point the operators were listening to more than one hundred separate audio alarms – a situation that ultimately would interfere with their task at hand.

Trust

We saw above that feedback also has an emotional element. Another area where this emotional element plays a part is in the accuracy of the feedback. Sometimes a system will communicate something to the user that they do not know, but sometimes the feedback will communicate something that the user already knows. In human–human interaction this happens all the time as part of the bonding and confidence building process, or as just idle chat. 'It's cold outside, isn't it?' 'Gosh, the server is running slowly, isn't it?' If the system gives this sort of feedback and it happens to be wrong then there is a breakdown of trust between the system and the user. The system has said something and the user knows it to be incorrect; how can the user trust the system on the other things that it is communicating?

I once worked in an institute where the office computer had a problem with the internal clock. It worked OK, but every time you switched it on it thought it was midnight on January 1, 1980, or something. The problem was that the office suite we were using had been designed to be chatty and user friendly. It always started off with good morning, afternoon or evening, depending on the time. With the clock problem it always started with 'good morning'. As we were using the computer only in the evenings and we had a variety of new staff using it, it meant that the first second of the interaction was wrong and that the user knew it was wrong. It was difficult to make the users trust the rest of the feedback that the system was giving when the first bit was so blatantly wrong.

In chapter 4 on layout we saw how important it was to design layout for different situations with the content. The same is true for feedback. Feedback needs to be true and sensible according to the actions that the system has done. Avoid situations like this:

> **We have placed your order successfully and your order code is:** *Error 42 unable to place order.*

Exercises

Kids' stuff
Babies' toys are awash with brightly colored buttons and knobs that do things. An interesting exercise is to assemble a collection of such toys and have students guess what the buttons do without actually trying

WEBCODE
kids stuff

them out. Are there enough clues from the context and the feedback to make it clear what is going to happen. The 'don't touch' rule must be strictly enforced until everyone has discussed them and made a guess.

Checking orders

Earlier in this chapter I gave the example of an online system that allowed you to purchase something. I stressed that it was important that the user had a chance to review the order without actually placing it. How could you design an interface so that the user had this opportunity and it was clear that it was just a review of the order and not a placing of the order?

Everyday feedback

Take a very simple everyday task and examine it in detail with respect to feedback. Consider making a pot of coffee or getting the mail. Repeat the process for a task in a new media environment.

WEBCODE
checking
orders

WEBCODE
everyday

13

Structure

Structure and navigation

This chapter deals with designing the structure of information – 'information architecture' as it is sometimes known. The structure is how the information breaks down into chunks and the relationships between them; how they all tie together and follow on from each other, which chunks are related and which are not.

When we think of information structures in new media we immediately think of clicking and exploring them because that is the tangible face of information structures. In fact that side of the presentation of the structures – the pages, links and navigation – comes later. First of all we have to sort out the abstract information structure that is to be presented.

In earlier chapters we have seen how structure can be presented and communicated to the user. In chapter 3 we saw how text and headings can indicate structure; in chapter 4 layout was used to communicate the underlying structure. In new media design the information structure is usually far greater than can easily be shown on one page or screen; thus there are technical barriers preventing it all being presented at once. Also, the amount and complexity of the information mean that there is a mental barrier; the user would be overwhelmed by the information even if it could all be presented at once, using text and layout to indicate the structure. In such cases the information must be split up and presented as a collection of smaller units, and the user of the information must be afforded the ability to move around and navigate among them.

The final presentation of an abstract structure is usually a combination of all three methods. Some clusters of information are grouped onto one page, while others are separated by links that the user must follow to get between them.

The abstract structure is to a large extent defined by the nature of the information while the navigation is more of a 'user thing' and is dictated by the way in which the user will want to access and peruse the information. Having said that, a lot of the time the user will want some navigational controls to be able to follow the structure (e.g. if the structure is a linear collection of articles the user will probably want 'next' and 'previous' among the navigational controls).

Standard structures

Let us now have a look at some of the standard abstract structures that emerge in new media. The index of a book is always at the back and the table of contents is at the front. A film has the main titles at the beginning and a complete list of titles at the end. Each existing medium has its own recognized conventions for structuring the information, sometimes with an obvious reasoning behind the choice and sometimes just because everyone else does it in that way. A similar thing is happening with the way people structure web sites and other new media systems. The standards and guidelines for the coming generations are being established today.

A good new media designer should be aware of what is happening in the medium (as should any designer). They should not copy blindly but should alter and reuse ideas in a constructive and meditated manner. They should also try to escape from the constant use of the tree structure. Other structures are emerging and should be given due consideration.

Linear

Have you ever got lost in a train carriage? The usual reply is yes, but not badly. You can get confused about which direction the buffet car is and whereabouts you were sitting on the way back from the buffet car. But it is never really serious. There are two reasons for this; first it is a restricted area, so it is not like getting lost in the city of Chicago; you know that the train has only a limited number of carriages. Secondly, a train is an example of a linear structure, so you can only go in one of two directions. See Figure 13.1.

Linear structures also occur in web pages and on cd-rom-based new media. They are used for definite linear structures of information: items of information related in a one-dimensional way, related in a straight line as it were. Examples are things such as time lines: the history of the United States of America and the development of the fetus in the womb. There are

Linear structure of chunks of information

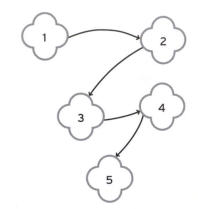

Linear path through a 2D space (Ikea)

Linear structure of ideas when writing a book

Figure 13.1: Three examples of linear structures.

also one-dimensional spatial subjects such as the houses along a historical street, the key sights worth seeing on a long-distance walking route, the events that took place on Christopher Columbus's voyage to America etc.

Real-world examples

In the real world there are many examples of designers being faced with a collection of things/resources and imposing a linear structure on them to assist users in getting around.

The European shopping chain Ikea has huge stores and each one has a pathway marked on the floor that visitors are expected to follow. For the company this is good because it ensures that visitors go past every product that is on offer, and for the visitors it is good because they know that if they stick to the path then they will not get lost. Tourist destinations sometimes do this as well: the Natural History Museum in London picks out a central axis of rooms and gives them a name and a distinctive color to create a linear path through the galleries. Although it does not go past everything like the Ikea path does, this central path does help visitors know where they are and if they stray from this path it is easy to get back on to it. It is a familiar thread running through the collection. The Anne Frank house in Amsterdam imposes a linear path on the rooms by putting barriers on some of the interconnecting doors, but the reason for this is more to keep a flow of visitors going through without their all getting in each other's way as they are going in and out.

If we look to conventional textbook publishing there is also the example of getting ideas down in a linear form – struggling with a large and complex structure that has to be condensed and presented in a linear one-dimensional form. Although it is presented on a two-dimensional page, the book, article or whatever is a list of units of information in a defined sequence. Despite the simplicity of presentation, the structuring of such documents is a complicated matter. The author is continually asking themselves such questions as:

- 'If I put this section here, will the reader have the prerequisite knowledge to be able to understand it?'
- 'How can I group the information together so that units that cover similar subjects follow each other in the text?'
- 'Should I begin with this section because it is the basic information, or with this section because it is an overview of the subject?'

I have heard it said that writing a book is an easy task; the difficult part is finding that initial structure to hang all the information on.

Linear with side-streets

Very often a linear structure is not enough. Maybe you have more to say about each chunk in the sequence. The way to do this is to have a linear structure with 'side-streets'. If we think ahead to the navigation, the user can follow the sequence and at any point choose to interrogate the information further before going on to the next chunk in the sequence.

A web site with information about pregnancy is a good example. The central thread would follow the development of the pregnancy and the user could choose to go down side-streets giving more information about that particular point in the development.

**WEBCODE
side streets**

This and the following structures are shown in Figure 13.2.

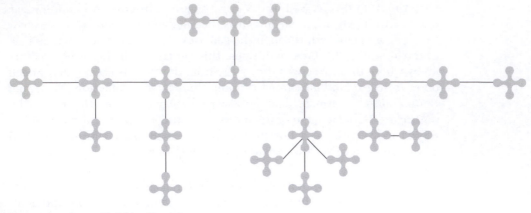

Linear structure with 'side-streets'

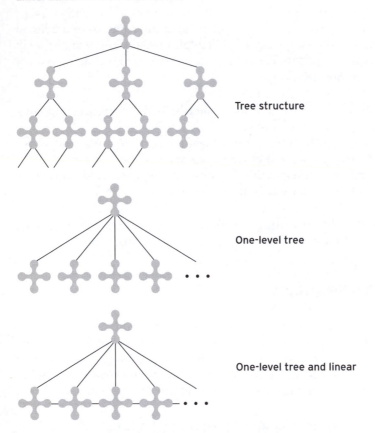

Tree structure

One-level tree

One-level tree and linear

Figure 13.2: Four structures for information.

Tree structure

This is the most common structure for organizing information. It ties in with the way that people deal with information in the real-world and in computer file systems. You have pages gathered together in documents, documents gathered together in files, files gathered into drawers in filing cabinets or into piles on your desk, and so on: clusters within clusters within clusters.

You see it everywhere in multimedia and on the web. The home-page offers a menu of choices and within each choice there are menus of sub-choices and so on.

One-level tree

A common structure that is a specialization of the above is a one-level tree. This has one central item of information with attached elements, for example a page describing the activities of the company and six or seven attachments describing each employee.

Tree and linear

A combination of two of the above structures that you often see is a one-level tree with linear sub-elements. For navigation the readers could step through the linear collection of elements or they could jump 'up' a level and get the overview of all the elements before jumping back into the sequence at whatever point they want.

It is best to use this sort of structure if the sub-items contain the same type of information, if there is a linear quality to the information and if the chunks of information would be useful on their own, independent of the others in the sequence – for example, a collection of articles or of student profiles.

No structure

There are of course times when there is no structure at all in the arrangement and interconnection of elements. Units of information are arranged in a sort of free association manner.

Such an arrangement is applicable if the user does not need an idea of the structure. Indeed there may be some applications such as games and interactive stories where it is vital that the user does not get an idea of the overall structure.

Which structure to use?

With all this talk about different standard structures and the fact that things are still so open on the web that many other structures are possible, the question of which structure to choose is a very important one. How should it be answered? Unfortunately there is no easy answer. You cannot say, 'Oh such-and-such a structure is always the best one to use'; it depends upon the exact nature of the project you are working on. Here are a few guidelines on deciding which to use.

Comprehensible structure

The structure should be easy for the user to comprehend. This is actually a two-fold point. Partly this depends on choosing a structure that is easy for the user to comprehend in the first place, a structure that is not over-complex and that is appropriate; partly, however, there is also an element of graphic design in that the information and the presentation of the information must help support the user in their comprehension of the structure. This can be achieved by such devices as the use of good labeling and titling and reliance on good contextual feedback such as color and style.

Structure implicit in the content

As I stated above, there is no best structure outright. However, there is often a best structure for the particular content that you are dealing with at that time. Analyze the subject material and choose a structure based on that. Information has its own logical structure with respect to sections, order and structure. This should be mirrored in the organization of the information within a new media system.

- If it is a description of the development of a product with argumentation for each change then it would best be structured as a linear sequence of documents with side-streets describing the changes.
- A monthly electronic journal suggests a sequential organization with higher priority given to the current issue (the 'head' of the sequence).
- A collection of profiles of the members of a design group suggests a one-level tree structure with the general information at the center surrounded by the individual information. There may be the ability to step through the member profiles without returning to the general information.

Hybrid structures

A key point in deciding which structure to use is the fact that large, complex new media systems are usually made up of several clusters of information at different places and at different levels. There will rarely be a situation where one standard structure will suffice. What will usually happen is that you get a hybrid structure; different parts of the system will adopt different structures, possibly with one key structure tying the whole thing together.

Internal company structure

Many companies already have a well-defined structure to their organization. This structure governs the flow of information within the company, the responsibilities for different tasks, the hierarchical command structure etc. This structure is so much a part of their thinking that it can sometimes dominate the structuring and presentation of information on the web for purely public consumption.

Such structuring of information for public consumption should be dominated by the public's perceived structure of the information, not by internal company structure. Thus if you were designing a web site for a publisher, the site should be organized not according to the different divisions within the company but according to the different subjects covered by the published material.

Think of a bookshop: this is not organized according to different publishing divisions or indeed to different publishing companies (except when they have a stand, for example devoted to the '. . . for dummies' titles). A bookshop is organized according to subject because that is how users think of books and browse and find books.

Look to the real-world for examples of structure

Above I stated that web designers should be aware of the trends in information structuring within multimedia and the web. For a richer source of information structuring ideas they should also develop an awareness of abstract information structuring in the world around them. How is the information in a bookshop organized? On a poster? In a city guide? A user manual? A chart of ice-creams in a café? From their observations they should try to extract general ideas about information structuring and attempt to apply these to their web design work.

WEBCODE
ice cream

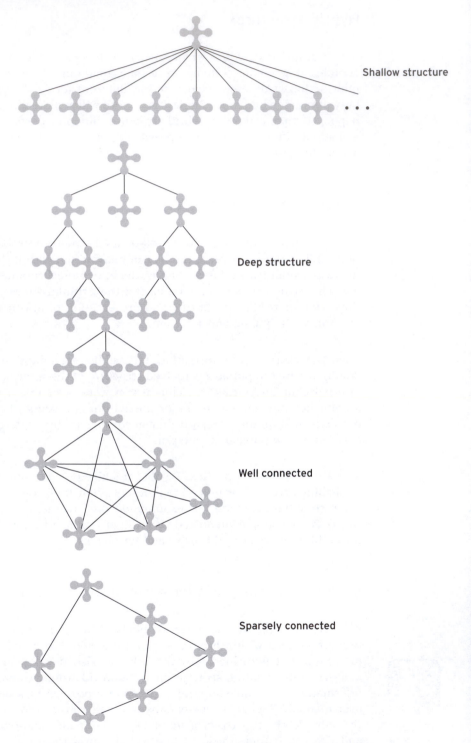

Shallow structure

Deep structure

Well connected

Sparsely connected

Figure 13.3: The issues of depth and connectedness in information structures.

Other structural issues

Although the designer should look to the information for the structure there is a degree of flexibility in the interpretation, and structures also contain an element of design in them. When designing the structure there are several important issues that need to be considered. See also Figure 13.3. We are starting to move into the area of navigation – how users move around the structure. This will be covered in even more depth in chapter 14.

Shallow structure

This results if you move all the choices up as near to the root of a tree structure as you can. The advantage of a shallow structure is that the reader has to make fewer steps to reach a certain item of information. The disadvantage is that there are many choices to choose from. Sometimes this can be too many.

The extreme is to have everything as a choice on the home-page – not a good idea. Everything is just one click away from the home-page, but what a home-page it is. It is about two meters long, takes five minutes to scroll through and there is no way of getting a good overview of what is available.

Deep structure

This is the alternative to the above. Each level has just a small number of simple choices and decisions. The advantages are that the structuring is more comprehensible and the user is faced with simpler choices, but there are many choices to be faced and the information can be reached only after a large number of steps in the structure.

Well connected

A similar story to the shallow structure mentioned above, but this is a more general idea. The idea is that everything is connected to as many other things as possible. It is quick to move to another part but difficult to get an overview of the structure. Even if this is done in a well-organized and logical manner it still means that there are many choices at each point in the structure.

Consider the parallel in buildings. From this room you can get to any other room in the building. 'Wow, great!' The only problem is that you always have 43 doors to choose from!

Sparsely connected

The structure is strict and clear, with few choices at each point in the structure. In the extreme this can be frustrating to the reader as they are forced to stick to the restrictive structure set by the author. They are repeatedly coming up against the limitations.

Structure for different users

The discussion above has been based upon the idea that a site is designed for one sort of typical user. In fact there are many different users of sites and sometimes a site is designed to cater for distinct user groups. The most obvious example is different languages, where a site is set up in more than one language and the user is able to choose which language they would like to view the site in.

In this particular example there are different structures for different users but the effective content is the same and the structures are the same. A user going through the information in French is probably going to want the same structure as someone going through it in English.

Where there really are different structures is where the underlying tasks of the users are different. For example a web site serving an academic institute of some sort would have different structures for students, staff, casual visitors to the site, prospective students, prospective staff etc. Much of the content would be the same but there would be important differences. For example, consider the information about a course. For a prospective student this would cover such things as employment possibilities with that course, how it tied in with other options and to what level it was taught. For an existing student it would cover such things as the timetable it followed, who was lecturing it, how many points the exam was worth and how it was examined.

Structure and content, which comes first?

Above I have said that the designer should look to the information for the content, but what happens if the designer does not have any content?

Which should they approach first? This problem occupied me while I was in the initial stages of this book. I wanted to tell the audience about new media design, but I also wanted to specialize and tell them very specifically about web design, since this is a new and important part of new media design. I had a large cloud of content and ideas and would constantly struggle to bring it together in different forms and structures. Sometimes I thought of two books, but then there was so much material that was common to the two. Sometimes I thought of one book, but then there was material that was relevant to web design but not to multimedia design.

It is almost as if there is a huge cloud of information floating around in some abstract space somewhere and that cloud has to be gathered together to crystallize around some structure. Some structures work partially, loads of stuff sticks and fits but then there is a huge pile left over that does not fit in somehow. If that bit that does not stick is well defined then a new part can be added to the structure to cater for it. If you choose the right structure then the cloud solidifies around it, binding to the sections and divisions within that structure.

There is a large overlap between the scope of a project and the issues of structure and content. The whole question of what is in and what is out. Does one embark on an archive exercise and gather a large amount of data and then postpone the act of designing a structure to fit it all in to, or does one start with the design of a structure and then gather content to fit that structure? (More on scope in chapter 9 on GAS analysis.)

If you are designing a 'clean sheet' system with an unlimited budget for filling content in later then you can easily start with the structure and then fill in with the content. However this is an ideal case. Often you are working with existing content, either through lack of resources to generate extra content or simply because the content is connected with what the client is about and therefore what the cd-rom or web site is about.

It is similar with the production of the actual new media system, where the detail of the design of the structure and navigation can only really be decided with a good knowledge of the content. What better way to build up that knowledge of the content than by actually starting to build it?

There is no ideal approach; it will always be iterative. What is important therefore is to ensure that that iterative process is kept as efficient as possible. Set things up so that large-scale revisions need to be carried out in one part rather than in 30 separate places. Test small sections for technique before applying that technique to the whole production.

Dealing with floating content

This is another quandary when dealing with a new media authoring process. The designer has a little chunk of content, a scene in a film, a chapter for a book, whatever, and it just does not fit in with the structure that they have chosen for the whole. In the new media world you could be working on a project where the content has been prepared earlier (digitized, optimized, classified etc.) and then you are trying to come up with an all-embracing structure. It is difficult. Sometimes you will find that there are large chunks of the content that just do not fit and then you are faced with one of three courses of action summed up below and in Figure 13.4.

- *Bend the structure*. You can bend or distort the structure, alter it so that it is not perfect but at least the extra content will fit into it.
- *Drop the content*. You can keep the structure 'clean' and just leave the extra content out of the project.
- *Redistribute the content*. Alternatively you could try to break the extra content up and redistribute it around the other sections of the system.

The situation has some similarities with trying to concoct a metaphor to describe a system. It is always difficult to find one that embraces all aspects of the system, and all too often some squeezing and bending has to take place. (See the coverage of metaphors in chapter 19.)

Structuring according to type of content

Within a web site there is much content of differing types:

- This information can differ with respect to *time*; some of the information is highly dynamic, changing daily or hourly while other information hardly changes at all.
- The information can also differ with respect to *detail*. Some is detailed paragraphs of text while other information is telegram style overviews or summaries of information.
- Also the information can differ according to the medium that it is realized in: text-only, video and audio, Flash animations etc.

The differing types of information are important to the user and as such the structure should go some way to indicating what the nature is, and areas of information of the same type could be clearly grouped together to indicate the similarity in type. That way regular visitors to the site can immediately make their way to the new information without having to read things that they may have seen several times before, and readers

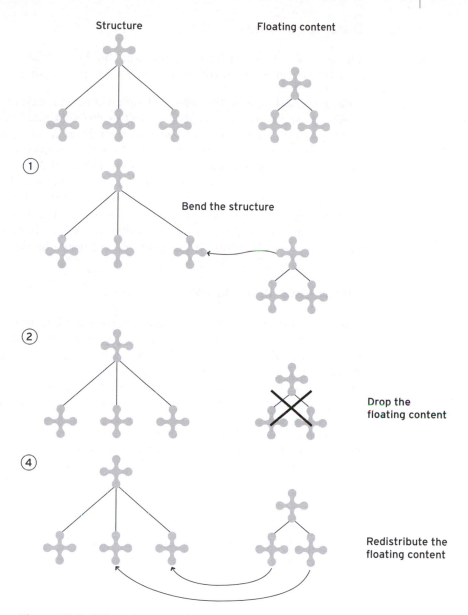

Figure 13.4: Different approaches to floating content that will not fit in with a chosen structure.

having a quick browse will not be confronted with huge blocks of text or long video downloads. However, this way of associating information can interfere with subject-related categorization. Chapter 4 on layout talks about grouping things in more than one set of groups.

Different sources

There are even cases where information should be differentiated in the structure because of the different sources it comes from.

One classic example of this was a cd-rom where one section was headed 'feedback' and contained feedback about events that had been organized by the producers of the cd-rom. The content of this section included reviews by national press, quotes from guest books at the events and quotes from the organization's own publicity. This was a mixture of two very different types of information, on the one hand impartial reviews and on the other self-written promotional material. To some extent they were both commentary on the events but the source, and thus the impartiality and value of the commentary, was very different and so it was decided to emphasize them by splitting them up into separate chunks.

Information distribution

There are two main options for handling the distribution of information in a structure. The designer may decide to keep the structure bare of information – there will just be the choices necessary to navigate through it and all the information will be at the 'end points' of the structure. The structure is clean and understandable, but the reader may find it boring simply making choices all the time before finally arriving at the information.

Alternatively the author may choose to spread the information throughout the structure, ensuring that each element has choices to go deeper into the structure but also has some information content. The result can be a more chaotic structure but more interesting for the reader.

For example an online catalogue with an option 'products' should not merely present the user with a choice list of sub-groups of products. There should be added information. This added information should not be promotional in nature but should assist the user with understanding what the product range is and how it is sub-divided. It may even highlight popular or new products.

Exercises

Spy networks
You have set up a spy network using a one-level tree structure. Mr Big is at the top of it and he is in charge of recruiting new members and passing

on orders; see Figure 13.5. The drawback is that if he is caught then the whole network gets rolled up.

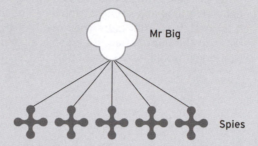

Figure 13.5: A rather bad spy network.

WEBCODE
spy network

Can you devise an abstract structure for a spy network? Each spy is connected to the others in different ways. Some connections will be anonymous (a voice on the end of a phone) and some will be known (a meeting can be arranged).

Once again test your design out by imagining key tasks that will be necessary with the network: recruiting new spies, repairing the network if someone gets caught etc.

Buildings and web sites
There are many parallels between the abstract design of buildings and the design of information structures such as web sites. Consider the following three comparisons and then try to find some others.

Duplicating important items
In a building there are certain key features that are accessible from many points in the building: toilets, lifts, the outside world etc. Building designers solve this by making important things accessible from different points in the structure or by making duplicates of the important features. Similarly in new media design there are such items that need to be accessed from many different places, e.g. fill-in forms for requesting information, help information and so forth. They should be accessible from all the pages.

Screening important items
In many office buildings the director's office is screened by the secretary's office. You can only get to the director by first getting past the secretary.

WEBCODE
buildings

Is there a parallel to this in the world of interactive new media and web sites in particular?

WEBCODE
front door

More than one front door
Buildings have more than one entrance. Even houses have a front door and a back door. Traditionally in the UK, the different doors were used by different users. Important guests would call at the front door, people delivering food and services would call at the back door. With new media it is possible to offer more than one home-page or starting screen which leads to the information. Give some examples of web sites and cd-roms where you would have such separate starting points.

Navigation

WEBCODE
navigation

Introduction

To begin this discussion of navigation let us have a look at an example from the real-world. It is an example of navigation designed for use that is not related to a new media system.

Architects use many representations when designing a building: sketches of the appearance, engineering drawings of the framework and cladding of the building and so on. (This in itself is a good example of different specifications covered in chapter 20.) One form of representation used in the early stages is simple diagrams of the topology of the house. By 'topology' I mean that they are not concerned with the appearance, size or layout of the rooms, only the interconnections between them: How do you get from this room to that room? Is the director's office directly connected to the corridor or is there a secretary's office in between? Can the people get from the kitchen to the dining room or do they have to go through another room first? There is an example in Figure 14.1.

The abstract way of considering buildings described here has many parallels with the design of interactive structures and navigation since we are in effect dealing with the same concepts: units with interconnections available to the user.

Structure and navigation

In the previous chapter we talked about structuring information – identifying the separate chunks of information present in a system. Think of books in a series, chapters in a book, sections in a chapter. Think of breaking a collection of artifacts in a museum down for display in separate rooms. Think of gathering bullet points together to put into slides for a business presentation. See Figure 14.2.

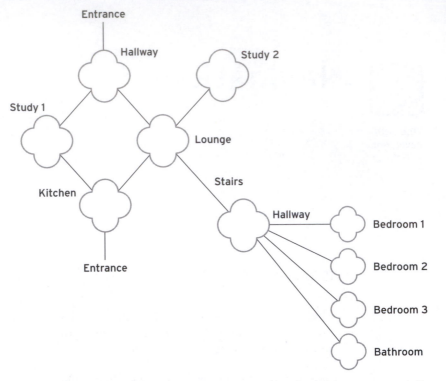

Figure 14.1: A topological map of a house showing the rooms and the connections.

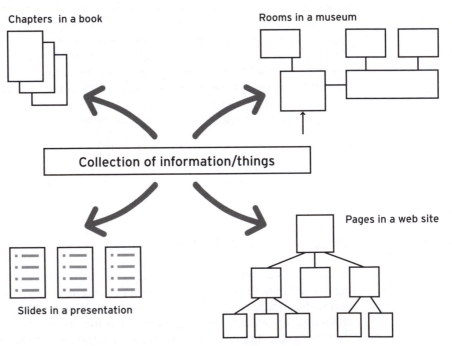

Figure 14.2: Examples of breaking a large collection into chunks.

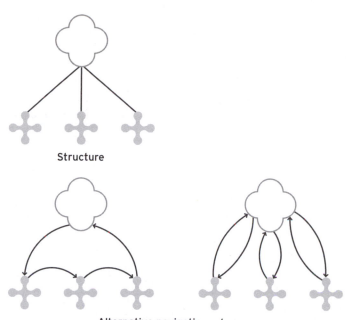

Structure

Alternative navigation schemes

Figure 14.3: An information structure can have different navigation schemes.

The structure is dependent upon the underlying nature of the information. The navigation, on the other hand, is more concerned with the user's relationship with the information: what they are trying to do with it, how they will want to access and use it; see Figure 14.3. Will they be reading a collection of chunks of information sequentially or will they be dipping in to the collection in a non-linear way?

With physical information carriers such as books and museums this getting from one chapter or room to another is fairly easy and direct (although I have had problems in some museums). With digital systems the ability to get around is more complex and requires more design. This is what navigation is all about. How do users want to move around in structures of information and how can designers help them to do so?

Structure and interaction

As well as getting around information structures, there is also navigation that is not primarily information-based. When a user interacts with such a system the user does things and the system does things, and as this all happens the system changes from one state to another. For example when I put money into a drinks machine the drinks machine has gone from 'a machine waiting for money' to 'a machine waiting for the user to

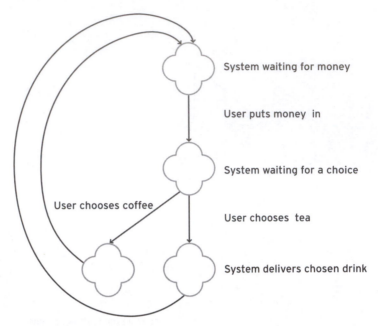

System waiting for money

User puts money in

System waiting for a choice

User chooses coffee

User chooses tea

System delivers chosen drink

Figure 14.4: An interactive system can be thought of as a structure of different 'states' connected by user or system actions to get to those states.

choose a drink', and this transition was caused by the user putting money into the machine, Figure 14.4. Or when I pay for a license and type the license number into my piece of demo software it goes from 'system in demo mode' to 'system in full function mode'.

Looking back to the building parallel above, the rooms are like these states and the doors between them are like transitions. The doors allow the users to move between rooms and transitions allow the user to move between states.

These doors or transitions are included by the designer on the basis of the typical tasks that the user will be performing. Take the house example. If we examine certain tasks that are part of daily living then we can see the need for a door connecting the two rooms. Consider the task of getting up and having a wash: we need a door between the bedroom and the bathroom. Or making the dinner and then eating it: we need a door between the kitchen and the dining room.

In a similar way we can add transitions to the states within an interactive system, although here the examples do not use as much common sense as doors in a house. The 'save a copy' option in PhotoShop is a good example of this.

The user is busy making alterations to an image using PhotoShop and at a certain point wants to save it in a certain format and then carry on making alterations. They used to have to save it in that certain format ('save as . . .' option) and then close that window and reopen a window on the old version in order to be able to carry on. Eventually this became such a common task that the designers of PhotoShop chose to support it by building in a more direct transition between the states.

What is navigation?

So, navigation is how the user gets around in some sort of interactive structure. It plays a part in information structuring and in interaction, but before we get too involved with the detail of designing navigation let us consider navigation in an abstract manner. The dictionary gives the everyday meaning as 'the act of locating the position and plotting the course of ships and aircraft'. We are dealing with it here on a far more personal level: the position and course of the user. Furthermore the usual meaning refers to spatial navigation in a spatial world (whether real or virtual), whereas we are interested in navigating through abstract structures created when clusters of information are linked together. There are similarities. Let us look at the key aspects of navigation in the real world and translate the ideas to new media. See also Figure 14.5.

Position

The first key aspect of spatial navigation is position: 'Where am I?' Where am I within the whole collection of information, where am I within the structure? What is my position in the whole?

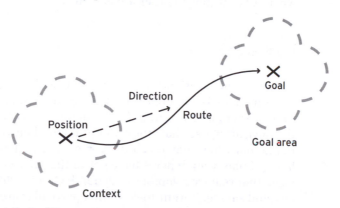

Figure 14.5: Position, route, goal and their less precise counterparts, context, direction and goal area.

Goal

Navigation is not just about being somewhere, it is about trying to get somewhere: the questions of 'Where do I want to go?' and 'What is my goal position within the structure of information?' Usually this is not to do with wanting to be in a certain place but more to do with what there is in that place that the user wants. The user does not say 'I want to be in the products section of the web site'; they want to be there to get something, some item of information.

Route

Having established where they are and where they want to get to, the next thing is the route: how to get from where they are to where they want to be, and ideally in the most efficient manner possible. Following a route can either be a matter of having a well-defined idea of exactly where you want to go or, as we shall see below, or it can be a vaguer process involving taking the first step in the right direction and then deciding what to do then.

These three are the precise items. However, each of them has a more 'fuzzy' version that also plays a part in navigation.

Context

The fuzzy version of 'position' is 'context'. Not so much 'what is my exact position in the whole' but more of a 'what part of the whole am I in?', what things are around me?, what is the extent of the area I am in?, where does it join to other areas?, etc.

Goal area

Similarly, the position I want to reach is within a general area that I want to be in. This is the area I want to get to, before I refine my navigation to the exact place I want to be. Sometimes this area is the only goal that the navigating user has: they do not know their precise goal and want to refine that when they reach the correct area. I have a better idea of what laptop I may want when I have got to the section of the web-based catalogue that relates to laptops in general. Or a tourist is navigating in a new city and saying, 'I want to go to this particular area of the city because it has old, narrow streets and good restaurants'. They then refine their goal when they have reached that area.

Direction

One can get from one place to another without having a precise route in mind to follow. As long as I set off in the right direction I can always refine the route as I progress. Again, in a spatial analogy in a museum, I ask which direction the Pre-Raphaelite collection is or what floor the café is on, and based on this first step I begin my journey. Similarly, on web sites users may navigate more on the basis of 'that looks like the right button to click', rather than having a complex model of the information structure in their heads and working out a precise and accurate path.

How do we navigate?

This is actually a very tricky question and is still the subject of continued research. We have pretty good in-built systems for spatial navigation in two dimensions. These can still be used when we move around in pseudo three-dimensional worlds such as different floors on the same building. Where things really start breaking down is when we try true three-dimensional navigation with no fixed up and down. That we find this difficult is no surprise since there is no evolutionary reason to develop the skill; however it will be important when we start inhabiting large space stations.

When we look at birds and insects there is evidence of primitive, low-level navigation systems hard-wired into the brains providing a sense of direction (which way they are facing) and a sense of place (where they are in relation to objects around them). There is also some evidence that these systems are also present in the brains of mammals. However, once we get to humans, memory becomes the main factor, although the other factors, if present, could be part of that elusive 'sense of direction' that some people have.

WEBCODE
nav research

Even if those first two primitive systems are present in humans they are so strongly linked to navigation in the physical world that they would only really be useful in limited situations such as totally immersive, virtual-reality-style environments depending on such visceral things as head direction, muscle movement in the legs and so on. For the rest of the new media world the fact that humans rely on memory for navigation is the key factor.

Designing to support navigation

In designed environments in the real world the main assistance that the designer can give to the user is to support the more high-level memory navigation functions. This support can be divided into two areas: implicit support and explicit support.

Implicit support

Implicit navigational aids are aids that are part of the context of the user and are used in a less conscious manner. They take the form of contextual clues and features; changes to the style of the direct environment that give the user support when navigating – such things as colors and details. There are some nice examples from the world of the built environment. Consider ferry boats ferrying people with cars across stretches of water. The journey will take several hours and the passengers will want to be entertained (and the shipping company can make money from them). We then have an interesting situation: there are many users most of whom will be there just for those few hours. We are not designing a building where people come to work for 10 or 20 years; we are designing a floating building where people will come once for several hours. They have to be able to find their way around very quickly, they have to be able to find the escape routes if anything goes wrong and they have to be able to get back to their car when the ferry boat arrives. All this has to be supported by the design of the environment. In some cross-channel ferry boats the different levels are given subtle coloring in the carpets and furniture, one floor red, the next one up blue etc. Car decks are labeled not with numbers but with colors and symbols, things that stick in the mind without the users having to make a conscious effort to remember them.

Details are an important visual clue to aid navigation and can be added to real-world environments either in a structured way or just ad-hoc to solve problems. A large science establishment had problems because all the floors looked the same and people were continually getting out of the elevator at the wrong floor. The solution? They simply put things outside the elevator on each floor. On one floor it was a model of an atom, on another it was a large waste bin. Simple but effective.

Landmarks

There is an old joke about a visitor to an English village asking for directions from a vicar and a farmer. The vicar gives all his directions in terms of the local churches and the farmer gives all his in terms of the local pubs: 'Turn left at the "Pig and Whistle", then go down towards the "Compass and Ball"'.

These are landmarks. Landmarks are elements in the environment that are easily recognizable by the person giving the directions and the person receiving them. They are a sort of common navigational language. They help with the navigation and they give a degree of reassurance in the following of the instructions. If directions were just given in terms of 'first left, second right, first right', there would be no indication of whether or not you were following the directions correctly. With landmarks there is a sense of confirmation. When you get to the 'Compass and Ball' pub as directed, you know you have been following the directions correctly.

Landmarks do not of course just play a part in the giving of directions. When you are retracing a journey you have made before, you make use of your own landmarks: things that you saw and noticed first time around and that you recognize this time around. The difference is that your own personal landmarks could be things that are very personal to you: you remember that bike chained to the fence because it was like the one your brother used to have. Landmarks used as part of giving directions have to be common to both parties. It would be no good saying, 'Well, you turn left when you get to a bike chained to a fence that looks like the one my brother used to have'.

Another interesting point in landmarks is that sometimes people, especially older people, give directions according to historical landmarks: 'you know that tall office building just past where the old cinema used to be'. They are giving navigation still in terms of a shared system of landmarks, but that shared system of landmarks exists only in their heads; it no longer exists in the real world.

Explicit support

Explicit navigation aids are things that are external to the actual context and depend on a higher degree of processing from the user. These are things designed as explicit navigational aids such as maps and room numbers.

Overviews and maps

A map is nothing more than an overview of a spatial area. Overviews are useful in many other contexts as well. A table of contents for a book is also a type of map: it is a smaller-scale version of the entire content of the book and can be used to access the whole and navigate through it.

WEBCODE
metro maps

Looking back to our breakdown of the key ingredients to navigation 'position' was first on the list. This idea of position is often given on maps by means of a 'you are here' arrow. Extrapolating this approach to maps of abstract structures actually leaves the author with a lot of freedom. The structure could be represented as a connected graph, a textual table of contents or some other more abstract representation. Just think of the typical metro map or other transport map for an example of an abstract map of a collection of connected things.

Another advantage of this approach when working with new media is that the maps can also be used for navigational actions. Simply making the map clickable enables the user to jump directly to where they want to go.

Labels

The example I used earlier of the vicar and the farmer is a good example of labels. Using pubs as landmarks when giving directions is a lot faster since pubs are in effect buildings with labels. You could communicate in terms of details – 'Turn left at the big white house with the two oaks in the garden' – but it is easier to communicate in terms of labels, since both parties understand them and they are short and quick to use.

There are also parallels here with the labeling of rooms in large buildings. The lack of detail and the repetitive nature of design in large office blocks mean that often the room numbers are all that there is to go on. In fact there is a whole science of labeling concerned with so-called way-finding in the built environment, using room numbers to encode other information such as which floor it is on etc. Contrast this with smaller buildings, such as homes, where there is more detail to navigate by, fewer options to choose from, and the user group (the family) is used to the set-up. The only labeling that usually ever gets done is to stick a 'bathroom' label to the toilet door when you are giving a big party.

Extra navigational structures

As well as the overview or map idea there are other structures that can accompany a system that assist the user with the navigation. As an example think of the world of paper-based publishing. There are many extra bits of explicit navigational information associated with texts. Consider the following and look at Figure 14.6.

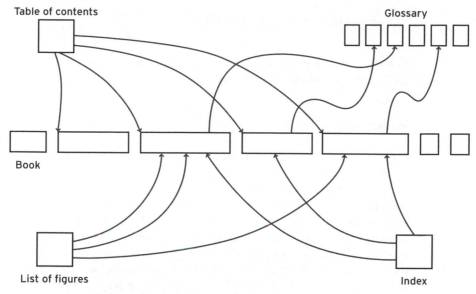

Figure 14.6: Extra navigational structures in a typical book.

The index, the table of contents and the list of illustrations are all navigational aids: overviews of the whole from different viewpoints, enabling the user to choose a point to go to within the whole structure. In a similar way references are also navigational aids, although they point to sources of information external to the book. Two interesting cases are glossaries and footnotes. Both of these are accompaniments to the main structure; they assist in navigation by removing extraneous information, thus leaving the navigation of the main thread of the structure easier and simpler.

In the world of the built environment use is sometimes made of structures external to the building. By incorporating large numbers of windows into the structure the designer can ensure that users are very aware of the outside environment and can use this to support their navigational tasks within the building: 'Oh, my room is on the side with the view over the car park'. Contrast this with so-called 'blind buildings' – buildings with very little contact with the outside world, resulting in the navigational behavior of users being based purely on what is within the building: 'Oh, my room is near where Frank's room used to be, you know, near the fire extinguisher down the corridor from the canteen'.

WEBCODE
outside
contact

Supporting navigation in designed and built environments is a very rich area. For the purposes of this book we shall leave it there and instead focus more on navigation within new media systems.

Navigation in new media

Before reconsidering the navigational topics dealt with above let us first look at the key differences in navigation in the world of new media.

Pages and stages

First, a comment on the inherent 'paged' nature of the web and multimedia. Interaction can be seen as a succession of steps, each step mirrored by a page of information/options. This very quantized manner of looking at things can result in a very quantized, step-by-step chain of pages supporting that interaction. This is especially so if it is coupled with a designer from a predominantly graphic design background who seeks to mirror each step by a uniquely designed individual page or screen. Furthermore, some technologies such as HTML (and long before that, HyperCard) are based on a model where this 'one-page-per-step' idea is an inherent part of it.

Cd-rom-based multimedia, and to some extent broadband web services, can use a more 'stage-based' approach to interaction. Instead of the interaction following a sequence of separate pages, the focus of the interaction is a screen or page that functions as a stage. It is a screen with fixed elements such as background and control bars, and the 'players' who come and go on this stage are extra bits of functionality that pop up (dialog boxes), get pulled down (menus), slide in (Apple's wonderful little control bar) or fade.

The user is left with less of a feeling of navigating around a network of interconnected pieces and more of a feeling of not getting lost because they are not actually going anywhere. They are just staying put and watching and interacting with things that come and go in the context that they are staying put in, Figure 14.7.

Although it seems like a golden solution to the problems of navigation, the approach is not without its own unique problems. Usually the design of a new media system embodies elements of both approaches. To some extent the page-by-page navigation in web pages is offset by having navigation bars that are always present. They become the 'familiar frame' to the rest of the content and as long as they are in the picture the user knows how to get back to familiar places in the web site.

Also we are not talking solely about navigating through large collections of interlinked information. The user also undertakes navigational actions as a 'side-effect' of interacting with complex systems. Finding the 'delete

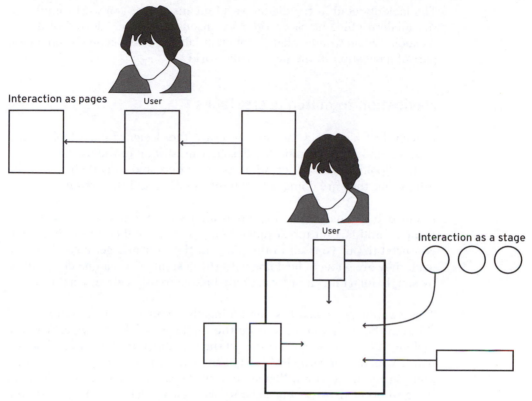

Figure 14.7: The pages or stages way of designing interactions.

filter' command in a large image-manipulation package is often a case of navigating and retracing your steps through a large menu structure. Although seemingly different, such menu structures are also essentially information and the user must find what they want by way of navigating through the menu structures.

Position in new media

In the real-world there is much to define your position, your sense of place. There is everything from the things around you to the quality of the light, the smells and temperature of the air. When we move into the digital world there is a lot less. Your position in a new media structure is defined by the information that is there and the tools that are available to you at that point. In large web-based community sites it can also be defined by who is there (which other users are browsing that particular page or item).

The lack of detail in the digital world means that it is a world similar to the modern office-block corridor we discussed earlier, devoid of detail. As such it is no wonder that simple text labeling has become such a vital part of navigation in the new media world.

Navigation to match users' tasks

Previously I have said that for structure the designer must look to the content, and for navigation the designer must look to the user. When we do this 'looking to the user' what we are interested in is their tasks, the things that they are doing with the information and the system.

Detailed task analysis is an important topic, but it can become very complex and is a bit too advanced for this text. Suffice to say here that you need to put yourself in the place of the user and get a good idea of what they are going to be doing with the system. This can be done either by simply imagining it or by actually talking to users about what they do.

This awareness of tasks is something that you need to practise at all times in the design process, from the top levels of design, when you are looking at the user's global tasks, all the way down to the low-level detail, where you are concerned with what the user will be doing at a particular point in the interaction. You should not be saying, 'This is a really neat thing to do in the user interface to the new media system'. You should also not be saying, 'Wow, it is technically possible to do this, let's do it'. You should be saying, 'This fits in with what the user wants to do at this point'.

Search and browse

The consideration above of the user's tasks is a good introduction to the ideas of searching and browsing since they are two very different tasks in which the user can be involved in terms of fundamental navigation. As well as search and browse there are other novel approaches as yet unexplored; consider navigating through a new media system and being guided by some semi-intelligent agent.

Search

The first way of giving the user the information that they want is by allowing them to state what they are looking for and then to return chunks of information that best match their requirements. (To some extent one can ask if this really is navigation in the purest sense of the word.)

There is much technology related to the way in which the user states what it is that they want and in matching information to their needs but this is not really navigation and deeper consideration of this topic (and it certainly is a deep topic) is not appropriate here. I mention it only because it is an important accompaniment to navigating information.

Browse

The other way that users can get the information that they want is to lay the information out and let the user go through it finding what they want themselves. It is this part, this browsing, where the subject of navigation plays a role and that we shall be looking at further in this chapter.

A bit of both

There are of course methods that involve both of these approaches, filtering information and then allowing the user to navigate their through the filtered information.

Search and browse

It is possible to offer a search tool and then allow the user to navigate or filter the results according to other criteria. For example, an auction site might allow the user to search on a particular word and then, when the results come back, they can choose to look at the results for a particular category. Executing a search for 'kitchen table' could return many hits, some for real kitchen tables, some for doll's house kitchen tables and some for things for a kitchen table or cds from groups that happen to be called 'kitchen table'! If the user can browse the results and go to all the search hits that are in the category 'furniture' then they can more easily find what they want.

Browse and search

Alternatively, a user can navigate through the structure to a certain area and then execute a search within that area. For example an offering of educational resources could be broken down in terms of subject: once the user gets to the appropriate subject and sub-subject area they then do a search for a particular topic they are interested in.

If we are using a spatial metaphor then we can say that browsing a structure is equivalent to walking around it and exploring it. We can also say that search is like getting in a taxi and saying 'take me to a good hotel'.

Navigation for dynamic content

Earlier in the book we took the dynamic nature of content into account when we looked at text (chapter 3) and layout (chapter 4). Now we will consider it in the light of navigation. The navigational actions designed to be part of the new media system need to be applicable as the nature and amount of content varies. The designer needs to ensure that all the key actions remain possible and are as efficient as possible. For example displaying a list of search results on one page will be fine unless the search returns thousands of results; then the structure and navigation will have to be different. Similarly displaying the results in alphabetical order in a list headed with the letters of the alphabet will be clumsy if the search only returns a handful of results.

Even approaches such as splitting the results up into pages of 20 can still give problems if the navigation is not properly designed. As well as buttons for 'next page of 20' users also need to be able to jump straight in at a particular page number without having to hit 'next' 30 times.

Supporting navigation in new media

Earlier in this chapter we looked at implicit and explicit support for navigation. Let us return to those two topics in the world of new media design.

Implicit support

We saw above how populating a ferry boat with designed detail can help with the support of background navigation. Similar things can be done in the world of new media. It is possible to color code different parts of the new media system, adopting a similar style but different colors, or keeping to the same corporate color scheme but altering the way the colors are used. The key thing is that users appreciate that it is different, but not so different that they think they have gone on to a different site; it must all look like 'rooms in the same house'. For systems that cater for a number of different user groups this difference in the design of the different parts of the structure can be very pronounced. The part of a banking web site targeted at students will be very different from the part targeted at business customers.

Landmarks

These are pages in the structure that you can easily get to and have cause to visit frequently: a home-page, a search page, a table of contents, a personal page, a page giving an overview of a particular subject. Such pages must be visually distinct, well connected and have a good reason to be frequently visited. There should also be a clearly visible route back to them (in effect a button) throughout the site. Landmarks give readers a warm feeling of security: they know where they are, they have a fixed point to explore from and to come back to.

The central role that these pages play means that they should be designed to help the user with their navigation as much as possible. Buttons should be as close to the top of the page as possible, otherwise the user will have to scroll the page to see the choices. Furthermore the page should be quick to load; it is very frustrating if the menu of choices is displayed below a big high-resolution logo that slows down each navigational action from that page.

Explicit support

Overviews

Giving a good overview of the structure is one goal in supporting navigation. One way is as a very detailed, independent overview or site-map. However, having such a useful resource one click away is not as good as having some overview present in a permanent navigation bar on the page. The drawback with this is the amount of space it takes up, and it is always a compromise between how much detail to show and how much space to take up.

One approach is to have navigational overviews that collapse, that is only the top levels are shown and the sub-levels are revealed in response to some user action (mouse over, click, whatever).

This design decision, like many others, is a question of compromise between different advantages and disadvantages. Having collapsing overviews makes things more manageable but it puts the burden on the user to click through all the collapsed collections of choices to find what they are looking for. It is similar to the difference between having everything nicely filed away and having everything spread out on your desk. One is disorganized but everything is close to hand; the other is well organized and everything can be found, but it takes time to do so.

Labels

The labeling of pages or screens of information leads on to the idea of breadcrumb trails. As the user 'drills down' through successive levels

WEBCODE
breadcrumb

of detail (e.g. HP site, products, printers, laser printers, model HP 6L, printer details . . .), the trail they have taken is displayed in the page, and they can see where they are at all times within the structure. Furthermore, by making the separate items on this breadcrumb trail clickable, the user has navigation as well to take them back to the upper levels of the structure.

The only problem that arises with this approach is when the structure is exceptionally deep and the titles are very long. You can quickly end up with a trail that is longer than one line and once the trail starts wrapping round onto another line it is more difficult to interpret.

Extra navigational structures

The examples of extra navigational structures we saw in the world of the printed book can easily be reproduced in the world of new media. The tools can be more powerful because users can go directly to places with just a click of the mouse; they do not have to follow page number references. This opens the door to all sorts of new structures and navigational possibilities beyond those copied from the print world.

As well as extra navigational structures to support new tasks there is also extra structure that is added to help to supplement existing tasks. Consider dealing with long lists of items, such as are returned by a search of some sort, or an e-mail inbox full of mail. The underlying structure is simply a list. It could be shown to the user one element at a time but it is better to provide them with an overview listing of key information where the user can click through to the full information of the element if they so wish. For the e-mail example the user sees a list of each e-mail's subject line and sender and can click through to read the e-mail in full.

These lists can be very long and presenting them to the user in one go could be slow or overwhelming. So the user is often provided with functions such as 'next page' and 'previous page', referring to elements of the structure that are not an integral part of the content but that are part of the way that the content is displayed.

An even simpler example is the extra navigational structure added to make a list into a loop. The linear arrangement of information occurs in real-world information organization as well as in new media; think of books or card indexes. The abstract nature of the computer, however, allows us to alter it in subtle ways. One such is to connect the two ends of the sequence so that the elements are arranged in a loop. This means that, when you are navigating through the sequence, you never come up against the end of the sequence. It avoids backtracking and thus makes access more efficient while remaining comprehensible.

Links

On a more detailed level there are a number of issues directly connected with the navigational links within a new media system. Consider the following.

Links for places and for actions

When navigating around a new media system, there are links associated with two key things (Figure 14.8). The first is links that are directly connected with moving around the information structure and the second is links connected with the performing of certain actions, not so much 'go there' but 'stay here and do this'.

Multiple links

Do not put multiple links to another page in a web page, especially if they have different buttons or texts. The user will be confused into thinking that there are more links than there are.

Multiple links are sometimes necessary to maintain consistency. Consider the navigational buttons in a sequence of articles: 'Back to first article', 'Next' and 'Previous'. When the user is on the second article then

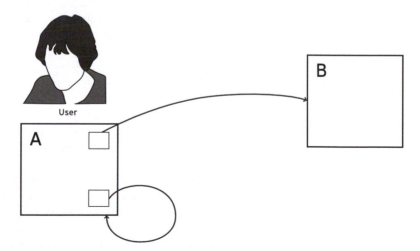

Figure 14.8: A link to go somewhere and a link to do something.

'Back to first article' and 'Previous' will in fact point to the same article. However, this is all right as they are both logically correct. The problems arise if there are two links to the same thing and the user has to do a lot of thinking or clicking to realize what is going on.

Non-working references

There is nothing worse than coming up against a reference in a web document or cd-rom that says, 'See the home-page for more information on this'. The user has to sort out where the home-page is and get to it themselves. The technology of new media allows us to always provide the user with a link. There are one or two situations where it is justified though. Consider encouraging the user to get accustomed to links that are a permanent part of the on-screen navigation. The help or introduction pages may then say, 'To see the options at any time just click on the "show options" button in the left-hand navigation bar'.

Cross-links

Cross-links can lead to getting lost especially if they are crossing branches in a tree structure. The user is reading about a particular book, for example, and the name of the author is a link. They click that and jump across into the branch of the overall structure that deals with author information. Then they are stuck in the author information and must find their own way back up the structure and down into the book information, or resort to the back function of the web viewer. It would be better if there were reciprocal links in both parts. Thus as well as click for author information there should also be a link in author information saying click for information about the book this author has written. This would enable the user to return to where they were.

Links within one page

With the web it is possible to keep a text as one long page of text but introduce a clickable table of contents at the top of the page that points to separate items within the rest of the page. Accompanying this with links to jump back to the top of the page from within the text is a good idea since it can be disconcerting for a reader to click on an entry in the table of contents and then end up stuck in the middle of a huge file where their only way of getting back to the top is to scroll upwards.

An important point is that the links should explain that they are taking the user to points further down in one big document, otherwise the user can follow the link, assume that it is a separate chunk of information and get very confused if they start scrolling and find themselves in among the whole collection of such chunks. It is best to avoid 'in page linking' unless you do make it very clear to the user what is going on.

Dead ends

It is bad practice to lead the user to a page and then provide no links from that page (you see this occasionally on 'thank you' pages when you have filled in a form on a web site). Wherever possible you should support the user in getting back into the flow of the interaction.

It is true that there is a 'back' button in the browser but when a reader is busy with the pages for a particular company or institute you do not want them suddenly taking a step away from your site and concentrating on the workings of the browser. You want them to be unaware of the browser in much the same way that the lights are dimmed in a cinema so that you are unaware of the hall.

Conclusions

That final section on designing individual links within pages just goes to show that navigation is an area of new media design that stretches across the whole range of detail of design, all the way from high-level, user-oriented questions about the user's behavior down to individual questions about what links to put where on an individual page. So, whether you are designing on the broad scale or on the small scale, an awareness of the navigation and where the user will want to go is always important.

Exercises

House design

Remember the opening example of designing a house as just a collection of rooms with interconnections? Imagine you have just won a fortune and can employ an architect to help design your new mansion. All you have to decide is what rooms to have and how they connect together. As well as the ordinary rooms to do with day-to-day living, there are all the extras like wine cellars, swimming pools, jacuzzis, roof terraces and so on.

This exercise is best carried out as a group project; you quickly get all sorts of rooms and all sorts of strange connections between them

WEBCODE
house design

according to people's perceived tasks ('I would like to be able to get up in the middle of the night and write a few ideas down in my study so I need a door between the bedroom and the study').

When the design is complete, try to imagine it in use. You are in the swimming pool and you need to get out and shower; you are in bed and you need a drink; you are in your study writing a book and you want a quick dip in the jacuzzi.

Family trees

WEBCODE
family tree

Imagine that you are called in to design the navigation for an interactive family-tree system. How would you design it? What exactly is the underlying structure in a family tree and what sort of navigational options would the user be interested in?

Experiment with different designs and also with different ways of writing the designs down on paper.

Navigation for an online journey diary

Imagine that you have been on a three-day hike through a national park, walking gently through some beautiful nature. All along the route you have been making a few notes and taking plenty of photos with your new digital camera. Finally, you get some time to put together a web page about the journey. As well as your notes and the photos, you also have a map of the route and have researched a bit of the animal and plant life of the area.

WEBCODE
journey diary

You have this collection of resources and now you must put them into an interactive structure of some sort and give the user navigational tools to move around in the information. Design a suitable structure and navigation scheme. What different approaches are there and which approach do you think is best and why?

A presentation

WEBCODE
presentation

Design a system where users can put together presentations. Concentrate not on the tools for adding text and graphics to the separate slides but on the tools that would be required for the sequencing of the slides, both during the authoring and during the presentation itself. Are there any metaphors that could be used in the design?

Standard navigation patterns

WEBCODE
standard
navigation

For each of the standard information structures described in chapter 13 on structure devise some standard ways of navigating them. For example a chain could have all the states linked together with 'previous' and 'next' transitions etc. Present your ideas in terms of diagrams with arrows indicating the navigational paths.

Narrative

15

Introduction

We have dealt with the structuring of information and the associated user navigation and interaction. Let us now move on to the role that narrative plays in it all.

In the early days of interaction design, when absolutely everyone was getting involved, there was a part played by those involved in the scripting of more conventional dynamic media: film and television. These players brought their scripting skills to the world of interaction. However, writing down a script for an interactive system or service is not about describing a linear course through time, as with a film, it is about describing *all* of the possible linear courses through time. In effect it is the act of specifying the complete interface, something that is so complex it has its own chapter, chapter 20. It is a vital part of interaction design, but it demands other skills and specification methods than those used in more conventional script writing.

Having said that, there are many aspects of conventional script writing that are powerful if they can be effectively migrated from the one medium to the other, in particular narrative and engagement. Brenda Laurel was the first to realize this, and wrote a very interesting book about it.

The critical phrase there is, 'if they can be migrated'. Film and theater are essentially linear forms of engagement; the author is involved in telling a story that captures the viewer and that evolves over time. How can this be the same as creating something where the user is in control and directing what happens next? Either the user has interactive control or they do not; if they do not, they are following a story and if they do then they are effectively writing it.

What is narrative?

For the purposes of this book, narrative is the telling of a story, but there is a lot more to it than just that. It is telling a story to someone. A story is not a story unless there is someone listening to it.

A narrative, then, is communication, but not just the communication of a lone idea; it is the communication of something that evolves over time – the ongoing communication of an evolving situation or collection of ideas.

Simple communication of an idea is successful if the idea is transferred to the mind of the listener. For narrative to be successful it must not only communicate the ideas but it must also keep the user's attention throughout the evolution of the plot: it must engage the user, draw them into what is happening, make them forget the world outside the interaction. It is not just transferring an idea, it is building a world and inviting the user to live in that world.

With film, the skill of narrative design is of such a high order that one rarely sees a film that has a bad story line; when was the last time you saw a film that was so bad that you actually walked out of it? In contrast, the ideas of narrative and engagement have yet to make an appreciable impact on the world of interaction. Interaction is seen as very functional. This is why there are often interactions that lack this feeling of engagement and development.

Narrative in games

Interactive games are at the forefront of narrative design for new media systems. The ultimate goal is to create a game where the playing of the game has the same feeling as watching a good movie; to have a narrative where the user is in control of what happens but the author still has scope to tell them a story. Combining the two is difficult (maybe even impossible).

Set-'em-up-and-shoot-'em-down games can be unsatisfying: in the middle of a huge battle you get hit and killed and the game ends. True to life, but how often do you see a good film end like that? Alternatively you win: after a ten-minute struggle with sweaty palms and a slippery joystick you finish off the alien and it is the same story: 'Game over, do you want to play again?' No, I don't! I want to bask in the glory of winning for a bit first.

As the area of games design matures, new approaches and ideas mean that interactive games are taking the first steps in presenting a mix

WEBCODE
narrative mix

of narrative and interaction. Game design is learning from film design and the newest clutch of games have clever techniques to enhance the narrative effect. Admittedly they are sometimes just glorified ways of saying 'game over' but that is what narrative is all about; it is connected with development and change in time. Sometimes a message is more powerful and enjoyable if it is communicated in ten minutes rather than in one.

Narrative in new media

Narrative is a fascinating subject, vital for film and theater, important for computer games, but does it really serve a purpose for interactive new media? One can appreciate that certain parts of new media information have a narrative element: the company history, for example, or how to get from the station to the head-offices etc. Even a presentation has a narrative element with recaps, development of ideas, plots and sub-plots, but what about everyday interactions? Surely the last thing an ordinary user wants when they try to delete a file is the computer to start in with 'Once upon a time there was a little file . . .'. Is narrative useful in terms of task-related interaction in a new media system? Telling a story in that way is not appropriate, but there are many other ways of telling a story. Deleting a file in conventional desktop environments does have a certain narrative element to it: you pick the file up, you carry it to the trash can and drop it in. In some set-ups you can hear it drop in and the icon changes so that you can see that the trash can has got something in it. You can then empty the trash or rummage through it at a later date to get things out. This is in effect a story, a chain of events that are linked in which the lead players are the file and the user. There is a strong sense of continuity and persistence of existence and things happening.

Micro-level narrative

This is an illustration of where narrative can play a part, if not at a macro-level then at the micro-level – stories built into the smaller events that make up a new media system. It may not be possible to tell the user a story on the grand scale of an interaction since you have no idea where the story is going. On the micro-level, when a user goes to throw a file out, you do not know why they are throwing the file out, but you do know that they are throwing it out. For this part of the interaction you can supply narrative; you can supply continuity (more about continuity later in this chapter); and you can give narrative-oriented feedback in the form of animation (more about animation in chapter 8).

Narrative in scenarios

I should mention that there is another area where narrative and new media design overlap, and that is when one is using scenarios as an aid to designing or presenting a design. A scenario is nothing more than a little story, but it has to be a good story: the reader has to remember it, enjoy reading it and empathize with the lead role of it (have a look at scenarios in chapter 21 on prototypes and demos).

Hidden agendas

Some stories have a narrative that is open and plain to see while at the same time running a hidden narrative, a hidden agenda or message. Aesop's Fables were entertaining stories that came with a moral at the end. In a similar way church sermons tie up a topical story with a biblical message. Novels sometimes couple a good yarn with a hidden message; consider allegorical novels such as George Orwell's *Animal Farm* or Arthur Miller's *The Crucible* considered a thinly veiled commentary on the communist witch-hunts of the McCarthy era. Robert Heinlein's *The Puppet Masters* is an anti-communist counter message from the same era.

This idea can be migrated to the world of new media design where a narrative can be chosen that satisfies two demands. The first is the demand of the user for information or entertainment or getting a task done. The second is the demand of the supplier of the system. Perhaps they want to get the user to make use of their product, or they want to channel third-party advertising at the user. These demands form a sort of hidden agenda to the interaction, although often it is not hidden at all.

No narrative

This discussion of narrative would not be complete without mentioning systems that have no narrative. Sometimes a system will have so many other rich facets that the narrative takes a back seat. The atmospheric graphics of some advanced computer games invite the user to forget about the story and just have a look at the scenery. Alternatively some games are just set-'em-up-and-knock-'em-down games which also invite the user to forget about the story.

Similarly there are films where the action and special effects are thought more than enough to compensate for a lack of story-line. These examples have a lot in common with the old idea of a 'mystery tour', a day trip to somewhere: you do not know where you are going, and to some extent you do not really care as long as the scenery is good.

Who is in control?

Let us get back to the wider picture of narrative, starting with the idea of control. Control in interaction revolves around the question of who is directing the course of the interaction, who is telling the story? The alternatives are the two parties to the interaction; either the user can be controlling the flow of the interaction or the system itself can be controlling it. Let us look at both cases in detail.

User in control, system passive

This form of interaction is typified by many systems and interaction styles: web browsing, drawing programs, basic word processors. No clever technology is needed; the system does not need to guess what the user is doing or try to lead them through things, it just sits there and responds to whatever the user is doing. It does, however, need to be clever in terms of giving the user good feedback about what is going on so that they can make informed decisions about what they are doing.

Conventional browsing of information falls very much into this pattern. The information is a landscape through which the user browses and navigates with the system only 'speaking when spoken to'. Fill-in forms that resemble tax returns for the IRS also typify this in that they have a large number of questions on one page and the user can go through and answer them in any order that they like before submitting the completed form.

In narrative terms there is very little of a 'story' being told. Some narrative style games seem to be in this mold; the user must go about of their own volition in a certain landscape and try to find out who carried out the murder (for example). In actual fact the narrative is already there; what the user is doing is actively finding the elements of that narrative and putting them together.

System in control, user passive

There are many instances where the new media system is in control. You may be familiar with the idea of 'wizards' when interacting with your computer at home. When you are faced with a complex procedure for setting something up, the computer will 'hold your hand' through the interaction. This 'hand holding' takes the form of a chain of little screens, each helping you with one small aspect of the set-up. You just have to deal with the screen being displayed at that moment and subsequent screens are shown based on your responses.

Similarly, one can find many other examples of systems where the interaction is orchestrated in this way. It is easy to design and develop because there are no unknown factors, no unpredictable users; you write the score and the user is forced to follow it.

Which is best?

There is no easy answer to this one. It depends on the technology being used, the nature of the user's task and the skills of the user. It is once again an example of 'look to the user, look to the context'. In terms of helping the user through a particular interaction certain users may know about what is going on and just want to get on with it themselves, whereas other users with less experience will want the 'hand holding' offered by a wizard-style system. In terms of narrative any system or game that wants to tell a story must be of the form: system in control, user passive.

Joint control

Sometimes the control of the new media system is shared between the user and the system. However, this is usually just a mix of the first two options but with the turn-taking happening at a much more detailed level of granularity. Instead of the system being in control for ten minutes and then the user, we have a finer granularity sharing where the system does a little bit, then the user, then the system etc.

WEBCODE
the sims

A good example of this are the simulation-type games, games such as 'The Sims' where the user sets up the environment and then things happen within that environment; the user does a bit, then the system does a bit.

Another, lower-level, example is the so-called 'snap-to-grid' function used in CAD programs. The user moves the cursor and the end of a line they are dragging follows the cursor but is always snapping from grid point to grid point. The user is the active agent but the system is not quite passive; it is interpreting the user's actions in some way to yield a different behavior. A similar thing happens when you are moving furniture in the Sim's household or moving icons on the desktop of some computers where the icons snap to an imaginary grid that keeps them in neat rows.

Control in existing technologies

If you look at various technologies in terms of who is in control, you see that conventional media are polarized toward one or the other extreme. A book is passive technology; the user must actively go a point in the book and start reading. True, the book determines the chain of developments in the story, but the users can choose when and where in the book to begin reading. The radio is 'user passive' technology: I often do other things while listening to programs and, although I am visually and physically busy elsewhere, the 'user passive' nature of the radio means I can still concentrate on the content. Television is rather different, especially now that there are so many channels. Watching television becomes a hybrid medium. Zapping around the channels is very much passive technology: the user is in control and flicks around until they find something worth watching; at that point it turns into active technology and the user settles down to watch a bit of the program. The web up until now has been passive technology with the user doing the browsing and reading (in a similar way to zapping the television channels). However, as more dynamic media (video, audio, animation etc.) begin to get used, it too is starting to shift towards the 'user passive' paradigm.

Granularity of control

How much you can lose yourself in the narrative of an interactive new media system also depends on your depth of interaction; how much of yourself is in the interaction, moving and controlling parameters.

Consider 3D games where you choose from four or five preprogrammed directions and the system moves you a fixed distance in that direction (typified by the original 'Myst' game). Contrast this with free-roaming games where you control your free movement through the 3D world (typified by games such as 'MechWarrior'). The former may have more detail and better graphics but you still feel that the system is moving you around in restricted directions according to your requests. Instead of begin able to roam free, it is as though you were sitting in a wheelbarrow being pushed around the landscape.

Who *thinks* they are in control?

Just as important as the question of 'who is in control?' is the question of 'who *thinks* that they are in control?' It is possible to set up systems where the user thinks they are in control when in fact the system is running the narrative. For completeness I should add that the converse – a system where the user thinks that the system is in control but in actual fact the user is in control – is not particularly useful and is more difficult to achieve.

Having the user think that they are in control is used in a number of real-world systems: there are examples involving heating systems with dummy thermostats where the user feels happier with the temperature because they think that they can influence it (this could be an interaction designer's urban legend).

I was once involved in the production of an online game revolving around penalty kicks in English-style football. You clicked the mouse to shoot a ball at a goal. In the final version many factors influenced the shot on the goal, and when it went online it had a discussion page attached to it. All sorts of theories started being evolved about how to score. Users recounted strange rituals of twirling the mouse around the ball, approaching the ball from a certain direction etc.

People like to feel that they are in control when they are doing things, and will often convince themselves that they are in control when in reality they are not. This applies to many other aspects of life than computer games.

Continuity

In the film industry one of the many credits at the end of a film is that of 'continuity director'. The narrative of a film is broken down into separate blocks for the purpose of efficient filming and so shots that appear to follow each other in the film are actually filmed at completely different times and places in real life. Someone has to make sure that, when one shot finishes and the other one starts, all the visual details of the first one are present in the second one. The hero has to have the same cut on his lip, have his collar set in the same casual manner and have the same buttons missing from his shirt.

Continuity is an essential ingredient for narrative; it keeps it all together. It keeps the threads running through the interaction and it ensures a credible flow to the whole story. Continuity can be broken down into different levels – from the low levels of visual continuity up to the high levels of continuity of belief. Let us start with the low levels and work upwards.

Visual continuity

The manner in which the eye interprets motion is a complex one. Suffice to say that when a flow of still images is shown to it and if there are enough still images shown per second (as with the separate frames of a film) then the eye is tricked into seeing the images as motion. Similarly if the lights in a chain of lights are flashed briefly on then off one after another the eye will interpret this as a single light moving along the chain of lights (you may have seen this sort of thing with Christmas decorations; it is called the Phi effect). This is the very basic level of visual continuity, making the eye and brain believe that separate things are in fact the same thing moving.

Continuity of existence

A higher level of visual continuity is the act of stringing events together so that they look as though they are all joined up in some form of progression. If a ball is rolling from left to right and goes behind another object, then, assuming it has not radically changed its behavior while out of view, it should appear from behind that object on the other side going at roughly the same speed and direction. This visual continuity helps the user build up the story about what is going on, albeit a very simple story: 'ball rolls behind something – comes out other side'.

This sort of thing has parallels in the new media world when you are trying to get some sort of interactive widget on to the screen. The simplest approach is just to have the user do some action and make the thing you want suddenly appear as if by magic on the screen. This is rather a jarring jump in the 'narrative'. To make things smoother for the user things need to appear in an understandable and coherent manner, just as in the real-world. The menu or panel of buttons could slide in from off-screen, or it could fade up from nothing, or unroll from a thin line like a roller blind or expand/zoom out from a dot of nothingness etc. The converse is also true; they should be disposed of in a similar way. In fact on-screen widgets should be treated like characters in a play; they should not just appear magically in the middle of the stage (on the screen), they should have a history, they should come from somewhere and, when they leave, they should go somewhere.

Continuity of narrative

This is continuity in the user following what is going on. On the lower level it is just making sure that they know what is going on at that particular moment. This involves camera angles and composing the shot so that they can see the important parts. For example many confrontational situations – interviews, football matches etc. – are filmed in strict adherence to the '180 degree rule'. Any camera angle is allowed as long as it is always within 180 degrees of the line joining the two parties, i.e. the camera positions are always confined to one side of the two facing parties. Although this is connected with narrative, it is basically good feedback, telling the user what is going on. On the higher level, continuity of narrative is about establishing and maintaining a good thread to the story so that the user follows the story as well as the immediate events.

Continuity of belief

Finally there is a big difference between being able to follow what is going on in a film and believing or feeling empathy with what is going on in a film.

When the hero leaves the heroine in the haunted house with all the gold and goes off, on foot, to make a phone call in a call box ten miles down the road you can follow exactly what is going on; the continuity from scene to scene is great, but the whole film has suddenly blown its credibility. Immediately you are saying, 'Oh, that's stupid, no one would really do that, it's obvious what's going to happen', and you start thinking about stopping the video and making a cup of tea instead. This may not seem to be be applicable to the world of interactive new media until you consider that much of what happens in the world of new media also depends on a certain level of credulity from the user's side.

When dealing with large amounts of data and complex tools there are going to be times when the user thinks, 'Well, I think I did that right. I haven't got time to check all the stuff I changed so I'll just have to trust that the system did it all in the way I wanted'. The user has to believe in the new media system; they have to have watched the system at work doing things and believe that the system is credible in terms of what it is doing.

Start to finish

I shall move on now to look at the different general aspects of a piece of narrative from an interaction design point of view. Once again the complexities of the subject mean that I shall restrict myself more to narrative on the micro-scale. As we are dealing with narrative it seems to make sense to deal with the different aspects in the same order as they occur in a narrative structure.

Start – the first five seconds

I have heard it said that the first five seconds of any relationship are the most important. I think it was said in the context of human–human communication but it is also true of interactions between users and new media systems. It is also true of many other media-related engagements – plays, books, especially stand-up comedians – I can remember one commenting, 'You can tell in the first ten seconds whether it's going to be a good evening or not'.

The same rule is true with media: the 'setting of the scene' in a film or a play, the impact of a book jacket, the opening bars of a piece of music, the first few lines of a newspaper article, a cd-rom and nowhere is people's attitude to media more fickle than on the web. If the first eye-full of a page does not hold their attention then there is a whole world of information just one mouse click away, and if the first five seconds are spent waiting for some huge unnecessary graphic to download then the relationship is flawed right from the start. That is the worst calling card there is, and is equivalent to a door-to-door salesperson having the door of a house opened to him and then saying, 'Oh hang on while I just go and get something out of the car'. Or a band coming on stage, being introduced and then saying, 'Sorry, you'll just have to wait while we unpack our instruments'.

The first five seconds establish many things about the forthcoming interaction. Furthermore, those first five seconds govern how the following five seconds are interpreted and so on. Negative and positive tend to snowball in this way: if things are bad then the user gets more fed up and more critical as time progresses, and vice versa.

During any new media design project try to empty your thoughts and sit down to use the system you are designing/building as though you were coming to it for the first time, just as all your users will be. Alternatively, sit someone else in front of it who really is seeing it for the first time and gage their reactions to the opening part of the interaction.

Making progress

It is important that the user always feels that they are making headway with the interaction. They should be aware of the narrative moving along. In the real world it is sometimes better to walk to an appointment rather than getting a cab even if it does take longer. Even though time is passing, you feel that you are actively making progress, in comparison with sitting in a traffic jam getting nowhere at all.

In the new media world you can often do clever things behind the scenes while the user is otherwise occupied, for instance pre-load large pictures while the user is reading text rather than having the user select something and suddenly saying, 'Right, for that we need to download a huge graphic, could you just wait a bit?' Sometimes it may even be worthwhile to build in unnecessary or spurious chunks of interaction simply because the user may find that more acceptable than having to wait for the next bit.

Where you are in the story

In many presentation and linear-style narratives it is useful for the user to be aware not only of progress, but also of how much further there is to go. This is typified by 'page 2 of 7'. A much simpler way of presenting the same idea are the progress bars you often see during interaction with computers while moving or processing large amounts of data.

I remember going to a presentation by a usability expert who started off numbering the lengthy points he was making with A, then ten minutes later with B. When he got to F we realized he was going to do the whole alphabet, so, thanks to his well-designed feedback as to where we were in the progression, we were able to intervene to tell him to hurry up.

Interrupting

Any dynamic interaction has a certain flow to it within which the user becomes immersed. This happens if the user is mainly passive and the system is spinning some sort of story or if the user is engrossed in doing something, assisted by the system.

Interruption to this flow, this narrative, is disruptive. Such interruptions can come from the external environment where they are beyond the control of the designer. However they can also come from within the environment. Consider the following:

- The user is engaged in an interaction and is interrupted by a pop-up window for advertising.
- The user clicks on a button labeled 'tell me more' and another window is popped up in front of the window where they were busy. After reading the contents they have to tidy up the window themselves.
- A video narrative allows the user to choose between three different endings: at the key point when the user is deep in the story a dialogue box pops up with 'choose your ending!'
- Just at the crucial point in the film the cinema lights go up and it is the interval.
- You are watching 'The X-files', Mulder is just about to go through the door in the top-secret lab when . . . 'to be continued'.

The best approach is to avoid interruptions from the system altogether. If they are unavoidable then make them as low impact as possible, and always provide contextual information so that the user can pick up the thread again after they have been interrupted.

The 'twister'

When the narrative 'thing' is approaching the end there is usually some way of rounding off the interaction in a holistic way. Sometimes it is very well thought out and intelligent and structured. In short stories and articles you often see the piece finishing off with some reference to the subjects covered at the beginning, revisiting the opening ideas and giving a new or funny light on them. Pieces of classical music sometimes have the musical structure of the opening theme repeated with a new interpretation at the end, a so-called 'reprisal'. Pop songs have a 'twister', that last little bit where the refrain and the title are repeated in some sort of odd way as the whole thing fades out.

Finishing off

Finally there is the actual end of the narrative. The end and the begining are both key points in any narrative. This is especially true of live performances where applause is expected of the audience: it will be hesitant or non-existent if the audience are not sure if it has finished, so a clear ending is vital.

Some narratives are of course written with the intention that it is *unclear* if the end has been reached. The unclear nature of the end thus becomes a subject of consideration as much as the content of the piece. For example, if *2001: A Space Odyssey* had ended with a scaly purple creature shaking Dave Bowman's hand and saying, 'Hi Dave, welcome to Jupiter' it would have been a more well-rounded narrative, but the film would not have provoked the interest and discussion that it has enjoyed over the years since it was made.

Which, coincidentally enough, is a good point at which to finish this particular chapter of the story.

Exercises

Internet radio
On the subject of user or system in control I mentioned that the radio was user passive technology; it directed the interaction by delivering information in a stream that the user has to follow. What would happen if you had a 'radio' that browsed the internet and read out web pages? What about if you gave the user a few controls: what forms would the interaction take and who would be in control of it?

WEBCODE
internet radio

WEBCODE
ring tone

Sound and narrative

I used to work in an office where one of my colleagues had a faulty telephone; the ring-tone was quavering and changed in tone as it rang. The first ring was low in tone, the next ring was higher in tone and so on. When it rang, the ring-tones would form a scale of increasing tone. By the time he got to answering it, we were all laughing.

Why was it so funny? Explain what was happening in terms of narrative and user models.

Narrative diagrams

The author Kurt Vonnegut did a wonderful study of narrative diagrams, basically charting how well things were going with time. The classic example is Cinderella. Things start off bad, stay bad for a while and then start getting better in steps (the fairy godmother's wishes). This goes on until all of a sudden everything is thrown away (it is midnight and Cinderella flees the grand ball). However, the prince finds her and they marry and suddenly everything is great again – even better than before in fact.

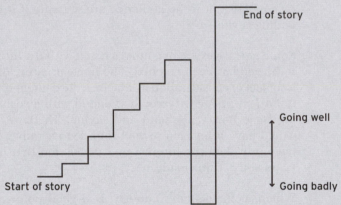

Figure 15.1: A 'Vonnegut style' diagram of how well things go for Cinderella in the fairy story.

WEBCODE
vonnegut

Have a go at charting the narrative development of films that you know. What patterns emerge? Are there any standard patterns?

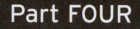
Part FOUR

Designing it

■ How this part relates to the other three parts

In the last two parts we dealt with the ingredients of new media design: the building blocks that are combined with one another and also the interactive structures and frameworks that bind those building blocks together.

In this part we shall look at what to do with those ingredients. This part gives some tools and approaches to the design of new media systems. There is little theorizing about how a designer designs, but there are tools for the practical side of new media design. I should add that they are not rigorous tools where you can just 'turn a handle' and get a design out; instead they are directions and methods; they are ways of thinking and ways of approaching design problems to ensure

Part 1: Setting the scene

Part 3: Interaction

Part 2: The elements

Part 4: Designing it

Figure Part 4: How this part relates to the other three parts.

that the designer does not get stuck or side-tracked and can consider as many avenues as possible and make rapid and informed choices between them.

The part covers the range from having inspiration through to rolling up your sleeves and putting together a prototype as part of the design process.

Generating ideas 16

Introduction: the Daleks

There is a race of famous science fiction creatures called the Daleks. (Don't worry if you've never heard of them, neither has my spell checker.) The creator of this evil race was the writer Terry Nation and in interviews he would often be asked how he came up with such a menacing name. The reality was that it just came to him 'out of the blue', but this was such a boring answer and so unsatisfactory to many interviewers that eventually he made up a source of inspiration. He said that he saw it on the spine of one volume of a set of encyclopedias; the first volume covered AAN-DAK and the second DAL-LEK. Everybody was happy.

That is one of the problems with inspiration: even the people who get it are not really too sure where they got it from. So, if no one really knows where to get it from, how can I tell *you* how to get it? Well the answer lies in a famous quote from the father of invention, Edison. He claimed that 'genius is 1% inspiration and 99% perspiration'. Having good ideas is not about sitting around in the sun waiting for them to come 'out of the blue'; it is about working hard to get them, trying things out, finding out about what is possible. That is the thrust of this chapter; I cannot tell you *how* to come up with ideas but I can tell you what to do to make things more susceptible to coming up with ideas.

Doing inspiration

So, you cannot force a good idea but you can set things up to increase the chances. Although people are unsure about the source of inspiration, they do know when it hits them. More often than not it happens when they are resting after a period of study or experiment, in bed, over a meal, or even in the bath (most famously with Archimedes shouting 'Eureka'). It seems that the brain needs a quiet time for reflection in order to sort and integrate all its new information. Certainly this is true of memory where it has been shown that recall increases after a short period of time before fading away.

Structured ways of thinking

Is it as simple as that; do lots of studying and then take lots of baths? In some ways, yes, but a further help is available in the form of structured ways of thinking. The most notable advocate is Edward de Bono. His philosophy is that we are taught to do many things, but the thing that we do the most of and that cannot be done by any other system is thinking. Yet we get no formal education about the best ways to think. He believes that it is possible to train people in simple, structured methods of thinking. (I wonder where *he* got the inspiration from in the first place.)

WEBCODE
de bono

It is worth reading some of his many books in the area. Not all of it is useful, but read it and extract those ideas that you think to be appropriate. One of his many books is *The Dog Walking Machine*, a book covering children's different approaches to the problem of a machine for walking a dog. It has got everything from a machine for waggling the dog's legs as it lies on its back through to a stick tied to the dog that dangles a bone down in front of the dog's nose.

WEBCODE
ibis

Another structured thinking method in this area is IBIS: a paper-based argumentation and decision-making strategy (now also on the computer). By plotting out discussions and argumentation in a rigorous way it helps avoid a lot of the unproductive 'noise' that can occur in normal meetings: repetitions, 'name calling', politicking, 'losing the thread'. IBIS supports and records the process for later and adds a welcome degree of structure to the process. In form it is something similar to the threads in online discussion groups but with extra structure and features added.

Where do ideas come from?

Ideas from technology

In today's world a key source of new ideas is new technology. New technology means new applications, and the explosion in mobile phones, lasers, computers and the internet has meant that there is a huge number of possibilities. Not only the development of new technologies but new combinations of technology lead to new ideas. The idea of document scanning coupled with the telephone yields the fax machine. The idea of GPS coupled with mobile phone leads to interesting spatial information systems.

The drawback with just basing an idea on new technology is that it is not guaranteed to be appropriate to the users and some new technological ideas clearly are not appropriate.

Tracking technology

Part of the skill of inspiration in the technological arena depends on tracking technology, on keeping abreast of new possibilities and new developments so that they can form a vocabulary for expressing new ideas.

What frequently happens is that at a certain point the time is ripe for an idea and the combination of technologies is so obvious that several people will have the idea at the same time. A classic example of this was the fevered speculation during the Second World War about who had worked out that the atomic bomb was possible and whether it was obvious given an insight into the technology.

Another nice example was a student project: a phone-based game involving navigating through a virtual sound-scape. Everybody I described it to would think a few seconds and then say; 'Hey, what you could do is use the number keys on the phone to navigate – up, down, left, right and so on! Have you thought of that?'

'Slow Glass' as an example

One of the exercises in this chapter concerns 'Slow Glass', a (fictional) type of glass that slows light down. It can be manufactured to produce any required delay, from a second or two to several years. With a delay of two seconds you could stand on one side and then nip round to the other side to see what you look like. Coming up with novel applications for this stuff is a good example of new ideas based on emerging technology.

Ideas from user tasks/new markets

You can also have inspirational ideas by looking in the other direction. Instead of looking to the technology, look to the users. Analyze what sort of things they are wanting to do or trying to do. Watch how they do things and talk to them about how it could be different. Ask them to come up with a dream system that would make their tasks easier. Also think of what you would want to do if you were in their place because sometimes users have difficulty thinking 'outside the box'.

This approach drives things the other way. Instead of having the technology and looking for an application you say, 'Wouldn't it be good if the user could do *this*?' and then you start looking to find or develop the technology that supports that.

Gaging the market

This approach depends upon being able to gage how useful your ideas would be: trying to get inside the head of the average user, trying to empathize with their needs and wishes. This can be tricky; one way of approaching it is to use focus groups – a small hand-picked group of people chosen to be a microscopic cross-section of the target audience.

Supporting idea creation

You cannot force yourself or others to have ideas, but you can make it easier to have ideas. Let us have a look at some of the ways of approaching this.

Physical context that supports it

To begin with we will consider top-level support. It is possible to encourage casual brainstorming by engineering places where people can 'accidentally' brainstorm. This could be having a central coffee or tea point or, in warmer climes, a water cooler. The effect of a coffee point can be increased by having a set time for the coffee break. One way is to have a coffee round where a coffee and tea trolley is brought round at a particular time; another way is to have a time when there are biscuits served or a fresh pot of something. Having a set time ensures that there is some interaction and also allows the length of the break to be regulated.

It is important to strike a balance between inspiration and procrastination. You must create environments that are comfortable and conducive to interaction, but not environments that promote snoozing. Chest-height tables with no chairs mean that people can drink and examine documents and sketch without being able to slump in a chair. Some companies even adopt this policy in their meeting rooms to ensure that meetings are as short as possible (and some fast-food restaurants adopt similar policies of making things uncomfortable enough so that clients will eat but will not hang around after they have finished).

Organizational context that supports it

Encouraging interaction around the coffee table or the water cooler is one way of encouraging discussions and ideas but it is difficult to tell how much real idea forming is going on and how much chit-chat is going on.

Active brainstorming can be better managed at an organizational level by adopting strategies such as arranging open ideas sessions or requiring staff to contribute one idea for the company per week. Some large organizations have an optional idea scheme with cash incentives for good ideas.

Physical tools

On a more detailed level there is also a lot that you can do to support brainstorming when you are actually having a session.

Support for brainstorming should include all the sorts of things that people normally need and one or two they do not, just in case: paper, pens, white board, Post-it notes, colored markers, ordinary paper, large rolls of brown paper. There is nothing worse than having a good idea and having to stop mid-flow because you cannot find a pen and paper.

Sand pit

As well as resources to help sketching ideas it is always useful to have some resources to actually try putting ideas together. This is of course easier for some disciplines than for others.

When inspiration hits, people have been known to resort to incredible improvisation in order to try ideas out. The familiar plastic net-bag that fruit comes in is produced by squeezing molten plastic between two moving plates with little gaps in. It was devised by a man who suddenly had the idea for its manufacture and immediately tried it out with two rulers and a load of mashed potato!

This sort of thing is trickier in the digital age. Despite the possibilities of the computer it is still difficult to prototype quickly on the screen. The fastest route remains pen and paper. Also it is good to have a photocopier somewhere near as this can save much repetitive copying of bits of illustration etc. (see chapter 21 on prototypes and demos).

Catalysts

With any creative process there are going to be moments when progress stops. At these points a catalyst is needed to kick-start the process again.

WEBCODE
brian eno

Various tools have been devised for this, one of which is the deck of Black Cards devised by that arch creative Brian Eno. The cards give new avenues of thought or new things to do with the problem and when the creative process grinds to a halt a card is chosen from the pack at random and its prescription is applied to the problem, in the hope that it will kick-start the creative process again.

Alternatively someone in the group can have the role of catalyst. They can monitor what is going on (and take part in it, of course) but have a collection of possible strategies that can be applied when things hit a dead end.

Groups

Group size

If you are organizing a brainstorming session one question is, how many people should you have? Extremes are not productive. One person cannot brainstorm effectively and numbers above 20 make it difficult.

You need enough to keep ideas and discussion coming but not so many that people get embarrassed at the attention and can easily play dumb in the background while everyone else continues to brainstorm.

Group members

It is a good idea to assemble a mix of relevant disciplines. However, you do need good communicators from each group, so no vague creative types who do not know what they are talking about and no grunting technicians who cannot be understood.

There are dangers in having a group that includes an existing hierarchy. No matter how informal and supportive the atmosphere is, it will be difficult to escape the existing power structures. Members may feel inhibited at having 'the boss' there and any suggestions made by 'the boss' are probably going to be supported disproportionately. One way of solving this is to have the brainstorming session in a 'non-work' environment, thus breaking away from the context that supports those power structures.

Group leader

You need someone to lead, but not from the front. They must not be 'in charge', merely a facilitator. They must prompt and keep the ball rolling, letting it roll when it gets going, steering it gently in the right direction without interrupting the flow and acting as a catalyst when things grind to a halt. This person must have the same qualities as a good meeting chairman. They should also come to the session pre-armed with various solutions to problems that may arise.

Group organization

As well as open group brainstorming involving the whole group you can try splitting the group into smaller 'buzz-groups' of two or three people. Then after exactly ten minutes split them again and re-form them into different groups in something akin to changing partners in square dancing. Ideas can be generated even in very short time-slots.

WEBCODE
Italian tiles

The early Italian tile industry is a classic example of splitting and re-forming in this way although over a longer time scale. It was composed of many small, competitive, but closely knit companies with a high changeover of staff. This arrangement ensured that skills and ideas were distributed throughout the industry very quickly.

When making buzz-groups it is a good idea to use random groupings in order to break up existing cliques. If you let people choose their own groups then the technicians will all get together and talk about technical ideas, and the group of baseball fans will just talk about baseball. One way is to use a pack of playing cards, assign one per person, shuffle them and form groups by picking the cards totally at random.

Supportive atmosphere

The key thing in group dynamics is a supportive atmosphere. This is an atmosphere where any idea can be voiced, no matter how unusual. When the ideas have been collected there will be a phase of evaluation and removal of inappropriate ideas. That will happen later; now it is time for gathering ideas, no matter how off-the-wall or infeasible they are, every idea put forward should be treated as if it is a working, possible, achievable idea and discussed as such.

WEBCODE
positive

Ideas can always be deleted later but they cannot easily be created later. Concentrate on creation in the brainstorming phase. Be positive! The reaction of others has a great effect on the presentation of ideas, so the person leading the brainstorming should ensure that a positive atmosphere is maintained. They should always be positive and they should ensure that all the others are positive and non-critical, even to the point of banishing members if they continue to criticize every idea put forward.

Recording sessions

A brainstorming session is only useful if it generates a list of ideas that can be edited later. Something tangible must always come out of the initial session, even if it is all thrown out at a later session. For this reason everything needs to be recorded.

The session can be recorded as a sound recording. However, this makes the material hard to review, since a two-hour meeting will take two hours to review. Furthermore people are self-conscious and are less likely to play an active part.

Paper-based recording methods are best. You need big sheets of paper and Post-it notes with some formal note taking to bring it all together. Any notes should be reviewed a little later to make sure that it all still makes sense and is decipherable.

As well as recording the end idea, you should also record why decisions were made along the way and why some ideas were rejected. Failure to do this can result in discarded ideas being rediscovered later and the entire analysis and rejection process being repeated.

Using it

Once you have the record of the session it needs to be reduced. All the noise and non-workable ideas need to be taken out. A small group of key personnel with different backgrounds could do this. Their brief is not to entertain the wild and wonderful possibilities but to decide what is realistic in terms of the resources at their disposal. The resulting ideas can then be pursued further for more evaluation or pursued to completion.

Exercises

Slow Glass

In the chapter I cited new technology as a source of new ideas. Any new ideas should be matched against users' needs, but would it really be useful?

WEBCODE
slow glass

A good example of such a new technology is 'Slow Glass', a hypothetical invention in a science fiction book by Bob Hughes. The hero of the story has devised a type of glass that slows light down. It can be manufactured to match any required delay, from a second or two to several years. With a delay of two seconds you could stand on one side and then nip round to the other side to see what you look like. With a delay of one year you could hang a sheet in the baby's bedroom and then a year later when it was 'full' send it to the grandparents to turn around and hang on their wall and watch the baby's antics over the last year. What else could you use it for?

Garlic press

Think of garlic presses. Think of the drawbacks. Design a new sort of garlic press. Work in small groups and try to record the process as it happens. After brainstorming several ideas, start being more choosy and narrow them down to one idea. When this is done, work back through the notes and follow the inception and development of that winning idea from start to finish. Where did it come from in the first place?

WEBCODE
garlic press

If a garlic press does not inspire you, then think of another simple design problem such as a corkscrew, an alarm clock, a desk lamp etc.

17

Top-down design

Introduction

WEBCODE
top down

One of the subjects I took at school was art, and one semester we were outdoors every week studying sketching. There was one particular day when the teacher got very excited because it was a bit foggy outside.

> 'This is a great day', he said. 'You can't see any of the detail. This will force you to draw the main things in the scene without getting distracted by the detail.'

He had often said that the best approach to sketching was to do the whole sketch first with just a few lines, get the structure and the main elements, then go over it all again with a bit more detail and to progress in this manner, gradually adding successive layers of detail until it was finished.

> Then, even if it starts raining half-way through, you will still have a complete sketch, completed to some level of detail. Don't spend hours working on one little corner until it's perfect, do the structure first and then add the detail.

This approach of successive levels of detail is at the heart of this chapter. It is an approach called 'top-down design': start with the big picture, the overall structure, and then add successive layers of detail, gradually building up to the required level of detail.

Another term for it is 'stepwise refinement': refining something step-by-step until you get to the end-product.

Areas of application

Top-down design is a very general approach and can be used for many complex design problems. To help with understanding how it can be applied to new media design let us have a look at how it is used in a few other areas.

Software development

This is really where the term developed. Top-down design was an approach that aimed to describe functionality at a very high level, then partition it repeatedly into more detailed levels, one level at a time, until a level of detail was reached that was sufficient to allow the design to be translated into computer instructions.

The approach of top-down design ties in very closely with the computer programmer's way of breaking the program up into procedures or sub-routines. Each successive level of chunking in the top-down development corresponds to a more detailed level of procedures, until at the end you are writing the actual computer code to do things. If you are not a programmer and do not know what a procedure is, then do not worry; this book is not about learning to program, it is about learning to design. Concentrate on that.

Writing reports and books

Working on large documents is usually best approached in a top-down fashion as well. First decide the top-level scope of the written project. Then divide it up into key sections. Within each section identify the chapters. Then within each chapter identify the main sections and top-level headings, and the sub-headings and summaries/introductions. Then add overviews of the content in telegraph-style bullet points, and finally the end detail – the actual writing of the paragraphs.

When carrying out a writing exercise like this, it helps to have paper-based tools such as Post-it notes and index cards, so that chunks of content needing to be written can be defined, moved about and grouped during the process.

There are computer-based tools to assist with this approach; word processors often have an outline processing mode enabling the author to look at headings and shift chunks of material around. They are useful for developing functional texts but as an approach to writing stories it works only for some people; when Jack Kerouac was writing he used to feed one end of a long teletext roll of paper in his typewriter and just start writing.

Advantages

As well as being generally applicable to a number of design disciplines, top-down design also has a number of advantages when used for new media design. Consider the following.

Maintaining a good overview

Right from the start you will have an overview because this is what you will work on first: the overall structure. In this respect top-down development is a very good management tool as it is a framework for all the subsequent activities. You can always see what bits are done and what bits need doing and can judge the time to completion more accurately.

Better focus

Dividing the design problem up into separate chunks as part of top-down design helps on a number of levels. It breaks the problem down into more manageable chunks. Psychologically, the whole task can seem easier if you stop looking at the whole and concentrate on a small sub-part of it. It is an efficient way of using resources, focussing them directly on just one part of the problem without getting distracted by other parts.

No wasted work

This should probably be entitled 'less wasted work' since there is no magical way to guarantee no wasted work. By delaying the filling in of detail until you know exactly what bits you will be detailing, you ensure that no chunks of detail are discarded later as a result of redesigning the main structure.

In effect you only put the investment in to the detail of a chunk when you know that that particular chunk is a definite part of the design. You should never have the situation where you spend ages working on one chunk and then decide that that chunk is not going to be a part of the overall solution.

Fewer errors

Defining the overall structure first means that the subsequent development work of repeatedly adding detail to each chunk of the system can be done within well-specified confines dictated by the overall structure. There is less chance of errors in working on the detail and less chance of errors in how they all fit together into the 'big picture'. Just spending a few minutes on the overall picture and then starting in one small corner with implementation is a sure way to run into problems later on.

Future extensibility

This is something a designer should be thinking about on the top level. If we are designing a new media system to deal with a particular design problem, then we also need to think about how that problem will change in the future and how the design will cope with this. This can be done only at the top level: it gives us a chance to take the 'long view' and consider the whole context before narrowing down to work on one chunk.

More open design

As well as being a tool for *thinking* about the future, top-down design is also a tool for helping us to *design* for the future. It allows us to chunk the design up in ways that correspond to how we think the design of the system could change. If the design is sliced up into the right chunks, it is easier to take a chunk out and replace it with another chunk that does something similar but that is better adapted to any changes that have happened.

Readers with experience of object-oriented programming will recognize elements of object-oriented ways of doing things here. Readers without that experience should not worry; this chapter is about object-oriented *thinking and designing*, not programming.

Better planning

Having the whole project divided up into chunks makes it easier to plan and manage the work needed to supply the detail and split things up into further chunks. Indeed top-down techniques are vital as a part of any planning process.

Bad examples

To illustrate the importance of top-down design here are two examples of where things went badly wrong without it.

An extra menu choice

Two students of new media design had spent a whole day tweaking the visual design of a pop-up menu in their system, adding one visual effect after another with PhotoShop until the menu was a fuzzy mass of highlighted chrome and 3D shadows. Then they realized that they had missed a key menu option off it. There was no way that they could add it without it looking wrong among the visual design of the other menu options. So they had to start all over again.

No delete function

This was a classic new media design mistake. Students were designing a digital Dictaphone, a digital version of the hand-held memo recording device. Being digital it could offer far more functionality. Designing this new functionality is a good exercise in underlying system model design (see the exercise for chapter 18). One of the designs submitted had it all, time coding, ordering options, everything. The only thing that was missing was a delete command. The result was a system that once you recorded something there was no way of getting rid of it. Very quickly the system would become so full of messages that the user would not be able to keep track of them no matter how many tools they had. Worse still, the user would be aware of a threshold for recording memos, and would have to ask themselves each time, 'Do I really want to record this memo, given that it will be a permanent fixture in the machine?'

Top-down design across mixed media

Top-down means starting at the top level, but how far up is that top level? A company doing a redesign of one of the features on its web site decided to rename it after doing a user survey of what they understood from various terms. Only after the initial development did they realize that the old term had already been used in printed marketing literature, meaning they had to either stick with it or change it and risk confusing users who were accessing the site after having read the marketing literature.

Doing top-down design

The list of advantages earlier makes good reading, but if we are faced with a real-world design problem how do we start doing top-down development? What is the first step? The designer is sitting there pen in hand about to start the design. They do not need textbook definitions that they can recite word-for-word; that might be useful for impressing clients and passing exams, but what about doing the actual design? They need to know what the first step is so that they can get started. See Figure 17.1.

Defining the problem

Taking the first step in the process has strong links with the GAS analysis that we dealt with in chapter 9. We are in effect defining the context of the design problem that we are dealing with. We are stating the problem, the direction of the solution and how we want to evaluate the solution when we are done.

Consider a web-based service which has an accompanying system for reporting and solving problems. Obviously this is a complex project, so we cannot just jump straight in and start chunking the problem up because this immediately raises questions about *what* we are chunking up: 'Right, the first chunk is a chunk where the system gets the user's name, e-mail and phone number; we will probably need that somewhere along the line,

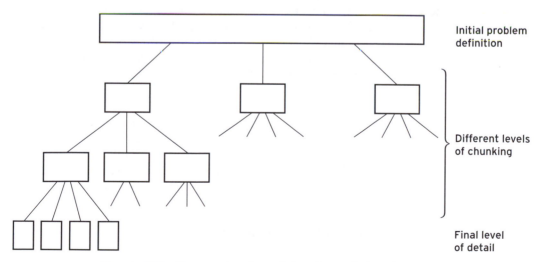

Figure 17.1: The progression of top-down design from the initial problem through to the final production of the solution.

let's get started with it'. Why do we need the name and address? What are the users going to be doing? What do we want to phone them about? First, we have to define who is using it, what they want to use it for, what the goals of the system are etc.

Chunking it

Having taken the first step of defining the context or parameters of the design problem, we now want to start dividing it up into chunks that we can deal with. To carry on with the problem reporting system, we can take a high-level chunking view and say that chunk one is a chunk where the user can report a problem and then there is another chunk where someone in the company can respond to the problem.

Or to use the example of a chunk that gets the user's e-mail and phone number, you may have a statement like, 'When the user clicks here they go to a screen where they fill in their e-mail and phone number'. You do not elaborate on the sub-system that interacts with them to get and check their details. You do not even define what those details are; that comes later. Who knows? Maybe before you get to working out the detail of that part you will have decided to do everything in a manner that does not require contacting the user directly.

Deciding the level of detail

When beginning on some sort of top-down development exercise you need to form an idea of the level of detail you are going to be using initially, either before you start or quite rapidly as you get going with the project. Are you just going to map out the bare bones of the idea? This is easy because you will not have much to do, but difficult because the less you decide to specify, the more chance there is that you will get distracted by the detail.

If you decide to go to some depth in specifying the detail then this could slow you down. Instead of tackling the high-level design of the main structure, you end up getting bogged down in detail that you have decided to include, perhaps filling in detail that you are simply going to get rid of at a later date.

Moving down to the next level

Once we have a framework of chunks that relate to one another we are ready to move down into those chunks and start dealing with each of them, breaking them down themselves into smaller chunks. This is where the process starts repeating itself. The whole thing is an exercise in iterative design: repeating a process and gradually getting closer and closer to the finished product.

Lowest level of detail

This repeated chunking continues until at the bottom level we are actually defining the interface elements. We are doing things such as asking the user to fill in the details of their problem. The level is low enough that we can simply say we do this as a text fill-in field of about 250 characters. When we start hitting this level we will have all the items that need to be displayed and we can hand the specification over to a graphic designer who will take our 'shopping list' of on-screen elements and give them a visual design: 'On this page we need a fill-in line of about 50 characters for the person's name, we show them their e-mail address and they can change it if necessary and we have a field where they can report their problem and a submit button etc.'. This visual design is then passed on to someone else who implements the front end of the system.

It is never that perfect

I should stress that this process, like any design-oriented process, is never as perfect as I have made out. In practice there will be times when detail is done at lower levels before the chunking is completely worked out, there will be times when the designers have to go back up a level and re-do the chunking that they already did, and there will be times when someone has spent a week defining a chunk only to realize that the whole chunk has just been thrown out with a bit of a redesign. Try to minimize these things, but do not lose sleep if they happen.

Drawbacks of top-down design

Now that we have described the method, we are in a position to look at some of the drawbacks of top-down design.

Chunking imposes assumptions on design

Breaking a design into chunks can impose assumptions on it by the very nature of the chunking. This can lead to run-of-the-mill designs or even errors. Questioning the assumptions that are made can lead to novel solutions. In the world of architecture we could be designing a new building and say, 'Let's break it down into the design of the bits above ground and the design of the bits below ground'. Immediately this imposes an assumption on the design: maybe we should think about designing it all to be below ground. One of the final-round contenders for Paris's Pompidou Centre was just such a plan.

In our example above we have chunked the thing up into a part where users can report problems and where people in the company can solve them. This immediately imposes assumptions on the solution. For example it would be useful to know how efficient this process is: are users having to wait hours, days or weeks for their solutions? In effect there is another complete chunk for managing the process which has been left out because of our initial assumptions and chunking activities.

Distraction by detail

There are some issues and problems related to the top-down approach. The main problem is not a negative side-effect of the approach, but rather a problem that you will encounter while trying to pursue the approach – that it is difficult to keep the big picture and all too easy to get side-tracked by detail.

The problem of distraction by detail keeps occurring and is the one thing that can really get in the way of successful application of this technique. All too often you sit down in a design meeting to sort out the high-level design. You decide that one chunk should get the user's postal address from them and then someone says, 'What about the different postcodes in different countries?' 'Oh!', says someone else 'We could have a record for each user of where they live, yeah, part of a profile that says which country they live in. What about if they want to edit it, what are the standard fields for a postcode? . . .', and so on.

One way to avoid this is to flag a chunk according to the need to discuss it further. If you say, 'Here's a chunk to do such-and-such' and everyone agrees, then that chunk is pretty much 'water-tight', but if consideration of the chunk looks like it is going to get bogged down in detail and problems, then you simply stop the discussion and mark that chunk down as possibly having problems associated with it. The detailed discussion is left until later. This is not merely a way of putting off the discussion. Leaving it until later has several advantages. First, the problem might just go away, as subsequent changes in the top level of the design may render that particular chunk of the design obsolete. Secondly, more will be known about the rest of the system and this will help with the discussion and possible solution of the problems. Finally, just letting the problem sink in for a while can help people think about it and be better able to solve it.

Lack of tangible work

I opened with the example of sketching by building up successive layers of detail. This means that at any point in the process you have a tangible end-product. If you stop early then it is a tangible end-product without much detail. With top-down design for new media it is a bit more difficult. As you are doing the real detailed implementation at the end of the chunking process, if you interrupt the process somewhere along the line, what you will have is an intermediate specification without much detail, but it is exactly that, 'a specification' – you have not actually started to build the thing.

In a commercial situation there is a need to show someone something that is working, be it the client, project manager, design team or yourself. This is certainly true with writing this book. I could not have done it by pure top-down design. That would have meant months of work before I had even written one word. With top-down development most of the tangible things are actually done in the last 10% of the time. Before that you are busy with the structure and the initial phases of the detail. Only in the last phases do you add the body of the detail that enables sections to be seen and interacted with. Getting things running up-front in the design process results in the partial implementation of the detail and usually involves building in things that would have been done differently had the product been designed from the top down.

It is more reassuring to mix the tasks; do some top-down design and then do some straight hammering out of the detail. The optimal approach is to use top-down development and combine it with appropriate use of prototypes and demos to make aspects of it tangible for presentation and evaluation. We shall be dealing with prototypes and demos in chapter 21.

Exercises

Defining the problem
For the following examples of design problems start off by defining the parameters of the design problem – the first step in top-down design. Do not go beyond this first step, do not start chunking the design problem up,

do not start designing the end-product, restrain yourself to a statement of what the parameters of the product are, who it is aimed at etc.

Do not be afraid of using pen and paper in the process, but do not let this distract you with any visual design of things.

- A portable computer (very general, what will it do? How portable is portable? etc.)
- A kite (what is a kite for?)
- A new media system that has a large collection of film trailers (What are they for? What will the user want to do with them?)

WEBCODE
define
problem

Chunking the problem

This exercise is similar to the one above, but this time you should specify the initial parameters of the design problem and then continue and chunk the problem up. Once again, pen and paper are useful design aids but remember that any sketching is not part of the design; it should just be helping you to chunk the problem up.

WEBCODE
chunk
problem

- A new media system for selling and buying houses
- An online collection of recipes
- A cd-rom with a collection of plant pictures for plant identification

Post/package tracking system

Imagine a system where you get a package ID number when you ship a parcel. You can go to a web site, key this number in and see what the parcel's progress is: if it has been collected, which depot it is at, if it has been delivered, whether that delivery was successful etc.

Start doing a top-down design of this system and go as far down towards the detail as time permits. If you can, work in a group and appoint one person to keep an eye on the level of detail. They must avoid getting too involved in the design discussions, but instead they must intervene whenever the discussions move too much toward the detail of the problem.

WEBCODE
package
tracking

The underlying system model

18

Introduction

The previous chapter dealt with designing a new media system using top-down design; starting with the 'big picture' and gradually working down to the detail. Part of the 'big picture' for an interactive new media system is something called the underlying system model.

What it is

The underlying system model is a 'user thing': it is the conceptual building blocks, the collection of objects and actions that are at the heart of the new media system. The user must think in terms of the underlying system model when they interact with it. When I say 'objects and actions' I am referring to abstract things, to the conceptual ideas that the user has in their head of the things that are in the system. The underlying system model is not connected with the underlying technology or software of the system. It is abstract and in the designer's head and the user's head.

For example, with my current e-mail system, I have the idea that there are objects (things) called 'e-mail messages' and other objects called 'folders' that can contain collections of e-mail messages. There are also actions: there is one to put an 'e-mail message' object into a 'folder' object, but there is no action to take an 'e-mail message' object out of a 'folder'. Instead I have to do the 'put an e-mail into a folder action' again, this time putting it into a different folder.

We also saw good examples of mistakes connected to the underlying system model in the previous chapter: remember the digital Dictaphone with no 'delete' function?

The underlying system model and the user model

In chapter 11 on user models we introduced the idea of the model in the head of the user (the user's model) and the model in the head of the designer (the designer's model). One of the goals of good interaction design is for the designer to design a system that helps communicate the designer's model from the designer to the user, so that their user model is the same as his designer's model. The designer builds things into the system that tell the user about the model he wants them to build up.

In effect the designer says, 'My idea is that the user should think that there are e-mail messages and folders to keep the messages in'; that is his designer's model. He designs the system so that the e-mail messages are called 'mail' and look like little letters, and the folders look like little folders.

Figure 18.1: The designer communicates an ideal user model to the user by means of the design of the system.

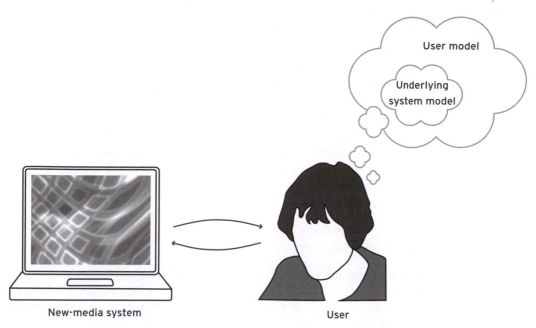

Figure 18.2: The underlying system model is a part of the user model of the system.

This is communicating his designer's model by way of the appearance and feedback of the system to the user. Then the user comes along, looks at and interacts with the system and says, 'Oh, I get it, these e-mails are like little letters and I can put them into these folder things'. The user has built up their user model of how it works and, thanks to good design and feedback, it is the same as the designer's model. See Figure 18.1. (Basically this is repeating what we covered in chapter 11.)

The designer's model and the user model are rich and complex, but one key part of them is the underlying system model, Figure 18.2. It is the part of the designer's model and the user model that concerns itself with what the basic building blocks of the system are and what the user can do with them.

As well as overlaps with the chapter on user models, there are some common ideas with the 'design vocabulary' discussed in chapter 2.

The underlying system model in detail

The underlying system model is one of those things where you can read definitions endlessly and still end up being not quite sure that you understand it. Let us look at it in a bit more detail.

TAO

WEBCODE
tasks

TAO stands for tasks, actions and objects. The key things in the underlying system model are the objects and actions that make up the system, and the user tasks that must be satisfied by these objects and actions.

Tasks

The study of tasks and task analysis is an important part of the rigorous study of the use of computer-based systems. If you are interested (and can cope with the abstract terminology) then there is much to read on the subject.

Within the context of the underlying system model I want to make the following observations:

- There are tasks in the real world; users are involved in doing things to achieve certain goals. Some of these tasks involve new media systems and some do not. Pinning down a task and a goal in clear terms can be difficult.
- For tasks that involve new media systems the user carries out their task using the objects and actions embodied in the system. For example, if my task is to sort through my e-mails I do it using the objects (inbox, messages, folders) and actions (move, delete, read) embodied in the e-mail system.

The simplest way to get some insight into the user's task is to imagine yourself in their place. For some common tasks (like the e-mail example) this is not too difficult. If the tasks are associated with an area that you are not familiar with (such as analyzing digital images of brain scans) then you need to talk to real users about what they do (jargon: 'knowledge elicitation') or select a group of real users to become more involved in giving feedback on the design process (jargon: 'focus groups').

Objects

In the world of designing systems 'object' is a word like 'system', and is used all the time to mean all sorts of things. Below are the objects I shall be discussing. See also Figure 18.3.

Real-world objects

In the real world there are physical objects, which are distinct things: sofa, cup, antelope etc. Then there are the conceptual objects that people have in their head. I have a conceptual object of a sofa and a cup and an

Figure 18.3: The different types of object that play a part in interactions.

antelope. Usually these conceptual objects miss some of the features of the physical object. My conceptual object for an antelope does not include what an antelope eats, because I have no idea what they *do* eat.

In certain situations the conceptual object has extra features. Consider a chess piece: my conceptual model of it includes how it moves on the chess board, and that information is nowhere to be found on the actual physical object. Conceptual objects are just in the user's head, nowhere else.

Digital objects

Now let us consider digital objects. These are not physical objects, although they can mirror or represent them. My personal profile is a digital object (on my computer) that represents a physical object (me). Digital objects can also be totally independent of the real world: my images folder is an icon on my desktop; I do not have an images folder in the real world.

Once again people have conceptual objects corresponding to these digital objects. I have a conceptual object of an e-mail message, this chapter in the book I am writing, the many folders in my to-do folder etc.

We saw that conceptual objects of real-world objects can have differences. The same is true with conceptual objects of digital objects. A digital object can have all sorts of features to do with the implementation of the system; it can have indexes, internal identities, position in lists etc. For example, in a list of e-mail headers in an inbox, each e-mail could have a number indicating its position in the list that is part of the program that drives the e-mail system: 'This e-mail is number 12, this is number 13 etc.' The e-mail system could present those e-mail headers purely as an unnumbered list of headers; thus as far as the user is concerned that number is not part of the conceptual model of an e-mail message.

Now consider a different e-mail system where users have to type commands in to do things to their e-mail. In this system the list of e-mail headers *is* numbered and users use those numbers to type in commands such as: 'Delete 12, move 13 to work folder' etc. Here the number is still part of the internal workings of the system, but now it is also part of the user's conceptual model of an e-mail message.

Conceptual objects

The thing that interests us as new media designers are these conceptual objects. It is not important how the system is implemented internally; what is important are the objects that the user builds up in their head and how they can use these objects and the accompanying actions to achieve their goals in as efficient a manner as possible.

Sub-objects and relationships
Each object can be composed of sub-objects. Some of these are properties of the object itself, while others are relationships to other objects. Consider the chess example again. In a computer version of a chess game, each chess piece would be a conceptual object with sub-objects defining things like what piece it is, what color (or more accurately to which side it belongs), position etc.

Actions

A world of objects is still a dead world. That world comes to life when the user can interact with and perform actions on these objects. The definition of these actions is also a part of the underlying system model. To draw a parallel with language in the real-world: objects are the nouns and these actions are the verbs. These actions are the building blocks of the tasks that the user will want to perform. Just as a set of instructions to make a cup of tea will involve certain nouns and verbs, a set of instructions to describe a task within a new media system will involve the objects and actions. The actions should be atomic enough to afford many different combinations, but complex enough to be useful. In effect we are looking for the 'lowest common denominators' of the tasks.

When thinking about actions it is useful to think about them in terms of the objects that the actions apply to, what objects are needed in order to carry out a particular action. To return to our e-mail example, the 'delete' action needs to be told which message to delete. The 'put in folder' action needs to be told two things: which message and which folder it is to go in.

Building the underlying system model up

Building the underlying system model up in the user's head means communicating the model efficiently. This depends upon two things: a good underlying system model and good communication.

Good underlying system model

Even if you were a brilliant communicator, if the message you were trying to communicate is not a sensible one then people will still not understand it. Thus, the first thing is to have an underlying system model that is as simple, logical and coherent as possible. Then when it is communicated efficiently to the user, the user will understand it and take it on board as part of their interaction with the new media system.

Good communication

Secondly, it depends on good communication, good design of the interaction and good feedback (see chapter 12), good choices of terminology, icons and dialogues.

A bad example of this was the spreadsheet program that had a rather terse help function. When asked for help on the 'retrieve' function it said:

Retrieve – this transfers a file from hard-disk to main memory

This is explaining the action to the user in terms of objects that are part of the technical realization of the system, but not part of the desired user model. In other words it is talking to the user in a vocabulary that the user is not expected to have. Even if they have the vocabulary, then what is being said is not particularly useful. So? If the file is in memory instead of on the hard-disk, what does that actually mean in user terms? Can they do more with it, or can they do less with it?

Designing the way the user builds the model up

As designers we are interested not only in the end point but also in the process. How does the user build up the model? Obviously it cannot happen all at once, so which bits come first? Also it may be possible to use the system with a reduced user model so the final user model can be broken up into user models that are nested one inside the other.

Presenting the objects

I have stressed that the conceptual object that the user has may not contain all the things that are part of that object as it is in the computer. The object in the computer may contain extra hidden features, and that is the key thing; hidden features should stay hidden. If you have a list of things in a system and you add numbers next to each, then there should be some reason for doing so; if the numbers are not part of the designed underlying system model, then they should not be there.

If you present things that are not part of the underlying system model they will at best lead to unnecessary 'noise' at the interface and at worst they will confuse the user should the user try to integrate them into their conceptual model of how the system is working.

The converse is acceptable: hiding some of the elements of an object when you present it to the user. Each time you present an e-mail, for example, you do not want to present the whole thing. Certain tasks that the user is performing will require only certain features of the object to be presented. When you list the e-mails in your inbox you list the key details of each one; you do not have each e-mail in the list in its entirety – that would be ridiculous.

Presenting the actions

Presenting objects is fairly straightforward since they are things and things are usually tangible in some way. Presenting actions is a bit more difficult (this is also dealt with in chapter 5 on icon design). If they have a name, then what is that name going to be? If they are presented in some non-textual manner, then what form should that take? What is the feedback connected with the action, and at what points in the course of the interaction are actions possible? Some commands are 'global': always available and always meaningful. Think of 'undo' in software or 'contact us' on a web site. Other commands are very context specific. Some commands are a mix of the two, globally accessible but with a context-specific outcome (think of context-sensitive help for example).

Some examples

To illustrate all that discussion and explanation let us now have a look at a few examples, starting with one from the real-world.

Cassette players

User tasks

With a cassette tape the user tasks are pretty simple; users want to listen to the stuff that is recorded and maybe navigate their way around what is there to select something to listen to. (Obviously, there will be a small number of users who will want to do other things, such as play sections of music backward, record separate stuff on the separate stereo channels etc.)

Key objects

Similarly, the key objects of the underlying system model of the music are the same for almost all cassette decks. It consists of the two sides of the tape and an idea of how long the tape is (for simplicity I am not treating the two stereo channels on each side as separate objects).

Presentation and actions

What is different in some cassette players is the presentation and actions that form the rest of the underlying system model. Different decks provide different controls to the user. These controls embody the actions and the key thing is that the user's goals are achievable with these actions. Consider 'rewind'; standard decks offer a rewind action. Contrast this with in-car cassette decks where the cassette is inserted sideways with quite a large part of it sticking out and the deck only engages with one of the sprocket holes. These decks only have the actions 'play' and 'fast-forward'. To rewind they need to be able to spin the reel that is sticking out of the deck. To achieve the user goal of rewinding a cassette, a composite action is required, namely, 'turn cassette over' and 'fast-forward'. Thus the design has fewer actions but still allows users to achieve their goals.

Another less common example is the child's cassette deck that my daughter has (and that I frequently borrow for lectures). To achieve the goal of playing at different volumes it does not have a play action and a separate volume control but has three distinct actions/buttons: 'play quietly', 'play normally' and 'play loudly'. Different actions, but the same approximate goals are achievable.

There are some tape decks on the market that allow the user to put a cassette tape in and then play either one side or the other without taking the tape out. In some ways this is a great idea, but in other ways it is a confusing one; the underlying system model immediately gets a lot more complex. In particular if you are listening to the 'other' side, the fast forward and rewind buttons do not make any sense since the directions are reversed. I do not want to invest too much time explaining this; basically, it is too complex an underlying system model, exemplified by my difficulties in explaining it here.

CD players

Each physical media carrier has its own underlying system model about the way the data are organized. We saw that a cassette tape had two sides (and a duration); in contrast, an ordinary VHS video tape only has one side (and a duration). When audio CDs came in there was a much more logical model: one side which contained a number of tracks in a sequence and each track had a duration. Figure 18.4 shows these different underlying system models. This richer range of objects immediately gave rise to a richer range of associated actions. Some of these were a necessary part of the user's task of listening to music, such as 'play from the beginning of the CD', 'play a particular track' and 'fast-forward/rewind within a track'. There were, however, other actions that were possible because of the richer structure of the underlying objects and these corresponded to new user tasks. Consider the 'shuffle play', where the tracks on the CD were played in a random order. Or 'play intros' where just the first few seconds of each track were played.

A Macintosh file

The Macintosh file is an artificial model. Each file is not a reflection of some real-world object but it does have some similarities with real-world

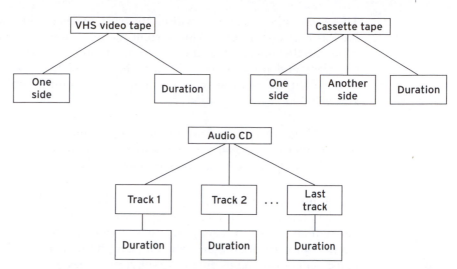

Figure 18.4: The underlying system model for different examples of audio and video media.

things since it is part of the desk-top metaphor based on a real-world desktop. What elements and relationships does it have?

- Position (relative to the containing thing, the desktop or an opened folder).
- Visual form (the icon).
- What type of file it is (an image file, a Word document etc.).
- Date of creation.
- Date of modification.
- The size.

There are quite a few more besides and in multi-user environments there are even more, such as who owns the file, who has access to it. I have actually missed one very important element out from the list above. Can you guess which one? The textual title of the file.

An e-mail system

Long before you start deciding what color the buttons should be and what font you are going to use to display the message, you must first decide: what is a message? It must certainly include the text of the message, but what else? The date? The date of sending or receipt, or both? A subject heading? Should that be obligatory or can it be empty? And is there anything else . . . ?

There are other elements within the system that could be incorporated as part of the underlying system model. They exist and are properties of the object, but the question is, should they be brought to the front and presented to the user as part of the system or should they be left 'behind the scenes' as part of the internal operation of the system?

One such factor is the size of the message. This could play a useful part in a number of user tasks such as sorting out and clearing up old e-mails or finding old e-mails based on whether they were big or not.

This example also shows how the design of the underlying system model can be governed by the established structures of shared things, in this case e-mail messages. The structure is already defined; I cannot suddenly decide that part of an e-mail should be a photo of the person sending it, since people use many different e-mail packages few of which would be able to deal with my photo idea.

A real-estate system

There are many web-based systems to aid in the selling of property, but the underlying model has to be well thought out first. What is a house? A house can be described in so many ways, but if you are putting together a new media system to support the selling of houses then you need a model that is comprehensive, easy to input, and matches the sorts of things that house hunters are looking for.

A house is
Number of bedrooms
Detached or Semi-detached or Terraced
Number of other rooms
Size of garden
Garage or not
Description of the town it is in

Other aspects of the underlying system model should include its status as far as the system is concerned:

Date entered into system
For-sale or sale-in-progress or sold

WEBCODE
real estate
agent

Is there anything else that the user may be interested in that should be part of this underlying model?

An image manipulation program

This is an interesting example of users carrying out a user task that was not part of the underlying system model. The designers had overlooked this common task and so it was up to the users to work out a 'trick' way of achieving what they wanted to do using the existing objects and actions within the system. Users could apply actions to two images, and they could also choose which image to show on the screen. Unfortunately there was no function to say, 'Show the differences between image A and image B on the screen'. So some creative users built their own version of the action using the underlying system model offered by the system. They wrote a script that did this: 'Show image A, Show image B, Repeat'. This caused image A to be shown on the screen, then image B, then image A again and so on. The effect was that any differences in the two images looked as if they were blinking on and off.

Designing it

We have established what the underlying system model is and looked at a few examples, but understanding what it is is only half the solution. The next question is, how do you go about starting to design it? You have a brief from a client or from yourself and you have to start on the first steps of designing the underlying system model.

The approach

1 User groups, goals and tasks

Identify the tasks that the user is doing or wants to do. Start with high-level tasks and work your way down to lower-level tasks.

For example you have to design a system to run e-mail advertising campaigns; who are the different users and what do they want to do? On the high level, what are the key tasks? – set up the campaign, set the campaign in motion, evaluate the campaign . . .

2 User vocabulary

What are the things and actions that the users are dealing with? What are they talking/thinking about in terms of objects, structures, concepts and relations?

'We want to send out e-mails to our selected customer base, after all the marketing people have okayed the text. We want to give each of the customers a login and offer them free information online that's available for a limited period of time. We want to see how many of them log in to the page after getting the e-mail; those that don't we send a follow-up e-mail after a week or so' etc.

3 Technology audit

What is technically possible. With the emphasis on 'what is possible at the interface', not 'what is possible deep within the system where the user can't see it'.

'Maybe some of them haven't got e-mail but have got a fax, could we send them a fax instead?'

4 Supporting the tasks

Design a set of objects, relations and actions that are related to the user's vocabulary and that support the user tasks.

List of contacts, contact's e-mail, name, style of address. An e-mail campaign is a series of e-mails separated by time periods etc. An evaluation is a measure of what percentage of the recipients reacted to the e-mail in some way (logging on to a web site, sending a reply).

5 Add detail

What is an object?

A contact can be new (never had an e-mail from us), existing (has had previous e-mails), inactive (our e-mails come back undelivered) etc. An e-mail message to be sent can be rough (still being written), finished, approved (everyone says it is good to be sent), sent.

What is the structure of the interaction, what does the user see when, and how do they see it?

6 Interface surface

Finally, design the surface: the detailed behavior and the visual side of the interface. What it all looks like, the layout, the feedback, the names of things etc.

General guidelines

The process above is not very well defined. You are not guaranteed a good design if you follow the six steps I have outlined. There will be plenty of feedback and iterative design (designing in loops). To try to make the process easier here are some informal guidelines and a list of useful questions.

Talk about the ideas

Talk about the system with the design group or with the users, but be careful when you discuss things with users: try not to use terms that you favor. When two parties are involved in discussing something for which there are no names, there is an effect in the communication called 'convergence', which means that the two parties start using each other's vocabulary in order to make themselves understood. So if you want to find out what the user calls 'little markers that they can set in the flow of a piece of video', and you say, 'Right let's discuss the *video-markers*', then you have already planted your terminology in their mind and they know that you understand that term and so are going to be more pre-disposed to using it.

You should be careful what you say. Try to use very neutral terms or very verbose descriptions to force *them* to come up with their own terms for the objects. Sometimes this will happen easily, but sometimes there will be a struggle. In these cases it could be that it is a familiar concept but difficult to put a label to it or it could be that it is an awkward or non-useful concept and you should think about taking it out of the system.

Explain the ideas

If you have a good way of organizing the interaction and interface simply and clearly, then you should be able to explain it to someone else, either someone in the design project or a potential user of the system. If you cannot explain it then something is wrong. Either you are not good at explaining things (which is a worrying trait for someone designing systems that explain themselves) or the underlying system model is a confusing or inappropriate one.

Explaining an idea will give you an indication of whether it is an easy concept to get to grips with or not, and it will also help in refining the best way to present the concepts: the best vocabulary to use, the best way of starting with certain concepts and developing them.

Use top-down design

Think back to the previous chapter on top-down design. The design of the underlying system model is a good example of this. You want to get the big things sorted out first before focussing on the detail.

Be aware of Matrushka user models

When a child learns to ride a bike, they first learn with training wheels (or stabilizers as they are called in Britain) and then they learn without. This breaks the learning to ride down into two stages. A similar approach can be adopted in interactive systems. This helps the user to learn to use the whole system in steps, but it also means that users who do not want to use the whole system can just learn the first step and then get down and use it. The simplest example of this are the software systems that offer the options of 'long menus/short menus'. The user can use the system with all the options or with a pre-defined sub-set of options.

You see hardware versions of this idea with complex video recorders having extra functionality hidden behind flaps. Or simple remote controls with more advanced functions on the TV itself. There are digital examples as well, on-screen panels that mirror this flap idea with an expanded view of the actions available. There are also menus that can show either the basics or the full suite of options.

(A Matrushka doll is one of those Russian dolls that come apart to reveal another doll inside and that one comes apart to reveal another and so on. With digital systems you can have as many of these steps as you want. You are limited only by what the user can understand.)

Qualifying the object

Can the object be qualified in some way that the user would find useful? For instance in the e-mail example earlier an e-mail has a sender. In these days of junk mail it might be useful to qualify the sender as recognized or not. A recognized sender is one whose e-mail address is in my address book or one who I have sent an e-mail to.

System sub-objects and user sub-objects

Some sub-objects can be defined by the user – titles for example. The user thinks one up and keys it in. In contrast some sub-objects are defined by the system. These system sub-objects are parts of the underlying technical system that can be brought up from below to be part of the underlying system model and hence the user model. Consider the size of an e-mail message. This is a technical property and it would be possible to design an e-mail system where the size was completely hidden from the user; in other words the size was not part of the underlying system model. It would also be possible to incorporate it into the underlying system model and to present it in some way to the user so that they could be aware of it and use the information to support their tasks.

The key difference is that user sub-objects require effort from the user. The system can either make them obligatory and risk the users getting frustrated with having to do them each time, or the system can make them optional and risk the user not using them at all.

In contrast, system sub-objects are extra information 'for free' for the user. The user does not have to do anything. The danger with them is that because they come from a technical source they may not be appropriate for inclusion in the underlying system model.

The range of applicability

Users should be able to do everything that they want to do by combining the objects and actions in the system. Think back to the cassette player example earlier in this chapter, or the Dictaphone with no 'delete' action in chapter 17.

Evaluating ideas with scenarios

Once you have a first version of the objects and actions it is a good idea to test them out. Obviously you cannot test them out for real since they are not yet part of a working system; however, you can analyze how appropriate they are by using scenarios.

Imagine a typical task that the user will want to do and then work out how they can do it, or indeed *if* they can do it, using the suite of objects and actions offered by your design.

Changes in the system as the user interacts with it

Earlier in the book, in chapter 4 on layout we said that layout had to be designed to deal with dynamic content. This is also the case with the design of the underlying system model. When the designer designs the underlying objects and actions for the system under normal circumstances, they must also think of how those objects and actions are going to work in *non-normal* circumstances. The object and actions may work well if there are a few of a certain type of object in the system, but do they still all fit together well when there are none of those objects there? What about if there are hundreds of them?

In my e-mail system I have hundreds of e-mails just left in my inbox, but the system was not designed for this. Also, most of my e-mail is junk mail. There are times when I simply want to say, 'There's nothing useful come in today, just delete all of today's e-mails'. But I can't; I have to say, 'Delete this one, delete this one, and delete this one'. It takes ages, every single morning, all due to a bad set of underlying objects and actions because the designer did not think about how things would change once the system was actually in use.

Question list

As well as the guidelines above, it is useful to have a list of 'pertinent questions' to guide you in some of the things that you should consider during the design of the underlying system model.

User tasks

- What are the user's existing tasks, either with the current digital system or with a non-digital system?
- What are the ideal tasks that the user is trying to perform?
- Does the use of a new technology suggest any new tasks that could be carried out?
- Are there any ways of combining technologies so that new tasks are created or old ones are automated? (One example is the coupling of stock prices with the internet allowing users to set triggers so that they are informed of prices crossing thresholds they set.)
- Are there any duplicate tasks or parts of tasks that can be unified in some way?
- Think of the different ways that a user may want to organize the information (sort it on a particular property – name, date, size), leave bits out etc.
- As well as tasks, ask yourself what should happen if the user makes a mistake with an action or does an action and then wants to do it again a different way (or not at all).
- Look for creative uses of existing systems that suggest new functions.

Actions

- Think of general purpose actions to apply in different contexts: next, previous, new, delete etc. (Apple used 'copy' and 'duplicate' to mean the same thing in different contexts.)

- For every action or low-level task ask yourself if there is an opposite task that is also necessary (create/delete, mark/unmark, send/receive etc.).
- Where an object is made up of (or contains) sub-objects, a suite of actions is needed relating to them. It must be possible to add and remove them, re-order them (if there is an order), move them from one 'parent object' to another etc.

Objects

- When you discuss the system, what terms do you use?
- Do you use terms from another system? (Could you perhaps use it as a metaphor?)
- Have you had to invent terms or redefine terms?
- Are there objects that are so similar that they can be unified into one object?
- If the system relates to a real-world system, then what are the physical objects that are used and what are their properties/sub-objects?
- Which sub-objects are actually useful to the users?

Exercises

Query tracker

You have a web service with a wide user base. It is a complex service and often users have questions. You want to design an accompanying web-based system to allow them to submit queries and then feed these queries to staff members who can solve them.

Come up with an underlying system model. What is a 'query'? What are the types of users who will do things to that query? How will the status of that query change?

This could get quite complex, so make sure you sort out the terms you are going to use while designing it, get a lot down on paper, and use scenarios to help with the design (see chapter 21).

WEBCODE
query tracker

News system

Design a web-based news service covering news about a company, a college or anything else. The content is updated throughout the day with new articles. Design the underlying system model for two versions of the system.

WEBCODE
news system

The first is for everyone to use and does not work with user identification. In other words you access the information and do not have to log on. The system does not know who you are or whether you have been to the site before; everybody sees the same information.

The second, more sophisticated, design is one where the user has (or can have) a login. They are given a user name and password combination and they enter the site using it so that the system knows who they are and what they have done before on the site. This enables all sorts of interesting operations and tracking to be carried out.

Think of the user, think of the way in which they would use the service, how often would they access it, what nature of information would they be interested in?

Restaurant reservation system

WEBCODE
restaurant

Design the underlying system model for a restaurant reservation system, to be used by restaurant staff for placing reservations. What are the key objects in the system? What are the user actions?

If you are designing it in a group see if there is anyone in your group who has worked in a restaurant accepting bookings. What sorts of tasks did they have to deal with?

How could you make the system help with adding reservations to the system? Here are a couple of scenarios to help you think:

- All the tables are booked up for the early evening and someone rings up to book a table for two in the late evening.
- The largest table seats 8 people and someone rings to book for a party of 12.

Meeting booking system

WEBCODE
meeting
booking

A large company has an online system to allow employees to book the meeting room for internal meetings. Design the underlying system model for the system. Hint: Start with a few scenarios of use, then think about a few scenarios where things go wrong: 'I've just booked a meeting, but now Frank says he will be at a client's all that day, so the meeting is off!'

Digital wallet

WEBCODE
digital wallet

People are talking about 'digital wallets', like Apple's iPod. This is a hardware unit where users can store huge amounts of music (or photos or anything else digital for that matter). Here you can store not just your favorite tracks for the day but your entire music collection – that whole shelf of CDs in one unit. This is interesting because it breaks down the entity of 'an album'. You can apply a shuffle function to your entire music collection and get all sorts of strange combinations of tracks from different artists and different genres. It is something like having your own radio station playing, but with music from your own collection.

Design a suitable underlying system model for this idea.

Problems with the USM

A user orders two DVDs from a web site. The web site has a clear simple design for ordering. In fact it is so simple that it is only possible to order one copy of the DVD. The user wants two and so he has to go through the order process twice.

In the company offices the order for the DVD comes in, and then straight away another order from the same user for the same DVD. 'Obviously,' say the people in the company, 'he has clicked twice on the order button, or done a reload or something'. They send out one DVD to him.

Explain what the possible assumptions of the designers were and how the problems that arose could be solved by altering the design.

WEBCODE
two DVDs

The digital Dictaphone

Until recently the miniaturization of portable systems has been a struggle with miniaturization of the internal technology. Now, however, we are reaching the point where the technological barriers have been passed and we are up against a new and very different barrier: the interaction problems that miniaturization brings. Keyboards below a certain size are unmanageable for large volumes of text input, handwriting recognition has not yet reached acceptable levels and small LCD screens struggle to display complex data in a space the size of a credit card.

Imagine a Dictaphone where the sound is stored not on tape but in digital memory (these are already on the market and, as memory prices drop, their capacity rises). The big difference this will make is that the sound is not constrained to a linear tape but can be structured in new ways (for example the user could record many small, separate 'sound-bites'). Couple this with simple voice-recognition of a limited number of commands (the system must learn the commands during a repetition/training phase, thus the number of commands must be kept to a minimum) and you have a 'hands-free' Dictaphone with complex and flexible sound structuring possibilities. You could even package it into a pen shape and wear it in the collar of your sweatshirt like Albert Einstein (something akin to Philips 'Magic Pen' in their *Vision of the Future* book). Advances in this area will start to speed up as storage prices drop and the Dictaphone market merges with other related areas such as the MP3 players.

Design the underlying system model and interactions for such a digital Dictaphone. Since the machine is voice controlled and all feedback is audio feedback you will have to think of the design of the underlying system models and interaction and not concern yourself with the external visual and tactile design of the product. There must be no buttons, no lights, no screen – just pure interaction design.

WEBCODE
Vision of the
Future

WEBCODE
digital
dictaphone

19

Metaphors

Introduction

WEBCODE
metaphors

Metaphors are difficult things to pin down. If you try to define them you get side-tracked very quickly into discussions about metaphors and similes and definitions and philosophy. Such precision is not important here; we are concerned with the ideas behind a metaphor and whether that idea is a useful one in new media design. Let me start with a nice example: Marlene Dietrich singing 'Falling in love again'. Here is a line from it:

> 'Men cluster round me, like moths around a flame'

This is a good metaphor. It gives a good comparison and people can extrapolate the metaphor to help them understand other things about the situation. The metaphor does not just tell the listeners that men cluster around her; it tells them that men are drawn inexorably toward her, and once drawn they remain buzzing around her, unable to escape from the attraction.

Marlene could just as easily have sung:

> 'Men cluster round me, like chairs around a table'

That would have described the simple fact of men clustering around her but it would not have supplied the extra information that the first metaphor did. It would not have allowed the listener to use the description she gave to reason about things that she did not give information about. That is the key thing about metaphors: they allow the user to get to grips with something without having to tell them all about that something; they allow the user to use what they know to understand something new.

Using a metaphor is using something that people are *already* familiar with to describe something that they are *not* familiar with. It goes without saying that the metaphor should be a good description of the unfamiliar thing that you are describing. Metaphors are powerful because, as we saw above, they can quickly give the end-user a richer understanding of something. Metaphors are a key high-level aid for the designers and users of interactive systems. When used properly they can tame highly complex systems and make interaction much easier to get to grips with.

What does the user really know?

Previously in this book I have stated that, 'The user does not know what you know; they only know what you tell them'. Actually, that is not strictly true. The user does know a lot of what you know, maybe not about the system you are designing, but certainly about other things in your world, and you can take advantage of this shared knowledge in the design of the system. The tricky thing is sorting out what this shared knowledge is that you can take advantage of.

Metaphors and understanding

WEBCODE
benzene ring

As well as that Marlene Dietrich song there are several interesting examples of metaphors from history, most famously, perhaps, the benzene ring. Throughout the history of chemistry scientists have struggled with the structure of certain molecules. They know how many atoms must fit together but they must find the stable shape that is needed to fit them together. One of the most renowned was Friedrich August Kekulé trying to find the structure of benzene. How could this collection of atoms fit together in a stable configuration? It is said that he slept on the problem and during the night had a dream which involved an alchemical snake eating its own tail and he awoke with the answer to the structure of benzene: it was connected together in the form of a ring. To some extent the alchemical snake was a metaphor for the structure he was searching for.

This example of the dream of the snake prompting the realization that the structure of benzene was a ring is just one example of how the human mind learns things and describes things by applying things it is already familiar with to new situations. I remember Morgan, my daughter, seeing a small family of cows when she was four. 'Look!', she said, 'A mummy cow, a daddy cow and a Morgan cow'. She was using something she was already familiar with (our own family grouping) to describe and under-stand something new.

Metaphors and familiarity

We have seen that metaphors offer the user the ability to reason about things in a new media system that they have not been told. Another advantage is that by their very nature they are familiar to the user. They are not just useful as the user uses the system but when the user has first contact with the system they see things that they already know about rather than complex things that might scare them away. This lowers the learning curve considerably and reduces the trepidation of interacting with an unknown system.

More examples

Let us look at some other examples to clarify what sort of things are metaphors and what are not.

Explaining with cutlery

I am at a restaurant explaining where John's new apartment is:

> 'Well, it's near the café. Imagine this salt pot is the hotel and this knife is the foot-bridge over the river, now if this spoon is the shopping arcade . . .' and so on.

This is *not* a metaphor. I am using a familiar system (the cutlery) to describe an existing system (the buildings around the river) but I am not saying that the knife is a good model of the foot-bridge. In fact my explanations would be better if the person could completely forget that the knife was a knife.

Describing the internet

In the early days of the internet I would find myself present while other people tried to describe the internet. They tried to do so by evoking all sorts of comparisons:

> 'The internet is like a giant feast with some people cooking and some people eating . . .'

> 'It's like a giant library and everybody has a shelf . . .'

> 'Well. Imagine a giant fish . . .'

This is an example of metaphors. However, the internet is so unlike anything that has gone before that it is very difficult to find a useful metaphor for it.

The desktop metaphor

The name does give it away somewhat. This is the direct manipulation interface on the early Apple Mac computers which was later copied on other computers (and was itself copied from the Xerox Star). They were easy to understand and use: 'If you want to delete a file you drag it to the trash-can icon and drop it in'.

Most definitely a metaphor. An efficient one, and one with a fairly good correspondence between the metaphor and the real system (although I usually have my trash can and filing cabinet under my desk, not on it).

What sorts of metaphors are there?

A metaphor can be designed and realized in a number of different ways. Consider the following list. I should point out that there is no order or definitive categorization here; it is merely a list of types of metaphor.

Textual metaphors

Sometimes a metaphor is presented in a very simple way, purely in terms of the text used to describe things. Something is chosen as a metaphor and the wording and terminology of this metaphor are used in the labels in the interface. One could, for example, have a computer program that tests a system, the metaphor used could be test-piloting so the function that allows the user to set up the parameters of the test could be labeled something like 'pre-flight checks', the button to start the test could be 'take off', the results log of the test could be 'de-briefing, and so on.

There are simpler examples in digital systems. Consider the scroll bar. The word 'scroll' is itself somewhat metaphorical in that it conjures up the idea of an ancient scroll: a document without pages, just one long roll of paper which the user can unroll from the roll above and roll up on the roll below to read the bit in the middle. The underlying idea is a metaphor; the name does echo this and the basic functionality mirrors this as well, but the controls – the scroll bar and the arrows – look nothing like a scroll of paper.

Spatial metaphors

There are many metaphors that revolve around spatial relationships, either two-dimensional such as the desktop or three-dimensional such as three-dimensional museum simulations. (In fact, the two dimensions of the desktop are really two-and-a-half dimensions since objects can overlap and get in front of other objects, something that would be impossible in a truly two-dimensional universe.)

This is one area of knowledge that users are deeply familiar with. Through evolution we have evolved to navigate and deal with three-dimensional environments, and more recently two-dimensional (or semi-two-dimensional) environments. The hurdle with using these as metaphors is providing the user with an intuitive suite of controls to navigate and manipulate within this space. The best attempts are those seen in interactive games with a three-dimensional element.

Strong and weak metaphors

Metaphors are offered to the user to give them support in using a new system. The strength with which the metaphor is presented can have serious consequences for the design, implementation and use of the system. Above, we discussed textual metaphors – these are very weak metaphors. With the test-pilot metaphor, there is no suggestion that the user will suddenly think that they are test piloting an aircraft; it is simply terminology to help them with the concepts. When a metaphor becomes more visual it becomes more 'believable' and stronger; it no longer relies on reading and comprehending text, it taps into our familiarity with that metaphor. Finally there are metaphors that are more like simulations, in that they try to make the system *become* the metaphor. Early word processors were examples of this: some systems actually had screen displays that looked like pieces of paper in the roller of a typewriter (using the typewriter as metaphor). Some new media systems for playing sound files have controls identical to the controls on an audio cd or tape player etc.

Stronger metaphors are more powerful but, by their nature, they are more difficult. They require more investment in realism and programming and there is more chance that they will lead to problems either because they do not accurately match the system they are being applied to, or because the system is restricted by the limitations of the metaphor being used. This is similar to the discussion of offering an illusion and forcing an illusion in chapter 21 on prototypes and demos.

Choosing a metaphor

There are two golden rules that should be taken into account when choosing a metaphor.

The metaphor must be applicable

Consider using video controls as a metaphor for flicking through a collection of images. First it is not really all that appropriate; you use a video recorder for moving video, very different from still images. Secondly, some of the controls may make sense in this new context: play, rewind, fast forward and stop. But what about 'pause'? What does that do in this context, and what about 'eject'?

WEBCODE
shopping sled

Jakob Nielsen has a wonderful example from a web site selling winter goods. Instead of the conventional shopping trolly to gather purchases, the designers had stretched the winter metaphor and used a shopping *sled* instead. Tests showed that a large percentage of users had no idea what was going on!

The metaphor must be known to the user group

In chapter 5 on icon design I used the example of the traffic sign for 'no entry' being used on shop doors. This works because the metaphor is known to almost all the users of the shop. Also, to some extent the 'no entry' sign is not a critical part of the interface. If it were removed people would still be able to use the shop doors correctly by relying on cues such as the behavior of other users.

In museums the exhibits are sometimes accompanied by recorded information. Rather than creating a new product that users must get to grips with, these sound tracks are provided through telephone-like devices – either conventional phones with a cord in a fixed place or on things resembling mobile phones that you pick up when you go in. Since most people have used a phone this metaphor works well.

E-mail often uses conventional mail as a metaphor. Obviously some things are the same in abstract terms – sending and receiving and such like. However, more concrete visual references can be brought over, such as the American-style mail-box with a little red flag. One would think that this could cause problems in the UK where mail-boxes do not look at all like this. However, a colleague of mine once asked his 4-year-old son (who had never been to America) to look at the US mail-box icon on the computer, and he said it was a mail-box. The metaphor worked – but where had this 4-year-old child got the knowledge from? It turns out that mail-boxes of the typical US variety feature on a huge number of cartoons, from 'Bugs Bunny' to 'The Simpsons'.

Words of caution

Metaphors are similar to icons; they are a cool sort of idea and very attractive to designers; in short they are good fun, but be careful with them. Like icons, just having them is no guarantee of good design.

Things can be easy to use without a metaphor

To start with remember that metaphors are not the final word in interactive systems. There are many examples of systems that are easy to learn and easy to use without a metaphor. Most of our initial learning about the world around us is done without metaphors. In the digital world there are many examples. Scroll bars, as we saw, are only loosely based on ancient scrolls, something which your average user does not have much experience of anyway. However, they are very easy to get the hang of and use.

Metaphors can bring problems

Using a familiar metaphor from the real-world brings over lots of useful points of familiarity, but it is a double-edged sword, as it can bring over restrictions that exist in the real-world as well. One example is the messy desk syndrome with the desktop metaphor. My desk at the moment is a complete mess. I store stuff on it without filing it away. Often I end up with a similar thing on my virtual desktop: piles and piles of files and folders that have to be sorted out every month in a monumental clean-up. The desktop metaphor does not guarantee tidiness.

Or consider the idea of an Internet Shopping Mall, a collection of online retail outlets that the user can browse through to buy something. If I need something specific that is easy to define I do not go wandering around town on the off-chance I will bump into it. I ring round the shops until I find one that stocks it. That is why business pages in the phone book (the Yellow Pages) were developed.

Non-interactive metaphors in an interactive world

There are some metaphors from non-interactive media that may seem appropriate for including in interactive media, but be very careful. Much of the world of existing media is non-interactive; the user is passive and just watches things go by. With new media the user is in the driving seat and any sudden shift in this can be frustrating. (Refer back to chapter 15 on narrative.) Consider the title credits for a computer game. If you follow a cinema metaphor then you set them in a cool font and roll them against an equally cool background, but is that appropriate for an interactive system? Recently I wanted to find out if there was an interaction designer involved in the development of a computer game so I clicked through the menus to the titles and started watching them roll slowly, slowly upwards. After several minutes of silly names and nicknames and job titles that I was not interested in, I just gave up. Simple as that. I pity the people who were near the end on those titles as no one will ever hang around to see their names.

Another example are the ticker-tape type displays of text that you see on some news web sites. This way of presenting information is actually rather inefficient. You have four titles and you show them one character at a time. When they are displayed the user has only a short time to click on them before the ticker-tape goes blank and the next one starts slowly appearing: 'That looks interesting, whoops it's gone, I'll have to wait for it to come round again . . .' The key thing that this communicates is not the information; that could have been done far better with just a fixed list of the four titles. Its message is not the content but the fact that the site is highly dynamic and regularly updated.

Metaphors wider than system

Users can find it restrictive if the system does not do everything they expect from the metaphor. The Macintosh desktop uses the 'clipboard' concept, but you cannot do as much with their clipboard as you can with a real clipboard. In fact the only thing that the virtual clipboard does – holding things you have 'cut' before you do a 'paste' – is something that people never do with a clipboard in the real-world.

Metaphors narrower than system

Some metaphors do not quite match the system and there are still functions that fall outside the metaphor or have to be artificially 'squeezed in'. Consider the paper metaphor that is used in most window systems: the windows can overlap, the user can push windows to the back and pop windows to the front, they can delete them and so on. However, the extra possibilities offered by the digital world mean that there are more functions possible, some of which fall outside the scope of the metaphor, such as resize, iconize etc.

Half-hearted metaphors

I came across a web site recently for an international airport where the designers had adopted zones as some sort of metaphor copied over from the airport. 'Zone 1' contained one collection of information and 'Zone 2' another and so on. It was very difficult to use and remember, and to some extent the designers must have been aware of this because they used the metaphor very half-heartedly, which begged the question of why they used it in the first place.

'Really neat' ideas

Beware of metaphor ideas that seem 'really neat' at the time. Let them sink in a bit and test them on other people before you start basing designs on them. The shopping sled discussed above is a good example of this. An idea is only 'really neat' if you still think so a week later, and if you show it to test users and they find it really useful.

Exercises

WEBCODE
clipboard

Clipboard
Choose a better term and metaphor for the Macintosh clipboard mentioned in the chapter. More old-fashioned technical systems used to call it the 'buffer' or the 'cut buffer' but this is unhelpful for normal users.

WEBCODE
interest

Interest groups
In an online web site I can set up a profile and then sell things and chat to people who are interested in similar things to me. Think of a good metaphor for such a system. What extra things could be included by using different metaphors?

WEBCODE
language
choice

Language switching
In a cd-rom-based language learning system, I can choose two languages: the language that the system operates in, the help, buttons, instructions etc; and the language that is being taught in the system. Think of a metaphor to support this idea.

Interaction specifications

20

Introduction

When my first landlord built a shed for us students to keep our bicycles in he marked out a rectangle in the yard at the back of the house and just started building. No plans, specifications, models or anything. He just leaned a bike against the wall to make sure it would fit and started building around it.

It is, of course, easy to build small-scale projects in this way as the scope for errors and the cost of correcting any errors are low. Such an approach breaks down when applied to larger problems. You would not, for example, build an aircraft hangar by parking a Boeing 747 up against a wall and starting to build around it.

Specifications and prototypes

I should make the distinction at this point between specifications and prototypes. A prototype is a part of the design that is made tangible in some way: either it is actually built or it is mocked up in such a way that it looks and feels real. A specification is a representation of the system, or a part of the system. Rather than being a tangible representation it is represented in an abstract way. The language that it is expressed in is somewhat removed from the real thing.

What I am dealing with here are ways of describing interactive systems. Creating a specification requires less investment than building a prototype. All that is necessary is to describe the things you are going to build, instead of partially building them (or faking them) as happens with a

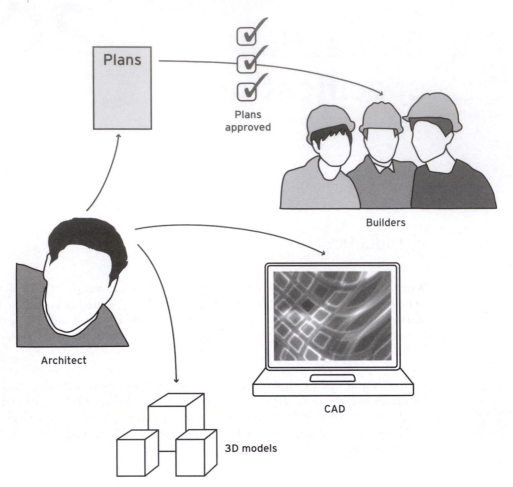

Figure 20.1: An architect realizing different aspects of the design.

prototype. Once you have the specifications and are pleased with them you arrive at the point at which part or all of it can be built.

Let us consider an architect designing a building as a parallel. The architect draws the plans to represent a proposed building. The drawings are the specification. Parts of the specification can be prototyped: models, CAD walk-through, even full-size mock-ups of certain key rooms. Finally, when the specifications are approved (by the designer, client and legislative bodies) they can be translated into the real building. See Figure 20.1.

In the new media world it follows a similar process. The designers spec up an interface design for a new media system. Parts of it are prototyped as paper-based prototypes, on-screen walk-throughs, story-boards etc. When the specifications are approved, they can be handed over to the technicians and producers to put the system together. See Figure 20.2.

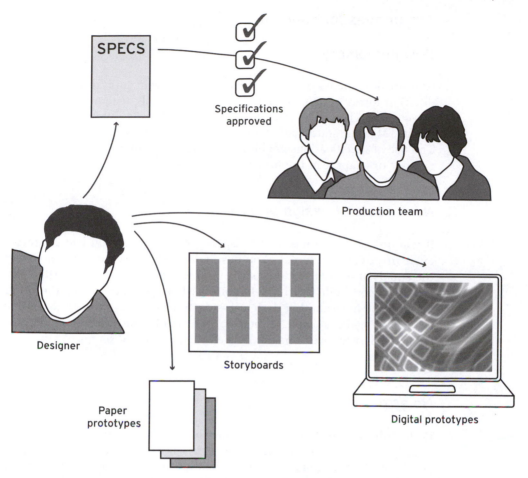

Figure 20.2: A new media designer realizing different aspects of the design.

But why bother?

This all sounds very time- and work-intensive. Why spend ages putting together complex detailed descriptions of the system. Wouldn't it be better just to do it all as you go along and adjust things as the project progresses? After all, that is how my landlord did the bike shed and it worked perfectly – he did not have rolls of detailed plans before he started.

In actual fact you can get away with little specification if the project is small scale (like my landlord's shed) and the people employed have a good deal of experience and insight into what you are doing, but the larger the project, the more the benefits outweigh the drawbacks of such an approach. Let us have a look at some of those advantages now.

Advantages for yourself

Design memory

Certain new media design problems return again and again in slightly different forms in new projects. This was certainly true of the first wave of web sites. They all had the same range of options: 'Contact us, Company profile, Mission statement, Products and services, How to find us', etc. The use of specifications enables the design team to capture a design and reuse it or adapt it in the future.

No repeats of design process

If you do not notate interactive aspects of the design you can get into a cycle of 'design and forget'. You have a brainstorm session, hammer out the details of several sections of the interaction and then by the time part one has been built you have forgotten what you decided for the other parts so you have another design session and go through the same routine again and again as each section is built. Each time there is a nagging feeling of 'haven't we done all this before?', but it still seems to take time to do it again.

No errors

Putting things down in detail on paper is an easy way to see if you know exactly what you are talking about. It is easy to convince yourself that you know what is going on but the moment that you try to pin it down formally, you realize that it has not been thought through sufficiently.

Evaluation of design

Specifications are usually drawn up as abstract flow diagrams of some sort and, although not everyone can understand them, it is still a useful way to get designs evaluated. The alternative is having to build a full-scale presentation every time you want to explain the ideas to someone.

Advantages for the producer

Planning and organization

The producers know best how to go about building a new media system. If they have a specification of the whole system, they can have a better overview and make more informed decisions about the planning and resourcing of the project.

Quality control

The producers of the new media system will also find a sense of reassurance in specifications written on paper. If the design team have put some effort into pinning the design down on paper then there is a good chance that they have evaluated and approved the design. This is a much better feeling than if the head of design rushes in and says, 'Oh, I think it would be better to have a help function on each page. Can you do it?' Chances are they will be back the next day to say, 'Hang on, it would be better not to have that help function on each page, but just the key pages. Can you go back and change it?'

A say in the process

All being well, the specification has been passed around the different people within the project group and the producer has had a chance to examine and comment on it. They should thus feel happier about producing the end result.

For the design team

Sometimes you will be designing as part of a team. As well as the advantages for a single designer outlined above there are additional advantages when specifications are used in a team context.

Shared memory

The point about design memory is relevant. Trying to recreate the results of a team design session without concrete specifications of the results will often require getting everyone together again as each person remembers different things about what was decided. Furthermore, the fact that we are dealing with more than one person means that there can be different versions of what was decided – a very dangerous situation indeed.

Focus for communication

Take a walk in the park and the chances are that you will not get into a conversation with a stranger. Take a walk in a park with a dog and chances are that you will. The dog acts as a focus point for chatting. In a similar way, having a tangible something at the center of a design discussion can help guide and focus the discussion. People taking part have a way of reviewing the design. Controlling the agenda of the discussion and the specification itself can support them in the discussions: 'What about this bit here? Couldn't we link that through to here?'

For the client

There are also advantages for the client and, of course, such advantages are indirectly useful to the designers.

Professional approach

Just the very fact that you are actually writing things down on paper is a plus point as far as many clients are concerned. It indicates that you and your company are approaching the task in a professional manner. Note, though, that the act of writing things down in itself is no guarantee of a professional approach!

Contractual specifications

I should add that this is more of an insurance exercise than an acceptance exercise. The client is unlikely to go through all your specs with a fine-tooth comb. However, in the event of anything going wrong you always have the fallback of saying, 'Well, this was all in the specification we gave you. Didn't you read it?'

Drawing up specifications

Before you do the specification

To start with, having applied the ideas in some of the previous chapters you should have a good idea of the parts of the interaction where the users interact and manipulate things. For these parts you should have sorted out the underlying system model: the objects and actions that make up that part of the system. For the parts of the interaction that are more concerned with interacting with large amounts of information, you should have mapped out the structure and the navigation that the user will need.

What is in the specification

The specification is a description of what the user sees and when they see it: what data and what actions are available to them; how the separate pages/screens link together. It is the flow of the interaction from beginning to end and including all the possible options that the user could take. It should also include what happens when the user's behavior or the information is outside the normal expected range.

The layout is not defined apart from functional groupings: 'These buttons are all to do with the user's profile so they need to be grouped together in this order . . .'. Terminology is not definitive; the terms are simply place-holders until a review of terminology can be carried out. This is best done after the design has settled down a bit. The last thing you want to do is to sort out the terminology early on, user test it etc., and then further on down the line add a new term to the list and have to do all the testing again on that one term!

After you do the specification

After the specification you will have a blueprint for the system that will still need design to realize the form of the parts of the interaction you have specified.

The terminology used in the specifications will have to be finalized and checked. The overall style and layout will have to be done, conforming to any visual house styles there are and adhering to the parts of the specification to do with the functional clustering and ordering of the buttons.

The user interface specification is usually . . .

Clear to the target group

Every time a designer does a specification it does not need to be a perfect presentation. The specification needs to be good and well thought out, but the actual realization of the specification, be it in text or as diagrams, does not always have to be top quality. The key thing is that the group that the specifications are intended for should be able to understand them. Thus if the specifications are just an aid to the designer, they can be as rough as they want as long as the designer can understand them several weeks or months down the line. If they are intended for the design group then the quality needs to be higher, since the whole group needs to be able to understand them. If the specs are still internal, but are interdepartmental, and are going to the technicians to be produced, then the quality needs to be good enough for the non-designers to know what is going on. The final level of quality is if the specs are going to the client as part of the pitch or acceptance process. They need to be good quality so that it looks like you know what you are doing.

Complete

The specifications need to cover all possible interactions between the user and the new media system, not just the most common route or the route where the user is being well behaved. The specifications need to cater for the situations where the user has typed in the wrong password, or does not have access to the content, or specifies an incorrect e-mail address.

If the designer does not fill in this detail in the specification phase then someone else will fill in the detail further down the line. This will usually be someone who is not a designer and who is very pushed for time, with predictably bad results.

Large in scope

Back to the garden-shed example. If the interface is small in scope then you probably do not need to specify it in the first place, although it is best to err on the side of caution. If you think, 'Oh this is obvious, I don't have to specify it here', the chances are that someone else will fill the detail in differently or that in two months' time you yourself will come back to the specifications and fill the detail in differently.

Low in complexity

A good interface must be simple to understand for the user, and it must also be specified in a simple way. If it is simple to understand and is expressed simply then the end result should be low in complexity. These two prerequisites imply that the interface is well designed and that the specification language is well matched to the interface it is describing.

For example, if the new media system has a link 'e-mail us' on every page then you do not want the specification to be a flow-style diagram showing all the pages in the system, each with a big arrow pointing over to the 'e-mail us' page. It would be sufficient to say, 'The link "e-mail us" always points to this page here . . .' and skip all the arrows.

Can have 'holes'

A specification does not have to be complete as long as it is obvious which bits are missing. These 'holes' in the specification can be filled in later. For example, you might have a hole where the user authenticates themselves in some way. The exact authentication method can then be left for further design work.

But should be unambiguous

Following on from the point above, 'holes' are acceptable as long as it is clear to the person reading the specifications that there is a hole to be filled and what sort of thing should fill it (this is in itself a form of specification).

Must be quick and easy

If a specification method has no tangible benefits it will not be used. Whatever the specification method chosen it should be as fast and as easy as possible without compromising the precision.

It is a useful exercise to incorporate the specification into some other task related to a new media system. This is especially so for a client-facing task, as it ensures that the specification does get done in the first place. For example it could be printed out neatly and incorporated into the client offer or presentation. Alternatively it could be rendered as an image or a structured web page and incorporated into the site as a site map.

Does not have to be too rigorous

There has been a fair amount of research on formal specifications of interactive systems, especially in the 1980s and early 1990s. Many different formal ways of specifying interactivity have been developed and used.

Established formal methods for interface specification are sometimes required by large corporate clients, but in general if you are specifying for yourself or a small group of designers/producers there is nothing that says you have to use an existing specification method.

Read up on them a bit, try to understand them and do not be afraid to pick and mix any bits that seem to work. Use methods that work for you and your design team, and use methods that work for the project in hand.

The medium of the specification

Specifications of user interfaces do not always have to be confined to flow-style diagrams. Consider the following.

Speech

If you want to be precise, a specification can be in any medium; it does not even have to be visual. Consider this:

'Listen; we could have two links on the home-page, one to a list of staff ordered alphabetically and another a list ordered according to their department, how about that?'

Strictly speaking that is a specification, as it is a presentation of a chunk of interactivity. Granted, the presentation is short-lived, imprecise and non-visual, but nonetheless it is a presentation of an idea that others can get to grips with and comment on.

Written description

Moving on to more rigorous and persistent forms of specification, it is possible to specify a proposed system by describing it in textual terms. Although this is more permanent than just talking about it, it still has the same drawbacks as speech in that the majority of interfaces are visual and spatial and text is not the best medium for describing them. However, the counter-argument is that text is a very easily accessible medium for everyone, especially those not well versed in the graphical world. So textual descriptions could be useful in certain situations, for example in specifying things to clients who can read text but are out of their depth with huge diagrams, or when specifying very text-rich new media systems.

Diagrams

This leads us nicely on to diagrams, simple visual representation of the steps in interactions and the screen presentations required. A balance needs to be sought, however, between informal sketches and diagrams based on some formal notation. Representing visual screen layout on paper is easy but representing interaction and dynamically changing information displays requires specific ways of setting things down on paper. All too often you will find yourself running out of paper, or drawing huge arrows from one side of the page to the other. Whatever you do, the specification will have to be redrawn neatly at the end, so start out with this assumption and do not immediately think you are trying to draw the final version.

Problems with diagrams

Specifying a web site on paper is difficult. Some people use long lists of numbered items, resulting in a document that looks good but that makes it very difficult to get any idea of the overall structure. Graphic connected graph representations quickly become unwieldy: it is difficult to show the content and structure in the same diagram and cross-links can leave the whole thing looking incredibly complex.

If you confine yourself to just one method of specification then a simple conceptual idea such as having the site in more than one language can result in an extra level of complexity that bears little resemblance to the simplicity of the concept.

Flowcharts

Sometimes people will use programming-style flowcharts to specify the user interface of a new media system. There are many similarities between conventional logic flowcharts and specifications of the interface: both are blobs joined together by arrows showing what happens with a system. The main difference is that flowcharts are more technically oriented and deal with what is going on within the system as well as what the user sees at the front-end to the system. Interface specifications are more concerned with the user's experience and less with what is going on inside the system. Having said that, if you can do a good flowchart then doing a good user interface specification should be easy.

Specification and prototyping

Specifying an interactive new media system focuses the designer on the design problem, and ensures that that focus happens before the implementation of the design is started. In that way specifications help enforce a degree of top-down design (covered in chapter 17). Specifications also help the designer to get a feel of the design, although getting a feel of the design by looking at abstract specification diagrams is somewhat difficult.

The next chapter deals with this issue of making parts of the design more tangible by creating prototypes and demos of new media systems.

Exercises

WEBCODE
simple spec

Simple specification

Choose a simple interactive device that you are familiar with, such as a cash-point, a ticket machine or a drinks machine, and try to specify the interaction on paper. Start with the simplest case by considering a well-behaved user who does everything correctly. Then move on to cope with errors, attempted fraud and incomplete transactions.

WEBCODE
web site spec

Describe a web site

Choose a typical piece of web site interaction, not simple navigation through a tree-structure of information ('our products, our company' etc.), but something a bit more complex such as purchasing a book or registering for a login. Specify it on paper. If you start hitting problems, have a look at examples on the web of how different web sites do it.

WEBCODE
finding gaps

Finding gaps

Choose a really simple interactive system to design. Get a specification down on paper. The focus should be on defining every possible user action and catering for it, even if it is just to say 'if the user does this then nothing happens'. Another person should concentrate on finding gaps in the specification. If the thing has two buttons, A and B, find out what happens if the user presses button A while holding button B down etc.

Prototypes and demos

21

Introduction: a *Star Wars* prototype

In the early 1970s, George Lucas, the guy who went on to create the film *Star Wars*, wanted to give his backers and crew a taste of what he was aiming for with the film. He wanted to give a demo of the ideas that were in his head. But how could he show them bits of the film he wanted to make without spending months and millions on it? What he did was to make a prototype, a demo, an interim version with low investment and fast turnaround that would make them say, 'Wow, I see what you're trying to make. Fantastic'. He made the prototype by joining together bits of existing films. He took bits of 'Battle of Britain' airplane dogfight movies, bits of swash-buckling pirate movies, and bits of other films and blended them all together to give the overall effect of what he was trying to achieve.

Terminology

We shall start off with some terminology. Throughout the software world and the new media world (and in fact in several other worlds) there is talk of simulations, prototypes and demos. The terms are used interchangeably and vaguely. For the purposes of this chapter let me define them in a bit more detail.

Simulation

A simulation is not a working version of a system; it simulates it. It pretends to do something that it does not actually do. It can be a simulation of a thing that has not yet been built. Or it can be a simulation of an existing thing that users use instead of the real thing because the real thing is too dangerous or too expensive. Flight simulators are a good example of the latter. You can try things out in a flight simulator that you would never dream of trying in a real aircraft. Although a flight simulator is expensive it is not as expensive as an airplane.

Prototype

The term prototype has a more complex history; prototype literally translates as 'first example' and that is exactly what it used to be, the first working version of something. In this book the term is used less precisely to mean an early version of some part of a new media system.

Demo

A demo is a demonstration; it is the act of showing how something works. You can give a demonstration of the first version of a system – a prototype – or you can build a simulation of part of the system and give a demo of that.

Specifications

The previous chapter dealt with specifying interactive system. There is an overlap with prototypes in that a prototype presents a part of the system and, when approved, that prototype is also a specification that shows what is to be built. Prototypes are more tangible than specifications and prototypes are less complete than specifications.

All of the above terms have a role to play in the design and development of interactive systems. In different contexts and different companies these terms will probably have different meanings. Indeed many design departments have their own words for these concepts: mock-ups, wireframes, I have even heard a designer be asked to 'give an idea legs'. The software world has its own terminology with version numbers and beta releases of software. However, these terms have more to do with the actual production and release of systems than with the design. What I am interested in here are the ideas that play a part in the design and development process.

Let me try to bring everything together in a diagram. The designer (or design team) has an idea for a system and during the development they build a prototype. The designers and also users interact with this prototype and through their interactions the designers can evaluate the design.

Through the course of design and development several of these prototypes may be produced, and when the prototype is the final one it can function as a specification for the production of the system itself; see Figure 21.1.

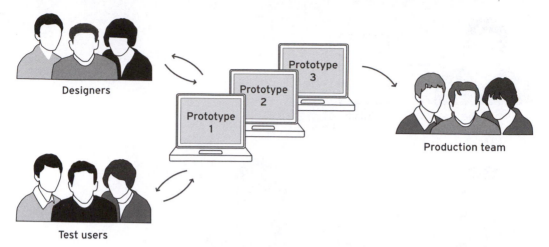

Figure 21.1: The part prototypes play within a design and production context.

Historical background

Now that we have mapped out what we are talking about, let us have a look at the history of simulations and prototypes, and the resulting separation of roles; see Figure 21.2.

Crafts-people production

Long before mass production, the link between the designer, the maker and the user of a thing was a lot more tangible. Often they would be one and the same person; the maker would be designing and making something to use themselves. Alternatively the maker would be making it for a friend, family or colleague with whom they were intimately familiar. They would be making one product and as they were making it they could alter the production process 'on the fly' according to the wishes of the 'client'. The design, the use and the evaluation were all happening at the same time. This was the case with the opening example of the bike shed.

Mass production

In the era of mass production the link between the designer, the maker and the user is more tenuous. The designer designs, the maker makes and the user uses, with very little communication between the groups. There

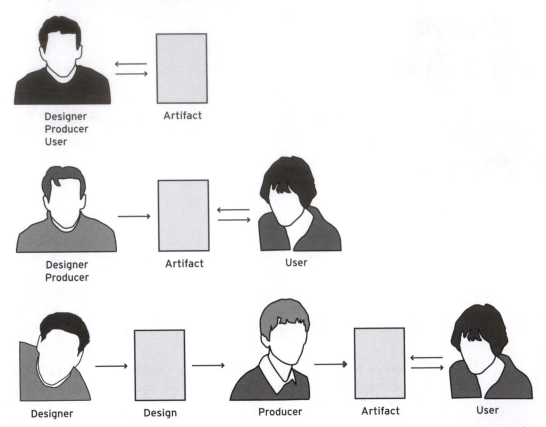

Figure 21.2: How the different roles in making things have become separated.

are no alterations in context according to the user's needs; there is no user involvement in the end-product. This is where the concept of a prototype was born: 'proto' – first; 'type' – example. It was an early version of a mass-produced product. The first of its kind, it would be evaluated and when all was deemed to be acceptable the mass production could start.

Marketing

In today's era not only is the design and production process fast and furious but the rate at which new products are appearing is also speeding up. In this context prototypes and demos play a vital new role in the marketing and publicity surrounding these new products. A prototype in this context is used to pre-promote a product or even to create and define a market that did not previously exist.

Prototypes in new media

WEBCODE
dyson

The importance of prototyping in physical products and new media systems is very different. Prototyping is important in physical products because there is usually a degree of mass production and thus any errors are multiplied a hundred-fold. Furthermore the fixed nature of physical products means that correcting a mistake involves the recall of all those thousands of products and a huge number of repairs/alterations at an incredible cost. James Dyson, the designer of a new sort of vacuum cleaner, made over five thousand prototypes before he was satisfied with his design.

With new media the same is true when mass producing and distributing complex interactive systems on cd-roms. Indeed many publishers have had problems with publishing cd-roms that turn out to have bugs in them that do not show up the first time around and so do not get caught by the testing before going to mass production. Correcting a book before publication is a different exercise from debugging a new media system on a cd-rom, and one wrong spelling in a book will never have the same impact as one bug in the code of some computer-controlled bit of new media.

With distribution channels such as the web, mistakes are less costly to repair. There is no mass production or copying; there is just one web site, and the fact that this can be easily updated means that any errors can be quickly put right. The downside of this is that the ease of correcting errors can lead to a 'gung-ho' attitude regarding updating and launching without testing or prototypes. There is always a feeling of 'if it's wrong we can just put it right later'.

WEBCODE
one dollar

There are even cases where prices have been incorrectly published on the web. A computer manufacturer and retailer once paid the price of an error on their web site where one model of laptop was on sale for just one dollar. Many people registered to buy one and although the company admitted the mistake it was still unclear what the legal situation was, forcing the company to make a deal with all those who had registered to buy for a dollar.

Building a prototype

The starting point of a prototype is deciding which aspect of the design you want to represent and evaluate. A prototype does not have to be a faithful reproduction of the entire system. This is an ideal and would cost too much in terms of investment. Different aspects of the design can be extracted and presented for different purposes. The designer has to decide what aspect is being focussed on and pull that one out of the design to be given form in a prototype.

Baby toys are an interesting example here. They have strong connections with the whole process of prototyping. With a baby's telephone, for example, you extract those essential features of a telephone – the dial, the handset and some sort of ringing bell. Throw in a few extras such as wheels and wobbly eyes and you have a telephone for a baby.

Prototyping an interactive system involves a similar process: extracting those features of the system that you want to evaluate and representing them in a perceptible form. If you are evaluating the visual design of a new media application you do mock-ups of a few individual screens. If you are evaluating the interaction you construct a prototype of the interactive structure with simple text menus and bits of text saying 'the help information comes here' and so on.

Film trailers are an example of non-product-related prototypes. The idea of a trailer is to present the atmosphere and high points of a film to prospective audiences without giving away too much of the plot. The designer of the trailer wants to present the 'essence' of the film in the trailer/prototype and make people go to see it. You would never get a trailer with a sincere voice-over saying something like this:

'Long Road Back, starring Ian Johnson: a powerful story of two brothers who die in the end'

Filling in detail

When you are demonstrating some aspect of a new media system in the way described above, the question arises of what to do about those aspects that you are not presenting in the prototype. You can either miss them out or you can fill them temporarily with something else. For example, if you are demonstrating on-screen page layout you can just fill the page with fake text. Latin is obscure enough not to distract the viewer with the content of the text. Or if you are demonstrating the structure of information in a web site you can set it up with minimal graphic design, just black text on white background, to show the viewer how the information fits together and how they can navigate through it.

The drawback with this is that viewers can miss the focus of the demo and home in on these unimportant details. Although I have yet to hear a client complain, 'Are we doing the whole site in Latin then?', I have often spent time debating aspects of the demo that were not the ones actually being demonstrated. For example, 'The structure is fine but the layout is a bit basic' and 'Oh, we would expect to have a lot more content than this'. Unfortunately there is no way around this except to explain to the viewer and to make sure that the unimportant filling-in is as low key and simple as possible so that no one will take offense and comment on it.

Balance of investment

There is a balance of investment between the people building the prototype and the people viewing it. If the people building it invest lots of work into it then the end result is likely to be very convincing and the people reviewing the prototype are likely to be totally taken in by it and sit there in amazement. Alternatively, if the prototype is shown as a collection of pen and paper roughs of screens which the person giving the demo has to keep moving around, then this demands a lot more investment in terms of imagination from the people viewing the demo. Obviously the balance depends upon who the demo is being shown to. You are not going to invest a few weeks' work on a slick demo if all you are saying is 'how about this idea?' to the design team; likewise you do not go into a client pitch armed with a pile of rough sketches on paper.

Different types of prototypes

We have seen that there are different ways of putting together a prototype of a new media system, depending on what aspects you want to concentrate on. There are also different types of prototype according to how it simulates the real thing. Let us have a look below and in Figure 21.3.

Forcing or offering an illusion

With any demonstration there is division of investment between the designers making the prototype and the people viewing it. This balance of investment is also tied up with the perception of the person viewing it. If the demo is life-like and convincing then they can easily believe in it, so the illusion is in effect forced upon them. If the demo is rougher and less complete then the illusion is merely being offered to them and it is up to them to believe in it. There are parallels with other forms of media. The credibility of a play or film is governed by how easy it is to believe in the illusion it is offering, whereas a magician must actively force an

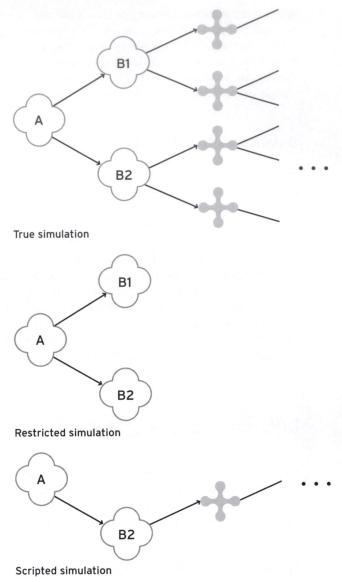

True simulation

Restricted simulation

Scripted simulation

Figure 21.3: Three different types of simulation shown as interaction/information structures.

illusion on the audience. It would be a poor magician who performed magic by offering an illusion:

> 'Right, in this hat is a rabbit but I want you to imagine that the hat is empty. Now, Abracadabra – I pull a rabbit out of an empty hat. Pretty fantastic, eh?'

True simulation

True simulation is the ideal goal, a simulation that is so close to the real thing that anybody seeing it or using it would not be able to tell the difference. Unfortunately, the amount of investment needed to achieve this is the same as that required to build the real thing so a true simulation is a bit of an abstract ideal. The exceptions are systems where a simulation has to be used because it is too dangerous or expensive to use the real thing.

Restricted simulation

If there are insufficient resources to construct a fully functional, interim version of the system then a more realistic scenario is to construct a system that offers most of the functionality, but in a restricted form. So, clicking on a button titled 'request a brochure' would take you to a page that said, 'Here the user can fill in their name and address for a brochure' or, if more detail is possible, a fake fill-in form where the user can fill details in (which are not used) and get a fake 'thank you' message in return.

Scripted simulation

A scripted simulation is one where the user is not free to click on whatever they want to for the simple reason that not much of it always works. The people who build the simulation decide on a script – a sequence of interactions that demonstrate the abilities of the system, and they build a sequence of screens to demonstrate those abilities. The exact sequence of interactions is well defined, hence the term script, and the demo must be given by someone who knows the sequence.

Making demos work well

Scenarios and stories

A demonstration should showcase the features that you want to tell the other party about (be it a client pitch, a user training session or an internal design group meeting) but a demonstration can be more than just a step-by-step journey through all the menu options. Make use of scenarios and stories to make the demo more meaningful.

A demo should not be long and boring

The key goal is that the demo should not be long and drawn out. If you want to methodically go through all the functional options within a system then perhaps you are better writing some sort of specification of the new media system (see chapter 20).

A demo should fit into the client's world view

If you have presented the demo as a scenario, make sure that it is a scenario that the audience can identify with. It should fit in with their world view and deal with the sorts of problems and situations that they are likely to be familiar with.

> 'This is a customer relation management system. Now imagine you have just been behind a stall in an exhibition all day and you have a huge pile of business cards of possible leads. What do you do? Stick them into a drawer and forget about them? Well, with this system you click here on "batch contacts" and then you get this input screen where you can fill in . . .' and so on.

A demo should be emotive and fun

A demo should not be dry and mundane. Give it a bit more life and substance and then the demo audience will be more drawn to it. For instance if you want a little scenario to accompany a description of web-based services, which of these two is the better?

> Mike is interested in sound wave interference and he wants to do some fast Fourier transforms, so he goes to a web site and downloads some software to help him.

> Mike is trying to work but they are constructing a new building right outside his office. Sometimes the noise is so loud that it might as well be *inside* his office. Two days in he asks the foreman how long it will take and he replies four weeks. Mike searches the internet for earplugs but finds something better instead – battery-powered, anti-noise headphones. He can even order them online. Four days in and Mike is blissfully unaware of the pile-driver that the builders have just brought in to do the foundations.

A demo should be memorable

To make a demo memorable try to make the story interesting. You could string together a sequence of real-world events but try to give it a humorous spin or a 'happy ending'. Perhaps you could bring a sequence of demos together into a little 'soap opera' style story. Chuck Berry was asked once about the timeless appeal of his song lyrics and he said that he always tried to make a song tell a little story. Try applying this to demos.

Presenting a demo of a prototype

One thing that will affect how you put the demo together is a consideration of what form the final presentation will take. There are several possibilities. See Figure 21.4.

A slide presentation

The most obvious is as a step-by-step presentation. This is a chain of several screens, each showing a step in the interaction and a 'next' button so that the user can click through and follow the interaction.

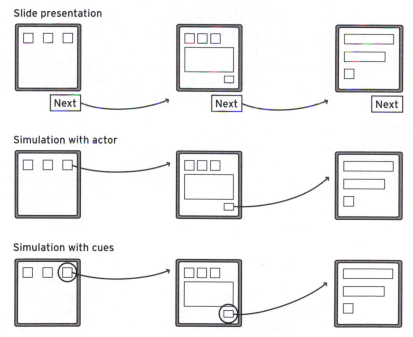

Figure 21.4: Three different forms that a presentation of a demo can take.

WEBCODE
slide demo

The realism of the presentation can be enhanced by anything that makes the separate screens look a bit more dynamic and interactive. They can use bits of animation, sound effects, even the inclusion of a simulated on-screen cursor moving and clicking on different things.

A simulation with an actor

WEBCODE
actor demo

A more realistic approach is to build the sequence of screens in such a way that moving from one screen to the next is achieved not by clicking on a separate 'next' button, but by clicking on the appropriate button in the screen. The demo can then be given by someone 'in the know' who knows which buttons they should be clicking to follow the script. 'We fill out login name and click on "done" and we get the welcome-screen'.

Such a simulation can be carried out only by someone who knows where to click. Alternatively it is possible to give the demo remotely, mount the demo on a web server, talk to the person receiving it on the phone and talk them through the interaction, telling them where to click.

A simulation with cues

With the method outlined above it is possible to get confused if you have not given the demo for a while. You may forget what the script is and where you have to click. Furthermore, any remote demo such as that described depends on the person viewing it having you on the line as well. This is fine for directed demonstrations but if you want to set up a public demonstration for anybody to use on a cd-rom or on the internet then you will need some other approach.

WEBCODE
cues demo

You could opt for the slide-presentation idea outlined above. Alternatively you could set up a 'simulation with an actor' as in the previous point, but as the actor does not know the script you could add cues to the interaction. For example, you could add a circle to each screen indicating where the user must click to move forward to the next point in the scripted interaction. As well as being useful for public demos this is also useful for giving demos yourself of scripted simulations you are not familiar with.

It is important that the cues do not get mixed up with the actual interface so they should be as distinct and different as possible. They should either be in a very different visual style from the rest, animated or blinking, or even be given in a different medium, such as text-based instructions at the bottom of the screen or spoken instructions: 'Welcome to this demo, imagine you are a guest to the site, click on 'guest login' to see what happens . . .'

Simulation in a video scenario

WEBCODE
video demo

A variation on the above is to have a scripted demo with an actor and to video the entire interaction. In effect this is a scripted play or advert where one of the players is the interactive system itself and the other is someone playing the part of the user. This approach can distract from the detail of the interaction but it can be useful to emphasize the context of use of the system and how it could fit into people's lives or work situations. Apple did this exercise to great effect some time ago with their Knowledge Navigator video.

Wizard of Oz methods

An overview of different demo methods should also include the 'Wizard of Oz' method, even though this is a method that requires a degree of investment not normally associated with interactive system design. The idea is that a person plays the role of the system. In the film *The Wizard of Oz*, the Mighty Oz is controlled by an ordinary person behind a curtain. This approach usually involves too much investment to do convincingly with digital means, but it is a good approach with paper-based prototypes, where a designer can move paper elements around in response to users' comments and directions.

Advantages of prototypes

Inspiration

Building a prototype is a good way of seeing if your ideas are good or not. Prototypes are also a good source of new ideas. While building or inter-acting with prototypes your mind is free to come up with new insights into the problem you are working to solve. You can sit round with the design group and discuss ideas based on the simulation; it acts as a sand-box, a focus, an inspiration for new ideas. That was the motivation behind the *Star Wars* example I opened this chapter with.

Make changes efficiently

A prototype provides the designer with valuable feedback about their design: is it good, will it work, will the user be confused? It enables aspects of the design to be evaluated at an early stage in the design pro-cess and, more importantly, it enables decisions to be taken at an early stage. The earlier in the process you can pick up mistakes and bad design and correct them, the better. There is nothing worse than coming up against a daft bit of design in the final stages of building. It threatens the deadline and it usually needs huge amounts of investment to put it right.

Convinces managers

Prototypes make things tangible. If you have a room full of designers working on digital design in a top-down manner it could be months before anything tangible appears. Managers and clients get nervous very easily. They like to see what is going on; they like to see progress. If you make a prototype for internal use, always show it to the managers/clients/other departments so they can see what is going on. Better still, make the prototype available on the web.

User testing

As well as evaluation within the design team, a prototype also enables you to do real user testing, either qualitative – 'this is great' – or quant-itative – 'this is 10% faster than before'.

Refines implementation

Having 'dry runs' at implementing parts of the system means that the people involved in building the prototypes can get a good understanding of the best ways to go about implementing the final thing. They can try out ideas in the prototypes and, if they work, they can use them in the final version.

Involves teams in decisions

Presenting prototypes to user groups, management, clients etc. for com-ment means that everyone can have their say. Even if their suggestions are declined there is still a feeling of 'consensus design' and people will usually be happier with the outcome than having an interactive system thrust upon them. And of course there is always the chance that a non-designer will come up with a good design modification!

Marketing

With the speed at which new media systems have to reach the marketplace it is not enough to wait for a product to be finished before it is showcased. Very often a prototype plays a part in the marketing of the product.

Useful in teaching environments

Finally, a word about prototypes and demos in the classroom. Prototypes such as those described are a key resource in learning contexts. Any new media should contain an element of hands-on design. Often, though, there are restrictions associated with such exercises:

- The user is not completely familiar with the technology (complex scripting languages etc.).
- The technologies that are appropriate are not easily available (technologies requiring that web pages are accessed on a web server as opposed to the local file system).
- There is not enough time for the development of a complete system.
- The student needs to practise design, not practise getting to grips with complex new media technologies.

To overcome such problems a teaching/learning approach involving a good deal of prototyping is ideal. Not only does this make complex projects possible, it also prepares students for using prototyping techniques in the real world.

Low-fi prototypes

The main drawback of prototypes is that showing a slick, digital prototype to the management or to a client can make it look so convincingly complete that they will have the impression that the project is almost finished. They may say, 'Great, it looks like it's almost finished, can we have it ready by Wednesday?' The design team is then left with the job of convincing them that, despite the amazing demo they have just given, with everything looking complete, there is in fact no way they could have anything ready by Wednesday.

A similar feeling of completion can also interfere with the presentation of the prototype to other designers and user groups. There can be a feeling that the system is now almost finished and so it is far too late to incorporate any comments that they may have. This hampers effective input into the design process.

Based on the comments above there is a case for building prototypes that present the essentials of what you want to present without looking too complete and slick. Other people can then get an idea of what you are working on, yet still feel that more investment is needed or that their comments can play a part.

WEBCODE
low fi

One elegant and fast way of doing low-fi prototyping is to make rough sketches on paper and then scan them in and assemble the prototype using the different elements. Presenting them on-screen supports the interaction so that users have a feel for more than just the visual side of the system, while the sketch quality of them encourages comments from the viewers since people are used to rough sketches being the language of early prototyping.

'Never play a note you don't believe in'

It is a nice touch to end a book about design in the world of new media extolling the virtues of pencil and paper, but that is a key thread in the whole of new media design and development. It is not about getting fixated on the technology and losing sight of the user, but about designing for the user and using only technologies and ideas that are appropriate to them.

A lot of good things can be done by looking at and using what has gone before. New media is new, but it exists in an old context and, although technology has changed quickly, people change slowly. So be creative and be brave, but do not lose touch with where people are coming from and who they are. Be true to them; only put things in your design that you know should be there, that you believe in.

The best quote to apply to this is that of the old Blues guitarist Ernest Banks. A young guitarist, Doug MacLeod, was visiting him and tried to impress him by playing a fast Blues solo, plenty of notes and full of technique. Old Banks then took the guitar and played a sparse progression that had more soul and feeling in a handful of notes than in all the flash notes that young MacLeod had played. When Banks was done he said, 'Never play a note you don't believe in . . . and live your life that way too'.

Further reading

For a good overview of books for teaching and practising new media design and all flavors of design for use the reader is referred to:

■ www.idhub.com

Index